EXPLORATIONS IN LOCAL AND REGIONAL HISTORY

Centre for Regional and Local History, University of Hertfordshire
and
Centre for English Local History, University of Leicester

SERIES EDITORS: NIGEL GOOSE AND RICHARD JONES

Previous titles in this series

FROM THE DEER TO THE FOX

The hunting transition and the landscape, 1600–1850

BY MANDY DE BELIN

UNIVERSITY OF HERTFORDSHIRE PRESS

Explorations in Local and Regional History
Volume 6

First published in Great Britain in 2013 by
University of Hertfordshire Press
College Lane
Hatfield
Hertfordshire
AL10 9AB

British Library Cataloguing in Publication Data
A catalogue record for this book is available from the British Library

ISBN 978-1-909291-04-1

Design by Arthouse Publishing Solutions
Printed in Great Britain by Hobbs the Printers Ltd

Publication Grant

Publication has been made possible by a generous grant from the Scouloudi Foundation in association with the Institute of Historical Research.

Contents

Figures

Tables

Abbreviations

CSPD   *Calendar of State Papers Domestic*
HCPP   *House of Commons Parliamentary Papers*
LRO   Leicestershire, Leicester and Rutland Record Office
TNA   The National Archives
NRO   Northamptonshire Record Office
OS   Ordnance Survey
VCH   *Victoria County History*

Series Editors' Preface

The series of *Explorations in Local and Regional History* is a continuation and development of the 'Occasional Papers' of the University of Leicester's Department of English Local History, a series started by Herbert Finberg in 1952. This succeeding series is published by the University of Hertfordshire Press, which has a strong profile in English local and regional history. The idea for the new series came from Harold Fox, who, with Nigel Goose, served as series editor in its first two years.

Explorations in Local and Regional History has three distinctive characteristics. First, the series is prepared to publish work on novel themes, to tackle fresh subjects – perhaps even unusual ones. We hope that it serves to open up new approaches, prompt the analysis of new sources or types of source, and foster new methodologies. This is not to suggest that more traditional scholarship in local and regional history are unrepresented, for it may well be distinctive in terms of its quality, and we also seek to offer an outlet for work of distinction that might be difficult to place elsewhere.

This brings us to the second feature of the series, which is the intention to publish mid-length studies, generally within the range of 40,000 to 60,000 words. Such studies are hard to place with existing publishers, for while there are current series that cater for mid-length overviews of particular historiographical topics or themes, there is none of which we are aware that offers similar outlets for original research. *Explorations*, therefore, intends to fill the publishing vacuum between research articles and full-length books (the latter, incidentally, might well be eligible for inclusion in the existing University of Hertfordshire Press series, *Studies in Regional and Local History*).

Third, while we expect this series to be required reading for both academics and students, it is also our intention to ensure that it is of interest and relevance to local historians operating outside an institutional framework. To this end we ensure that each volume is set at a price that individuals, and not only university libraries, can generally afford. Local and regional history is a subject taught at many levels, from schools to universities. Books, magazines, television and radio all testify to the vitality of research and writing outside universities, as well as to the sustained growth of popular interest. It is hoped that *Explorations in Local and Regional History* will make a contribution to the continued flourishing of our subject. We will ensure that books in the series are accessible to a wide readership, that they avoid technical language and jargon, and that they will usually be illustrated.

This preface, finally, serves as a call for proposals, and authors who are studying local themes in relation to particular places (rural or urban), regions, counties or provinces, whether their subject matter comprises social groups (or other groups), landscapes, interactions and movements between places, microhistory or total history should consider publication with this series. The editors can be consulted informally at the addresses given below, while a formal proposal form is available from the University of Hertfordshire Press at uhpress@herts.ac.uk.

Nigel Goose
Centre for Regional and Local History
Department of Humanities
University of Hertfordshire
College Lane
Hatfield AL10 9AB
N.Goose@herts.ac.uk

Richard Jones
Centre for English Local History
Marc Fitch Historical Institute
5 Salisbury Road
Leicester LE1 7QR
rlcj1@leicester.ac.uk

1

Introduction

Whittlebury, in Northamptonshire, lies at the heart of what used to be the royal forest of Whittlewood. The village pub is called 'The Fox and Hounds' and nearby a handsome sign has the name 'Whittlebury' surmounted by a depiction of fallow deer. This juxtaposition illustrates how central hunting has been to the locality. The sign represents the reason for the forest's existence: the preservation of the king's deer for hunting. The name of the pub speaks of the local importance of foxhunting in later centuries. This book is concerned with the transition from deer hunting to foxhunting, and the manifestation of that transition in a changing landscape. It focuses on Northamptonshire because that county contained the archetypal landscapes of both the old and the new forms of hunting.

Northamptonshire is perhaps more often thought of as an area of classic Midland open-field systems and parliamentary enclosure, but it contained no fewer than three royal forests. Whittlewood, Salcey and Rockingham originally formed part of a band of forests running from Oxford in the south to Stamford in Lincolnshire in the north (Figure 1.1). From the time of the Norman Conquest to the early modern period these Northamptonshire forests went in and out of favour as royal hunting grounds, but the machinery of deer preservation continued regardless. Of the venison supplied to Charles I for Christmas 1640 by far the largest consignment came from Rockingham Forest; the next largest came from Whittlewood, which tied for second place with the New Forest.[1]

By the nineteenth century the sport of hunting had been totally transformed. Foxhunting had replaced deer hunting in terms of both popularity and prestige; where the royal forests had once been the prime hunting grounds, this mantle was now worn by the grassland of the 'shires'. The great and the good hunted the fox in east Leicestershire, Rutland and west Northamptonshire (Figure 1.2). To hunt anywhere else was to hunt in the 'provinces'.[2]

---

1. P.A.J. Pettit, The royal forests of Northamptonshire: a study in their economy 1558–1714 (Gateshead, 1968), pp. 3–17; J.C. Cox, The royal forests of England (London, 1905), pp. 78–9.
2. R. Carr, English foxhunting: a history (1976; London 1986), pp. 68–71; E. Griffin, Blood sport: hunting in Britain since 1066 (New Haven, CT, and London, 2007), pp. 126–40.

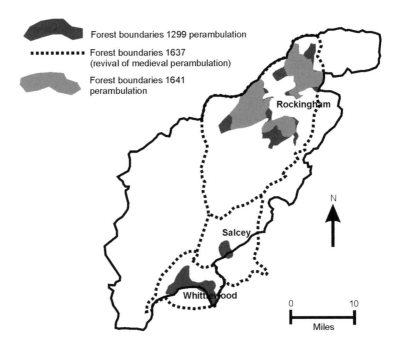

Forest boundaries 1299 perambulation

Forest boundaries 1637
(revival of medieval perambulation)

Forest boundaries 1641
perambulation

Rockingham

Salcey

Whittlewood

N

0   10
Miles

Figure 1.1 The Northamptonshire forests.

Hunting, of either the deer or the fox, was a sport that was intimately connected with the landscape. Both variations required suitable habitat for the preservation of the prey animal and the terrain across which to chase it. The traditional explanation for the decline of deer hunting and the rise of foxhunting has cited change in the landscape with an argument that could be generally summarised thus: forests, the traditional hunting preserves, came increasingly under pressure from 'improvement', which usually meant disafforestation, enclosure and even ploughing up for conversion to arable; and the wooded parts of the forests came to be regarded more highly for the economic potential of their timber reserves than for their provision of habitat for deer. The deer population was the victim of these two developments, and both hunting and preservation became concentrated in deer parks in the course of the sixteenth century. The aftermath of the Civil War saw greater depredations on deer herds as parks were broken and raided. According to some sources this was a blow from which the deer population never recovered and, subsequently, when the nobility and the gentry once more turned their attention to hunting, deer were somewhat thin on the ground. An alternative prey had to be found, and the fox fitted the bill on several counts, one of the

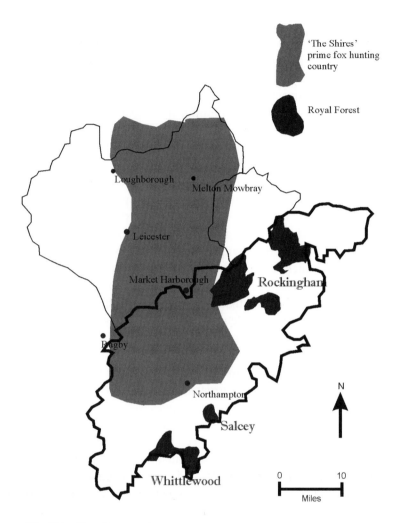

Figure 1.2 'The Shires' hunting country.

foremost being that it could be pursued at speed on near-thoroughbred horses across the enclosed pastures of the Midlands.[3]

One of the primary aims of this book is to question this account of the hunting transition. While there are few surviving figures for deer population in

3. The earliest rehearsal of this argument that I have found is in W. Scarth Dixon, *Hunting in the olden days* (London, 1912). This is repeated in later works: Carr, *English foxhunting*, pp. 22–4; D. Landry, *The invention of the countryside: hunting, walking and ecology in English literature, 1671–1831* (Basingstoke, 2001), pp. 5–6; M. Brander, *Hunting and shooting: from earliest times to the present day* (London, 1971), pp. 55, 60–61. Griffin, *Blood sport*, pp. 108–10.

the Northamptonshire forests, those that do exist illustrate a recovery in deer numbers following a mid-seventeenth-century crisis,[4] a pattern that is repeated for other forests across the country.[5] Even without taking into account the number of deer that were kept in deer parks, if the will to hunt deer remained there were certainly still deer to hunt. But, by the beginning of the nineteenth century, to talk of 'hunting' invariably implied foxhunting. If the growth of the new sport was not due to declining deer populations, its real causes still require investigation, including an examination of what was happening in the landscape in this period and what effect this had on the transition from one form of hunting to the other. If deer hunting simply 'went out of fashion' why was this so, and what made foxhunting such an aspirational pastime? In attempting to answer these questions, this study examines the landscape of the forests and parks of Northamptonshire over the period from 1600 to 1850, as well as looking for other developments that may have helped to effect the change, such as the growth of horse racing as a sport and the consequent revolution in the types of horse bred in England. The investigation of these subjects covers a wider geographical area.

Why is it important to investigate the transition in hunting practices? For a great many years there was a tendency to consider the agricultural and landscape history of this period overwhelmingly in economic terms. Some historians followed nineteenth-century agriculturalists in concentrating on 'improvement', sharing a belief in the continued progress towards perfection. While this approach has been questioned by more left-leaning historians, they still tended to think primarily in terms of economic ambitions: landscape changes were motivated by the desire to make money, or at least the desire to flaunt it once made. Accordingly, the royal forests in the early modern period have been largely ignored, and when they have been considered it has been as an anachronistic backwater in chronic decline. Little or no attention has been paid to the forests in the context of a hunting and recreational landscape.[6] Similarly, any effects that the rise of foxhunting as a sport

4. Although Whittlewood was reckoned to have been particularly hard hit by depredations of deer population, in 1828 it was still estimated to have a stock of around 1500 and could support the taking of some 120 bucks and 110 does per year. NRO, Grafton archive: G3982.
5. E.P. Thompson gives figures for Windsor Forest that show that, while deer levels never regained their pre-Civil War numbers, they had certainly recovered significantly by the eighteenth century owing to both breeding and restocking. E.P. Thompson, *Whigs and hunters: the origin of the Black Act* (London, 1975), pp. 55–6.
6. In his foreword to B. Schumer's *Wychwood*, H. Fox traced three main phases in woodland historiography. The first was primarily concerned with the history of royal forests, and, in particular, their legal and administrative aspects, and ranged from Manwood's *Treatise of the Forrest Lawes* in 1598 and continued through to Cox's *Royal forests of England* in 1905. The next phase, arising in the 1950s and 1960s, had historians concentrating on woodland as a negative type of land use, as a resource to be 'destroyed, tamed, converted into "more profitable" use'. Fox considered Hoskins and Darby to have been the most notable proponents of this view. The third phase, to which Schumer's work belongs, emphasised the management of woodland and

had upon the shaping of the landscape in the eighteenth and nineteenth centuries have been largely ignored.[7]

Increasingly modern society is reconsidering land use and deciding how to balance the needs of food production and recreation. We are in the process of changing from a mindset of ownership, exclusion and exploitation to one of access and preservation. In short, we are beginning to think of the English countryside not only as a factory but increasingly as a leisure resource.[8] Hunting with dogs is now banned (although it remains a contentious issue). Perhaps it is now possible to put aside moral judgements of the sport and consider the impact that it has had on the landscape over the centuries. Whether we approve or not, the hunting of deer and of foxes has been an important part in the recreational life of the nation which extended, as we shall see, beyond the social elite. The time seems right to examine the historical relationship between preservation, leisure and the landscape in the context of one of its most widespread recreational uses: hunting with dogs.

its preservation as a valued economic resource. Fox had Pettit's *Royal forests of Northamptonshire* as part of this tradition, with Rackham as its most prolific contributor. B. Schumer, *Wychwood: the evolution of a wooded landscape* (Charlbury, 1999); Cox, *Royal forests*; Pettit, *Royal forests*; O. Rackham, *Trees and woodland in the British landscape: the complete history of Britain's trees, woods and hedgerows* (1976; London, 2001); O. Rackham, *Ancient woodland: its history, vegetation and uses in England* (London, 1980).

7. Finch has questioned the disregard of the role of foxhunting in shaping the Midland shires in two fairly recent papers: J. Finch, 'Grass, grass, grass: fox-hunting and the creation of the modern landscape', *Landscapes*, 5/2 (2004), pp. 41–52; J. Finch, 'Wider famed countries: historic landscape characterisation in the midland shires', *Landscapes*, 8/2 (2007), pp. 50–63.

8. For a wider discussion of rights of access and new ways of using the landscape, see M. Shoard, *A right to roam* (Oxford, 1999).

2

Early modern deer hunting

In 1600 the deer was still considered to be the most worthy quarry, and the iconic landscape for the hunt was royal forest or private park. But, before looking at the royal forests of Northamptonshire and their provision of a hunting landscape, we need to gain an understanding of the methods and techniques of hunting deer, of who hunted deer and how they did it (and here evidence is drawn from across England, not from Northamptonshire alone). This is difficult territory: there was not a simple, straightforward set of rules regulating who could hunt what and where. Instead we have an overlapping, and sometimes contradictory, set of rights, with new sets of rules and means of enforcement arising as old ones declined. Added to this is the problem that there are about as many different interpretations of these rights as there are books that attempt to define them.[1] Consequently a (greatly simplified) narrative of evolving hunting entitlement up to the beginning of the study period might prove helpful.

The starting point is the Norman Conquest and the beginning of the Forest Laws. Forests were vast tracts of land where hunting was reserved for the king, his huntsmen and those to whom he granted (usually limited) hunting rights. Within the forest no one was allowed to hunt certain animals, most notably deer, without the permission of the king, even on their own land. Inside and outside the forests the Crown also had royal warrens: areas where it reserved the hunting of the lesser animals such as hares, foxes and rabbits. It is worth pointing out that, outside royal forests and warrens, the Crown also believed that it had the right to hunt anywhere in the kingdom regardless of actual ownership, but the real issue regarded who else was allowed to hunt there. This point is often missed: hunting rights hinged more on exclusivity than permissibility.

What hunting rights did the king's subjects have? The great magnates of the realm might have their own hunting grounds, known as chases, which were large and unenclosed. These were, in effect, private forests where they could reserve

---

1. For descriptions of laws and regulations affecting hunting, see John Manwood, *A treatise of the forrest lawes* (London, 1598); Cox, *Royal forests*; R. Grant, *The royal forests of England* (Stroud, 1991); C. Young, *The royal forests of medieval England* (Leicester, 1971).

hunting to themselves or grant rights as they saw fit. Ownership of a chase gave the magnates exclusive rights to hunt over the land of others in a manner similar to the rights of the Crown in a forest. (Historians often make the distinction that forests were royal and chases were not, but this situation is complicated by the fact that there were 'forests' in private hands and 'chases' in royal ones. For example, John of Gaunt held Ashdown Forest, while Whaddon Chase was held by the Crown.)[2] The Crown might also grant rights of free warren both inside and outside the forest. The grant of free warren gave its holder exclusive rights to hunt the lesser animals within their demesne land. Exclusivity is an important part of this grant because without free warren anyone could hunt on the demesne without the owner's leave, an offence punishable only under the law of trespass. Increasingly the monarchy and the wealthy and powerful would make themselves deer parks: enclosed hunting reserves for the enjoyment of themselves and their guests. In principle a licence to empark had to be granted by the Crown, but this requirement was by no means always observed.

All these private reserves were to some extent 'mini-forests'. The holder of the rights described above could prevent anyone else from hunting, and could, indeed, pass their entitlement on to their heirs. The difference between these rights and those under the Forest Law was that there was no dedicated legal system to enforce them. Redress against offenders had to be sought through the common law courts. Needless to say, the Crown exploited the granting of hunting rights in various ways in order to make money. It is also worth emphasising once more that in granting rights the Crown was, in effect, claiming control of hunting in the whole realm, not just in the royal forests. Theoretically, outside of the forests, chases, parks and warrens anyone could hunt anywhere. But in 1389, in the wake of the Peasants' Revolt, the first Game Law was passed. This stipulated a property qualification of 40 shillings a year for anyone wishing to hunt, even on their own land. Successive Game Laws tended to make property qualifications stricter. The Game Law enacted in 1610, for example, required different qualifications for hunting deer and rabbits, for hunting pheasants or partridges, and for possessing hunting dogs and nets. This was part of a process that sought to limit the pursuit of game to gentlemen and noblemen.[3]

Who hunted deer?

The discussion above sets out who, in theory, could hunt and where they could do it. But this is not quite the same as who did actually hunt. The forests had come into existence to act as game reserves and to provide sport for the kings and queens of England, but the popularity of such royal sport tended to wax and

2.   VCH Sussex, 2, pp. 316–24; VCH Buckinghamshire, 2, pp. 137–43.
3.   For more details on hunting rights and game laws, see Grant, Royal forests, pp. 10–32, and P.B. Munsche, Gentlemen and poachers: the English game laws 1671–1831 (Cambridge, 1981), pp. 8–14.

wane with the preferences of individual monarchs, which also governed their policies towards hunting rights and towards the forests and chases of England. The beginning of our period saw the death of Elizabeth and the accession of James I. It is part of the 'lore' of many books on the history of hunting that, with one or two regrettable exceptions, all English monarchs have been ardent devotees of the chase. Opinions on Elizabeth differ, however. Some portrayed her as a veritable Diana and others suggested that she was at best lukewarm to the sport, other than as a political tool.[4] The ambiguity seems to arise partly from differing attitudes to the type of hunting in which she took part. Elizabethan stag and buck hunts tended to be elaborate park-based pageants which, some maintained, were staged more to impress foreign ambassadors and other visiting dignitaries than to satisfy any 'genuine' sporting instincts. Even while Mary was still on the throne the Princess Elizabeth was the inspiration for elaborate hunting rituals. In April 1557 she was escorted from Hatfield to Enfield Chase by a retinue of twelve ladies 'clothed in white satin' and twenty yeomen in green, all on horseback, in order that she might 'hunt the hart'. On entering the chase she was met by fifty archers in scarlet boots and yellow caps, armed with gilded bows.[5] The writer 'Sabretache', with the eyes of a mid-twentieth-century foxhunter, characterised Elizabethan hunts as nothing more than 'colossal shoots with the crossbow'.[6] James I himself attributed the poor state of game preservation to the queen's lack of interest; he blamed this on her age, sex and lack of 'posteritie', which made her 'lesse carefull of conservation of that kind of Royaltie, which her progenitors kings of this Realme had maintained'.[7] But there are accounts of Elizabeth hunting deer 'by force' early in her reign, which was the method preferred by James himself.[8]

There is no doubt surrounding James's attitude towards hunting. His journey from Scotland to claim the English throne in 1603 took the form of a prolonged hunting expedition, with frequent stopovers to pursue stag, buck or hare.[9] Some portions of the journey were made more enjoyable for the new king by the laying of a trail with a 'tame deer' so James could hunt along the road as he travelled

4.   Rackham had her as 'the mightiest hunter of all English sovereigns', while Pettit believed Tresham's assertion that Elizabeth was not interested in hunting, suggesting that the Privy Council had to look after the interests of the deer in view of the queen's lack of real concern. Rackham, *Trees and Woodland*, p. 159; Pettit, *Royal forests*, p. 44.

5.   J. Nichols, *Progresses, public processes &c of Queen Elizabeth*, 3 vols (London, 1823), 1, pp. 11, 17.

6.   'Sabretache' (Barrow), *Monarchy and the chase* (London, 1948), p. 67. As was common with many hunting writers, Barrow adopted a pen name. A sabretache is the leather bag worn together with a sabre by Hussars.

7.   'Proclamation against Hunters, Stealers and Killers of Deare within any of the King's Majesties Forests, Chases and Parks', made September 1609, reproduced in E.P. Shirley, *Some account of English deer parks* (London, 1867), pp. 44–5.

8.   Nichols, *Progresses of Queen Elizabeth*, 1, p. 435. Hunting 'by force' is described below, p. 19.

9.   A. MacGregor, 'The household out of doors: the Stuart court and the animal kingdom' in E. Cruickshanks (ed.), *The Stuart courts* (Stroud, 2000), p. 86.

south.[10] So many of the early entries in the *Calendars of state papers* for his reign were concerned with warrants for the appointment of hunt staff and for the preservation of deer and game that the reader could be forgiven for thinking that James regarded his new kingdom principally as a vast hunting ground. Early in his reign James issued directives concerning the deer in the forests of Northamptonshire, and in August 1603 he appointed Thomas, Lord Burghley (later first earl of Exeter), keeper of Rockingham Forest, with particular instructions for protecting the 'much decayed and wasted' game and deer there.[11]

James's passion for hunting did not noticeably decline as his reign progressed. In 1624 Secretary Conway wrote to Lord Brooke, explaining that 'the French Ambassador and the Household have taken up all the time the King could spare from hunting'.[12] But while his ministers might pity him for how matters of state interrupted his pleasures, not everyone shared their sympathy. The interference with the business of running the state was remarked on by a number of foreign ambassadors. In 1606 the Venetian ambassador commented that the 'perpetual occupation with country pursuits', though 'possibly not distasteful to those who hold the reins of government', was 'extremely annoying to those who don't'. The same diplomat informed us that the king's subjects were hardly more favourably disposed to their ruler's obsession: 'The people too desire to see their sovereign. The discontent has reached such a pitch that the other day there was affixed to the door of the Privy Chamber a general complaint of the King.'[13] James clearly did not follow the advice he had given his eldest son that, whether hunting or hawking, he should 'observe that moderation that ye slip not the houres appointed for your affaires'.[14]

Next to the monarchy the group most commonly associated with hunting, and particularly with the hunting of deer, was the aristocracy. Accompanying the monarch as he or she hunted was a duty expected of the court aristocracy, and Elizabeth's elaborate hunting spectacles could hardly have taken place without their support. Even when the queen could not personally be present she could rely on her lords to host hunting extravaganza to keep visitors amused. An account by the private secretary of Frederick, duke of Wirtemberg, related how his master had been entertained after visiting the queen at Reading in 1592: 'It had pleased her Majesty to depute an old distinguished English lord ... to amuse him [the duke] with shooting and hunting red-deer.'[15] James also relied on the accompaniment

10. J. Nichols, *The progresses, processions and magnificent festivities, of King James the First*, 4 vols (London, 1828), I, p. 139.
11. *CSPD Elizabeth and James I, Addenda 1580–1625* (London, 1872) p. 427; *CSPD James I, 1603–1610* (London, 1857), pp. 32, 161.
12. *CSPD James I, 1623–1625* (London, 1859), p. 295.
13. Cited in MacGregor 'The household out of doors', p. 86.
14. King James, *Basilicon Doron* (1599; Menston, 1969), p. 145.
15. Cited in Shirley, *Deer parks*, p. 40.

of an enthusiastic aristocratic coterie. Another Venetian diplomat described a hunt in 1618 where the king was accompanied by 'a number of cavaliers riding the quickest horses'. After personally slitting the deer's throat, his hands covered in blood, James was 'wont to regale some of his nobility by touching their faces. This blood it is unlawful to wash off, until it fall of its own accord.' Any courtier lucky enough to receive this treatment was considered to have 'a certificate of his sovereign's cordial good will'.[16]

The nobility also hunted of their own accord. John Smyth, in his *Lives of the Berkeleys*, wrote about the dedication to the chase of Henry, Lord Berkeley (whose life began under Henry VIII and ended under James). When living in London with his mother, the same Berkeley occupied himself with 'daily hunting in the Grays Inne fields and in all those parts towards Islington and Heygate with his hounds'.[17] Later he spent every summer in 'a progress of buck hunting' around his various parks from Leicestershire to Gloucestershire, a practice he kept up for some thirty years.[18] There are also numerous examples of the Crown granting warrants to the nobility to allow them to hunt in royal preserves, such as that issued to John, Lord Mordaunt (later first earl of Peterborough), in July 1623 permitting him to hunt and kill a specified number of deer in the forests of Rockingham, Whittlewood and Salcey and the parks of Grafton and Ampthill.[19] The aristocracy kept their own packs of hounds and hunted both on their own lands and in royal forests and parks. The hunting of deer was clearly an important part of the aristocratic lifestyle.

So far the picture of hunting that has been drawn accords with the expectation that hunting was a pastime of the privileged, with the pursuit of deer and game restricted to the monarchy and those whom the king or queen authorised to hunt. But we should be wary of this interpretation, and contrast the situation in England with that in France and other parts of Europe, where hunting was restricted to the monarchy and the court aristocracy. Carr reckoned that the right to hunt had, in fact, spread steadily downwards and quoted *Moryson's Itinerary*, claiming that, at the end of the sixteenth century, 'every gentleman of five hundred or a thousand pounds rent by the yeere hath a Parke'.[20] We must consider such gentlemen, and the extent to which they hunted. Deer parks were, in many ways, an aspirational statement: a means of demonstrating one's wealth and status by setting aside a large acreage of ground mainly for entertainment and pleasure. Parks also demonstrated the gentry's ambitions to imitate their social superiors' interest in hunting. Not all contemporaries approved of the fashion: *Holinshed's Chronicles*

---

16. Cited in MacGregor, 'The household out of doors', p. 99.
17. J. Smyth, *The Berkeley manuscripts: lives of the Berkeleys*, ed. J. MacLean, 3 vols (Gloucester, 1883), 2, p. 281.
18. Smyth, *Berkeleys*, 2, p. 285.
19. *CSPD James I, 1623–1625*, p. 11.
20. Carr, *English foxhunting*, p. 19.

bemoaned the amount of early sixteenth-century land 'employed upon that vayne comodotie which bringeth no manner of gaine or profit to the owner', claiming that some twentieth part of the realm 'is employed upon Deere and Coneys already'.[21] There is ample literary evidence, however, that hunting was considered to be a fit and proper pastime for a gentleman. Many books published in the early modern period were either entirely concerned with hunting or had large sections dedicated to the sport. For example, there were two separate works entitled The gentleman's recreation; neither was entirely dedicated to hunting, but both gave it prominence as a gentlemanly pastime. These works, and similar ones, were revised and reprinted into the eighteenth century.[22]

It should also be noted that hunting was not an exclusively rural pastime. It was perfectly possible to be an urban resident and participate. When Henry, Lord Berkeley, hunted while staying with his mother in London he had 'the company of many gentlemen of the Innes of Court'. Smyth also adds, rather intriguingly, 'and others of lower condition that daily accompanied him'.[23] This raises another point: whether a passion for hunting had in fact spread yet further down the social scale. In principle, anybody below a certain level was forbidden from hunting legitimately by the Forest Laws or the Game Laws, and this has been taken as evidence by some that it was a pursuit of the elite. But such an interpretation ignores the fact that many people would have been needed to assist with the process of hunting, some of whom would have performed quite menial tasks. Yeomen could also share a common culture with gentlemen because their sons frequently became servants in the households of peers and gentlemen. Their role required them to become proficient in the occupations and pastimes of their masters, and able to entertain master and guests with table talk on such matters. In the Lives of the Berkeleys Smyth reproduces instructions regarding how the gentlemen and yeomen servants of the household were expected to conduct themselves.[24] In addition to household servants, specialist huntsmen would be employed and other, more lowly, staff were required to look after the hounds and the horses.

---

21. W. Holinshed, Chronicles of England, Ireland and Scotland (London, 1587), p. 205.
22. N. Cox, The gentleman's recreation (London, 1674); R. Blome, The gentleman's recreation (London, 1686); G. Markham, Countrey contentments (1615; New York, 1973).
23. Smyth, Berkeleys, 2, p. 281.
24. This touched on conduct in the house and without, including the following two strictures: 'That noe gentleman come into the great chamber without his cloake or livery coate; And when there are strangers, to bee all or most part in the dining chamber after dinner and supper, to shew themselves and doe such service as cause shall require', and 'When the lady shall ride abroad, the yeoman usher to discharge his duty Riding abroad in causing the yeomen appointed to ride to keep togeather, without tarrying behind their company and scattering abroade; And when they come through any Town, the yeoman usher to place them by two and two orderly.' Smyth, Berkeleys, 2, pp. 365–6.

Information about the personnel required for a hunting establishment can be recovered from the records of the royal hunts. In 1604 the officers of the privy buckhounds comprised the master, two sergeants, eleven yeomen prickers, six grooms and one waggoner. In addition to the privy pack, the royal hunting establishment included a hereditary buckhound pack, a harthound pack, an otterhound pack and a pack of harriers. There were also establishments for the keeping of the toils, which were nets and other contraptions required for hunting. The *Calendars of state papers* contain many references to the appointments and remuneration of hunt servants and also allow us to trace incidences of promotion. For example, Richard Brass was appointed yeoman pricker in November 1603 and in October 1607 became a sergeant.[25] Robert Rayne was one of five yeomen prickers added to the privy pack shortly after James's accession. By July 1609 he was a sergeant and in receipt of a commission to hunt in any grounds, parks, forests and chases belonging to the king or his subjects in order to train the hounds.[26] We get some clue as to the social standing of the staff of the privy pack from their listing in the pack's 1604 expense accounts: the master was an esquire, as was the sergeant, but grooms and yeoman prickers lacked this distinction. The master, Thomas Tyringham, was knighted soon after.[27] The privy buckhounds must be considered one of the most elite hunting establishments in the country, but there is evidence that professional hunters in other households enjoyed a privileged position. When a new steward was appointed to the Berkeley household the huntsmen and falconers were explicitly excluded from the instructions the steward was given for 'displacing whomsoever he found in his house disorderly'.[28]

Outside the formal hunting establishments the opportunities to participate could spread down the social scale in other ways. Some tenants owed their lords hunting services as part of their tenancy. The customary tenants of Sutton Coldfield, Warwickshire, owed labour services that included two days' deer driving for every yardland they held, and the burgesses of Bishops Castle, Shropshire, were required to drive deer three times a year or find a substitute.[29] Lacking first-hand accounts from those drafted in to help, we have no way of knowing whether such hunting duty was regarded as an onerous burden or a bit of light relief (the lucky tenants of Sutton Coldfield were given venison as an additional reward for their labour), but at least we do know that this was another way in which people took part.

In considering who did hunt around 1600 we have worked our way down from monarch to peasant, and have considered legal participation in hunting

25. *CSPD James I, 1603–1610*, pp. 53, 374.
26. *CSPD James I, 1603–1610*, p. 526.
27. J.P. Hore, *The history of the royal buckhounds* (Newmarket, 1895), pp. 98, 114.
28. Smyth, *Berkeleys*, 2, p. 364.
29. Cited in R.B. Manning, *Hunters and poachers: a social and cultural history of unlawful hunting in England, 1485–1640* (Oxford, 1993), p. 18.

whether under the jurisdiction of the Forest Laws or the Game Laws. People often disregarded the law, however, and we should also consider the question of who stole deer as well as who hunted them.

Illicit hunting

The *Calendars of state papers* furnish examples of deer stealing in Northamptonshire as well as elsewhere. In June 1609 the king wrote to Sir Christopher Hatton complaining of the state of game in Benefield (Rockingham Forest) 'being much spoiled by unlawful hunting'.[30] In July 1622 a warrant was made for the Lieutenant of Whittlewood Forest to 'search out suspected persons who, in warlike manner, with pistols, swords and bucklers, made spoil of the game in Grafton Parks'.[31] It has been suggested that illicit hunters came from all social groups, with the range of people displaying an equally varied range of motives, among which were: hunting to provide the commercial market with venison; hunting as an expression of violent feuds between gentry and noble factions; 'skimmingtons' in which a local community would attempt to punish possessors of game rights who they considered had overstepped the mark in some way; and hunting as an expression of discontent by those who considered themselves disenfranchised of some existing right to hunt.[32] The hunting of deer was a cooperative venture and many poaching gangs comprised men of mixed social standing, often led by a gentleman.

The history of the Berkeley family provides some accounts of hunting as an expression of feud and illustrates the mixed nature of such gangs. A dispute over the descent of the manor of Mangotsfield led to an almost comical episode between Henry, Lord Berkeley's mother, Anne, and his uncle, Maurice. Maurice, together with his brother-in-law and a 'riotous company of servants and others', entered Anne's park at Yate and set about wantonly destroying her deer. They decided to end a good night's work by setting fire to a great hayrick, but, unbeknown to them, there was 'another company of hunters – in the same park stealing also of this ladies deere'. Perceiving Maurice's band to be the stronger of the two, the other poachers had hidden themselves in the hayrick. On overhearing Maurice's incendiary plans, they decided their best course was to flee. Maurice's band mistook them for keepers and 'fled as fast another way'. This episode rather neatly illustrates a group out for revenge encountering another group presumably out for profit or enjoyment.[33] In our study area in the late seventeenth century a similar, but lower-key, expression of rivalry caused Edward, Lord Rockingham, to attempt to hunt the Lawn of Benefield without a

30. *CSPD James I, 1603–1610*, p. 518.
31. *CSPD James I, 1619–1623* (London, 1858), p. 432.
32. These arguments have been made in detail in Manning, *Hunters and Poachers*, p. 2.
33. Smyth, *Berkeleys*, 2, p. 268.

warrant. Lady Hatton, writing to inform her husband of the incident, reported that 'everyone says it was done as an affront to you'.[34] The seventeenth century also saw a feud over the enlargement of Stowe Park, near Whittlewood Forest, that involved the Temple family and their servants in confrontation with the Dayrell family and theirs. Episodes in the 1630s and 1640s saw the killing of deer in the park by intruders and the Temples' attempt to prevent deer that had escaped from the park from being hunted in the purlieus.[35]

Further illustrations of deer stealing can be drawn from Northamptonshire. Events at Brigstock in Rockingham Forest in 1603 demonstrate how people might have expressed their disapproval of some lordly action while simultaneously stocking their larders. Keepers of Robert Cecil's park at Brigstock were intent on pulling down the park pale and driving the deer into the forest. The villagers of Brigstock and Stanion considered this to be a bad idea (presumably mindful of the damage to their crops these extra deer were likely to inflict as well as the loss of common rights that they held in the park) and stood upon the pale to keep the deer back. Nevertheless, 400 or 500 deer were put into the forest and so the villagers tried to console themselves with venison. The people assembled apparently killed nine or ten deer and 'carried them by force to their own houses'. The list of deer stealers in the state papers included an underkeeper in Rockingham Forest and a sometime keeper in Brigstock Park: an incident of gamekeepers turned poachers, perhaps.[36] The Northampton Quarter Session records provide an example of an individual who killed a fallow deer in Whittlewood, but who was too poor to pay his fine. In 1699 Henry Jerome of Paulerspury was fined £30, of which £10 was to go to the poor, £10 to the informer and £10 to Captain Rider (who was the dowager Queen Catherine's tenant in her Whittlewood estates); but the constable was unable to recover goods to the value of £30, and so the unfortunate Henry was remitted to gaol. There is no indication as to whether he acted alone or with other, perhaps wealthier, people.[37]

Hunting methods

Before we can explore the relationship of hunting with the landscape, we need to understand what people were actually doing when hunting. Hunting in this period was a diverse process: the methods employed depended not only on what was being hunted but on where, when and why. In early modern England two species of deer were considered to be worthy quarry: the red deer and the fallow

34. NRO, Finch Hatton archive: FH4389.
35. Beaver used this conflict to illustrate the complex interrelationship between a politics of honour, status and reputation in this period and the role that hunting played in the drama. D.C. Beaver, *Hunting and the politics of violence before the English civil war* (Cambridge, 2008), pp. 32–54.
36. *CSPD Addenda 1580–1625*, p. 317. The CSPD wrongly dates these occurrences to 1590.
37. NRO, Quarter Session Records: QSR1/173/24. For more examples of poaching in Northamptonshire parks and forests, see below, p. 54.

deer (the roe deer had been hunted historically but its pursuit was not widespread or popular by 1600). There were distinct hunting seasons that were recognised and respected, at least by those hunting within the law. Male deer (red deer stags and fallow deer bucks) were hunted in the summer, generally from mid-June to mid-September. At this time the stags and bucks were fully antlered and in prime condition (described as 'in grease'). Hunting ceased as they entered the rut in the autumn. Female deer (red deer hinds and fallow does) were hunted over the winter. This ceased when the females produced calves and fauns, and during this so-called 'fence month', which occurred immediately before the opening of the male deer season, no deer were hunted at all. The answer to the question of 'when' a deer was hunted is likely to determine the sex of the deer being pursued.[38] As to 'where', the two principal locations were the forest and the deer park. We have already mentioned the popularity of the deer park in the sixteenth century. Private deer parks could be small, while royal deer parks could be very large indeed: there was some 1000 acres of parkland for Henry VIII to enjoy at Grafton in Northamptonshire, and, at around 4500 acres, Clarendon Park in Wiltshire was reputedly the largest in the land.[39] Nevertheless, given the confined nature of the deer park it was inevitable that the techniques used there would differ from those of hunting 'at large'. So far we have largely concentrated on hunting as a source of recreation and entertainment, but it had a practical side too: venison was both a useful food source and a valued gift. The Crown regularly ordered hunting in its forests and parks to harvest deer for these purposes, and James's state papers give numerous examples of warrants being issued to permit such hunting and the giving of such gifts.[40] Similarly, other owners of deer parks would have their servants take deer as required.

In discovering how men pursued stag, buck, hind and doe in forest or park, for fun or for meat, we can take advantage of the fact that hunting had always been a popular subject in literature. Several notable medieval treatises on hunting survive, both from Europe and from England. These include the *Livre de chase*, of the late fourteenth century, and Edward, Duke of York's *Master of game*, of the early fifteenth century. At the end of that century came Dame Juliana Berner's *Boke of St. Albans*, which was concerned with hunting, hawking and fishing.[41] Later works on hunting were produced in the sixteenth century by Gascoigne and by Cockaine,

---

38. Blome, *Gentleman's recreation*, pp. 77, 81–6; Cox, *Gentleman's recreation*, pp. 13–31.
39. *VCH Northamptonshire*, 5, p. 20; T. Beaumont James and C. Gerrard, *Clarendon: landscape of kings* (Macclesfield, 2007), p. 10.
40. For example, *CSPD James I, 1619–1623*, p. 278, *CPSD: James I, 1623–1625*, pp. 33, 321.
41. Gaston Phoebus, *Livre de chase*, commentary by W. Schlag (London, 1998); Edward of Norwich, *The master of game*, eds W.A. and F.N. Baillie-Grohman (1909; Philadelphia, PA, 2005); Juliana Berners, *English hawking and hunting in 'The Boke of St Albans': a facsimile edition of sigs a2–f8 of 'The Boke of St Albans'* (Oxford, 1975).

and in the seventeenth century by writers such as Markham, Blome and Cox.[42] The subject of hunting also made appearances in contemporary plays, figuring largely in those of Shakespeare, which has spawned a lively debate on the bard's own attitude to the chase.[43]

It was generally agreed that the highest form of hunting available to the Englishman in the late medieval and early modern period was the pursuit of the mature red deer stag (called a hart to distinguish him from younger and less worthy quarry). The hart should be hunted at large *par force des chiens*. The early modern sources follow the medieval ones in dividing such a hunt into distinct stages: the harbouring (or finding) of the hart, the rousing of him, the chase, the standing at bay, and finally the reward of the hounds (known as the *curée*).[44] Each stage had its own special rituals and considerations. The importance of the selection of the animal to be hunted should not be understated. The aim was to find a 'warrantable' hart: that is, one mature and impressive enough to command attention. The sources, from Phoebus to Blome, largely agree on the methods used to locate such a quarry. The men who were to harbour the hart (Figure 2.1) set off at dawn, taking a hound called a lymer with them (the nearest modern equivalent is a bloodhound). Ideally the searchers would be able to observe the stags as they grazed in the open, select a likely one, and then follow him back to his lair. They would be aided in this quest by their knowledge of how to sex and age a deer through his hoofprints (slots), his droppings (fumes or fewmets) and the marks he left when rubbing his antlers on trees. The harbouring served the triple purpose of finding a suitable animal, locating his hiding place and accustoming the lymer to his scent.[45] The whole technique relied on the hart being a creature of habit. Blome observed that, during the hunting season, the hart 'retires from feeding back to his layre, about sun-rising; and for the most part, if not always, to one and the same place'.[46]

The next stage was the rousing of the hart. This was accomplished by the lymerer and his hound accompanied, at some distance, by other unmounted men bringing couples of running hounds. In the meantime more couples of hounds would be posted with their handlers in 'relays' along the line it was predicted

---

42. George Gascoigne, *The noble arte of venerie or hunting* (London, 1575); Thomas Cockaine, *A short treatise of hunting* (London, 1591); Markham, *Countrey contentments*; Blome, *Gentleman's recreation*; Cox, *Gentleman's recreation*.

43. See E. Berry, *Shakespeare and the hunt* (Cambridge, 2002) and C. Fitter, 'The slain deer and politic imperium: *As You Like It* and Andrew Marvell's "Nymph Complaining for the Death of Her Fawn"', *Journal of English and Germanic Philology*, 98 (1999), pp. 193–218.

44. Edward of Norwich, *Master of game*, p. 29.

45. Edward of Norwich, *Master of game*, pp. 148–51; Blome, *Gentleman's recreation*, p. 82; Phoebus, *Livre de chase*, pp. 41–5. Phoebus suggested that the hart be harboured the day before the hunt, while Edward recommended the morning of the hunt.

46. Blome, *Gentleman's recreation*, p. 82.

Figure 2.1 *Unharbouring ye Stagg*. Illustration from R. Blome, *The Gentleman's Recreation* (London, 1686) © Trustees of the British Museum.

the hart would take. The company would keep in touch using horn calls, and when the hunters saw the hart break (and provided they were happy that it was the right animal) a signal was given for the handlers of the running hounds to let their hounds slip. The next stage, the chase, then began as the hounds picked up the scent and set off in pursuit of the hart. The mounted huntsmen followed the running hounds at much greater speed and helped to keep the hart to his course. If all proceeded according to plan, the relays would let the extra hounds go just after the hart passed in order to quicken the chase and reinvigorate the pack if it was flagging.

Eventually, it was hoped, the hart would be run to exhaustion and would turn and stand at bay. Blome suggested that, if it was early in the season and the hart's antlers were tender, he be allowed to stand until all the hounds arrived, as he was unlikely to gore those that held him. Later in the season the hart should be despatched quickly, by sword or crossbow, lest he injure or kill some of the hounds.[47] Once the hart was dead there followed a great 'undoing' as, with due ceremony, the hart was butchered where he lay. The portions were allocated according to a defined custom, with the lymer and running hounds being rewarded with the *curée* – portions of the carcass laid out on the animal's hide. The evening might see a feast in which participants in the hunt could relive the day's pleasures in their retelling.[48]

There are several points to note about the progress of the hunt as described by the sources. The importance of selecting the animal to be hunted and of pursuing that exact animal has been alluded to. The area in which the animal was to be hunted and the course it was desired that the hunt should take were, as far as possible, both planned in advance, taking advantage of local knowledge and an understanding of how deer behaved (for example, preferring to run with the wind, and liking to retreat to water).[49] The location might be a forest or a park.[50] The role of the hounds was paramount; medieval sources gave no consideration to the horse. Blome complained that, in his day, it was the horse more often than the hound that seemed to hunt the hart, signifying some shift in emphasis of which he did not approve.[51] Even though the horse was becoming more significant, it should be noted, nevertheless, that many of the hunt servants were on foot. Unmounted men continued to be vital to the sport.[52]

Fallow deer could also be hunted in this way, although a buck was generally accounted not so worthy a quarry. Blome reckoned that if you could hunt a hart

---

47. Blome, *Gentleman's recreation*, p. 84.
48. Edward of Norwich, *Master of game*, p. 180; Blome, *Gentleman's recreation*, p. 84.
49. Cockaine, *Short treatise*, p. C3.
50. Edward of Norwich, *Master of game*, p. 148.
51. Blome, *Gentleman's recreation*, p. 83. The importance of the horse in early forms of hunting is discussed in depth in Chapter 5.
52. Edward of Norwich, *Master of game*, p. 165.

or a stag then 'you can't hunt a buck ill'. The main difference lay in the start of the hunt, when the huntsman did not harbour a buck, but rather 'lodged' him. Both terms referred to tracing a male deer back to his lair, but a buck was not unharboured with a lymer in the same formal way, but rather roused with the hounds who were to chase him. This lodging did not apparently require the same degree of woodcraft as harbouring, as the hunter could simply follow the buck back to the lair. Blome expected the buck to be more commonly hunted in a park than 'at large' and asserted that the greatest skill was to keep the hounds from running counter (following the scent backwards) or changing to another beast 'in regard of the plenty of fallow deer which are usually in the same ground'.[53]

There were other methods of hunting too. Bow and stable hunting was popular under Elizabeth, but much derided by some later writers on hunting. The aim of such a hunt was to have a large number of harts running past a standing where hunters were waiting with bows at the ready to shoot them. Greyhounds were then loosed to chase and bring down wounded deer. The 'stable' was a group of men strategically placed to ensure that the deer ran the intended course, past the standings. Fewterers were required to take charge of the greyhounds (swift hounds who hunted by sight rather than by scent), and carters were needed to pick up the deer carcasses and transport them to the place of the *curée*. Here the hounds were rewarded, and the venison and deer skins divided among the hunt's participants.[54] This form of hunting clearly demanded less exertion from the occupants of the standings than did hunting *par force*, and was consequently popular as a form of entertainment. In Elizabeth's time it could be made even easier; when she hunted at Cowdray in Sussex some thirty deer were driven into a paddock to be shot from the standings. Elizabeth accounted personally for three or four of them. Later that evening the queen retired to a turret to watch sixteen more bucks being brought down by greyhounds.[55]

There is some question as to what degree the *par force* method was pursued in the Elizabethan period even by the social elite. There is evidence that they preferred less physically demanding methods, as so many allusions to hunting contain references to bows or crossbows. When Smyth talked of Katherine, Lord Berkeley's first wife, accompanying her husband hunting, he described the activity as 'delighting her crosbowe'.[56] In 1580 William, Lord Burghley, wrote to the earl of Leicester to thank him for a hound he had sent him and talked of 'a stagg, wch myself had strychen with my bow'. James I was fairly contemptuous of hunting other than by *par force des chiens*, however, commenting that 'It is a thievish forme of hunting to shoote with gunnes and bowes' (although there are accounts that he did

53. Blome, *Gentleman's recreation*, p. 85.
54. Edward of Norwich, *Master of game*, pp. 188–96.
55. Shirley, *Deer parks*, p. 40.
56. Smyth, *Berkeleys*, p. 285.

occasionally 'lower' himself to hunt in these ways).[57] It is worth considering that perhaps renewed royal interest led to something of a revival in hunting *par force*.

Blome also gave a description of the coursing of deer with greyhounds which, he said, was 'a great esteem with many of the gentry'. Coursing of deer could take place in paddock, forest or purlieu. The 'paddock', a formal, purpose-built structure, was most commonly taken out of a park, and needed to be about a mile long and a quarter of a mile wide, with 'the further end broader than the nearer'. The whole was enclosed within pales or a wall. At the start of the paddock were boxes for the greyhound, a box for the 'teaser' hound, and a pen for the deer. At the far end there was a ditch. The teaser (a mongrel greyhound) started the deer running, after which the greyhounds (usually two, but sometimes up to four) were slipped. Money was put on the outcome, with the winner being the hound that made the deer swerve (so long as this occurred past the 'pinching post' that was the halfway mark) or that first jumped the ditch after the deer. Some remnants of these deer-coursing paddocks survive, such as the 'pady course' at Clarendon Park and the viewing stand at Lodge Park, near Northleach in Gloucestershire.[58] In forest or purlieu two methods were apparently available: deer were either coursed 'from wood to wood' or upon lawns in front of the keeper's lodge. In the first method some hounds were thrown into the wood to bring out the deer, and the handlers waited to let the greyhounds slip when some 'worthy' deer emerged. If coursing on a lawn, notice was given to the keeper to lodge a deer fit for the course.[59]

There were many variations on the ways of hunting deer so far described that incorporated features from one or more of the methods. An account of hunting in the deer park at Kirtling, near Cambridge, in the mid-seventeenth century has 'the keeper, with a large cross-bow and arrow, to wound the deer, and two or three disciplined park hounds pursued till he dropped'.[60] This seems to have been a method adopted when the aim of the exercise was the taking of meat rather than the provision of entertainment. There were also variations on hunting *par force*: the duke of Saxe-Weimar describes hunting at Theobalds, in Hertfordshire, with James I, during which the king surveyed a herd of deer and selected the one that he wanted to hunt, after which the huntsman set dogs on and pursued that animal. (The duke was somewhat contemptuous of this exercise because, in the course of the whole hunt, only two animals were caught.)[61] This method accords

---

57. King James, *Basilicon Doron*, p. 144.
58. For a description of Clarendon Park's pady course, see A. Richardson, *The forest, park and palace of Clarendon, c.1200–c.1650: reconstructing an actual, conceptual and documented Wiltshire landscape* (Oxford, 2005), pp. 80–82. Taylor found evidence of a 'paddock course' at Stowe, presumably removed during eighteenth-century landscaping. C. Taylor, 'Ravendale Park, Derbyshire and medieval deer coursing', *Landscape History*, 26 (2004), p. 46.
59. Blome, *Gentleman's recreation*, pp. 96–7.
60. Shirley, *Deer parks*, p. 49.
61. Shirley, *Deer parks*, p. 46.

with the description of buck hunting in a park from horseback given by Thomas Cockaine.[62] In 1669 the grand duke of Tuscany described a hunt in the company of Prince Rupert where deer were driven into nets by dogs and then released. Nets were a favourite tool of poachers, too. A 1538 investigation of deer stealers in Kent found that one man was employing a net-maker in his house. Nets could be used to entrap running deer or to steer them in a desired direction. Other methods included the use of stalking horses to approach the deer (with bowmen firing from behind the horse), the use of fire to drive deer and even the use of a long-gun with multiple shot.[63]

The hunting of the deer was, thus, far from homogeneous in method. Some animals were pursued 'at large', but probably more were hunted within the confines of a park. Some animals were pursued on horseback, but all methods seem to have involved the participation of unmounted men. Most animals were pursued with dogs, but there were ways of taking deer without canine assistance. Some hunts involved elaborate ritual and considerable organisation and manpower, but where the taking of meat was the primary aim of the exercise the process seems to have been far more low-key and pedestrian.

Conclusion

The methods described above suggest that what deer hunting required was a landscape of the 'find', rather than a landscape of the 'chase'. All of the advice on the hunting of deer available in early modern England concentrated on the finding and flushing of the beast rather than on its pursuit. The best surroundings for the preservation of both red and fallow deer were considered to be a mixture of wood, wood pasture and open rough grazing (or lawns). These provided the deer with shelter, grass to graze and browse to help them through the winter.

Unlike later sources relating to modern foxhunting, our deer hunting sources contain next to no descriptions of the actual pursuit of the prey (other than for some royal occasions which tended to emphasise pageantry rather than place). Consequently we have no detailed description of the terrain over which such hunts were conducted. Even without explicit descriptions of the chase, however, we can infer from the available evidence that the pursuit of the deer was very different from the pursuit of the fox in a modern hunt. Chasing deer must have been a much slower affair if the men on foot were expected to keep up with the action. These men would doubtless be running rather than walking, but could not be expected to match the 20–30 miles per hour at which a modern horse could gallop. Such a slow chase could be effected in a variety of landscapes.

To summarise, the most important aspect of a deer-hunting landscape was the certainty of finding a suitable beast to pursue. The ability of the personnel involved

62. Cockaine, *Short treatise*, p. 10.
63. Manning, *Hunters and poachers*, pp. 25–6.

to select the correct deer was important because there were separate seasons for male and female deer, and also because only males over a certain age were deemed fit to hunt. While it may be true that, by the early modern period, hunting in a park was more common than hunting at large, the forest retained its importance as a breeding ground from which to stock the parks.[64] The study of the personnel involved and the methods and techniques that they employed outlined above gives us a much clearer idea of what we are looking for when we come to examine the Northamptonshire forests in the context of hunting landscapes.

64.   The CSPD for the reigns of James I and Charles I contain numerous examples of John Scandiver transporting live deer around the realm at the behest of the monarch. For example, see CSPD James I, 1619–1623, pp. 377, 488; CSPD James I, 1623–1625, pp. 408, 423.

3

The landscape of deer hunting

When thinking of royal hunting forests, Northamptonshire does not necessarily spring to mind. The county lies firmly within that area of England described as the 'central province' by Roberts and Wrathmell. There has been broad agreement among landscape historians as to the defining characteristics of this area, which ran in a north-east–south-west band from the North Sea to the English Channel. It is the landscape of the medieval open fields, overlain in the eighteenth and early nineteenth centuries by the straight, thin hawthorn hedges of parliamentary enclosure. This is the landscape typified as 'champion' or 'open'.[1] Many early writers followed Camden's example in describing Northamptonshire's open and populous nature in terms of the number of churches you could see from a single vantage point.[2] Morton went so far as to recommend certain viewing points, the best being between Great Billing and Overstone, from which you could see forty-five churches (including two in Buckinghamshire).[3] The county is characterised by gentle undulations, rather than precipitous climbs, and to see so many distant churches from a single vantage point would require an open landscape containing few trees and hedges in order to maximise the view.

A large swathe of Northamptonshire most definitely did not conform to the expectations of champion countryside, however. This was the band of royal forest that traversed the county from south-west to north-east. Although the bounds of the forests were much reduced by 1600, Rockingham, Whittlewood and Salcey still occupied a significant portion of the county and still contained a significant area of wood and wood pasture (as did the adjoining disafforested areas). Northamptonshire had a contemporary reputation for being a tree-less landscape, but early writers were keen to defend it from this, which Norden reckoned did 'most of all to blemish the shire'. He observed that many places were 'well stor'd',

---

1.   B. Roberts and S. Wrathmell, *Region and place: a study of English rural settlement* (London, 2002).
2.   W. Camden, *Britannia or a geographical description of Great Britain and Ireland*, 2nd edn (London, 1722), p. 511.
3.   J. Morton, *Natural history of Northamptonshire* (London, 1712), p. 22.

especially around the forests.[4] A century later Morton concurred: in woodland resources, the county was 'not so destitute as 'tis commonly imagined'.[5]

The Roberts and Wrathmell model builds on the work of landscape historians of the preceding forty years. These studies tended to dwell on the role of the countryside as a unit of economic production. Leisure and sport as shaping forces were considered as secondary aspects, if they were considered at all. It is time to examine the landscape of Northamptonshire, and how it developed between 1600 and 1850, in terms of recreation as well as of agricultural production.

The Northamptonshire forests

Studies of the Northamptonshire forests have stressed the duality of their position within the county. On the one hand, the forest areas had much in common with the rest of Northamptonshire: arable agriculture was practised predominantly in open fields, cultivated in common, and settlements tended to be nucleated rather than dispersed. On the other hand, the forest areas contained large tracts of woodland, which set them apart from the rest of the county.[6] None of the county's forests lay in particularly favoured areas. Whittlewood and Salcey were situated on a low (120 metres) watershed between the Ouse and the Nene and were characterised by surface geology comprising cold, intractable clays. Rockingham Forest occupied a more extensive area lying between the Nene and the Welland, where heavy clay soils again predominated. In many ways, woodland was probably the best use for these areas, explaining the persistence of woodland in places where land had been disafforested and alienated. But all of the forest areas were to some degree amenable to arable cultivation and to use as pasture; they were far from being tractless, uninhabited wastes. Recently, evidence has been found that arable cultivation predominated in the Whittlewood area in the Roman period, and woodland subsequently recolonised the area (and possibly was encouraged to do so by the designation of the area as a royal hunting ground well in advance of the Norman Conquest).[7] By 1600 the extent of Northamptonshire's royal forest was much reduced from its thirteenth-century peak, but the influence of forest status extended beyond the forest's recognised boundaries. Villages lying outside the forest perambulation still benefited from common rights to grazing, fuel and other forest resources, while holders of purlieu land were still restricted in terms of their rights to pursue deer that strayed onto their lands from the forest.

Salcey (Figure 3.1) was by far the smallest of the three Northamptonshire forests. At the beginning of the seventeenth century it occupied a total of some

---

4.   J. Norden, *Speculi Britannie pars altera or a delineation of Northamptonshire* (London, 1720), p. 39. (This was originally prepared in 1591.)
5.   Morton, *Natural history*, p. 12.
6.   Pettit, *Royal forests*, pp. 3–5.
7.   R. Jones and M. Page, *Medieval villages in an English landscape: beginnings and ends* (Macclesfield, 2006), p. 61.

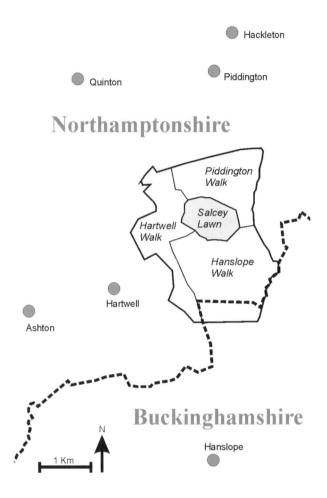

Figure 3.1 Salcey Forest.

1847 acres, comprising 1100 acres of coppice surrounding the open pasture of Salcey Lawn. For administrative purposes the forest was divided into four 'walks', with the lawn itself comprising one of them. Six villages enjoyed common rights in the forest, including the large Buckinghamshire village of Hanslope.

Whittlewood (Figure 3.2) was considerably larger than Salcey, with a total area exceeding 6000 acres. Around the year 1600 over 4500 of these acres were woodland. Administratively the forest was divided into six walks, two of which, Shrob and Handley, were detached from the main body of the forest. The villages enjoying common rights within Whittlewood were divided into seven 'in-towns' and nine 'out-towns', with the former entitled to a longer period of access to forest resources than the latter. Some of the forest villages lay in Northamptonshire and some in Buckinghamshire.

Figure 3.2 Whittlewood Forest.

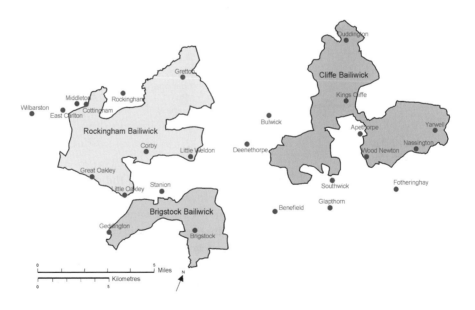

Figure 3.3 Rockingham Forest.

The largest of the three forests was Rockingham (Figure 3.3). The 1641 perambulation suggests a length of fifteen miles and a width of five miles. Such was its size that it was divided into three 'bailiwicks', which were further subdivided into walks. Cliffe Bailiwick was sometimes treated as a separate forest in its own right, and twelve villages enjoyed common rights within it. The other two bailiwicks, Rockingham and Brigstock, were more closely linked together both physically and administratively. Ten villages had common rights in Rockingham Bailiwick, while only three villages had such rights in Brigstock Bailiwick. Rockingham Forest also differed from the forests towards the south-west of the county in that more of its woodlands tended to lie in private hands, whereas in Salcey and Whittlewood woodland was royal demesne.

How far did the royal forests of Northamptonshire continued to fulfil their original purpose as hunting reserves at the beginning of the seventeenth century? Was the landscape of the forest still suitable for the preservation and nurturing of deer, and was hunting still actively pursued in these areas? What changes occurred in the forests in all these areas in the years 1600–1850 and, is there evidence of the shrinkage of deer habitat and population across this period? Although the purpose of this study is to look beyond purely economic explanations of landscape use, it would be foolish to ignore this aspect altogether. Wood and timber certainly had value, and early modern man was adept at woodland management.[8] It is important, therefore, to examine how economic exploitation was combined with preservation of deer and whether the two uses proved incompatible.

The forest landscape

In his *Treatise of the Forrest Lawes* Manwood described the landscape required for a forest to fulfil its functions. It must comprise 'a territory of woody ground, stored with great woods of coverts for the secret abode of wild beasts, and also with fruitful pastures for their continual feed'.[9] An eighteenth-century copy of a large-scale map of Whittlewood in 1608 provides the opportunity to assess the forest's provision of 'woody ground' and 'fruitful pasture', and its alignment with more modern notions of a forest.[10] The map shows the woodland within the forest area occupying one large area with Shrob Walk forming a smaller outlying section (Handley Walk was omitted from the map altogether). Closer examination of the map reveals the division of the woodland into coppiced compartments (variously called 'coppice', 'copse' or 'sale'). Coppicing involved cutting the trees down to their base on a regular cycle and then harvesting the shoots that grew when they reached a certain thickness. Low coppice was typically interspersed with 'standard'

8.   Rackham made this observation for the country at large and Pettit for Northamptonshire in particular: Rackham, *Trees and woodland*; Pettit, *Royal forests*.

9.   Manwood, *Treatise*, f. 1. Much more recently Rackham characterised the forest landscape as being primarily wood pasture: rough grazing with many trees. Rackham, *Trees and woodland*, pp. 164–83.

10. NRO Maps: Map 4210.

trees that were allowed to grow to maturity and then harvested for their timber. The Whittlewood map gave the names of the coppices and listed their sizes, which ranged from 20 to 100 acres with an average of around 50 acres. Coppices were vulnerable to grazing animals when they were newly cut and their shoots (known as 'spring') were young and tender, and so the coppices were worked in rotation. The chief regarders and preservators of the Northamptonshire forests were instructed that keepers be inhibited 'from putting any horses, beasts, sheep, colts, calves, swine or other cattle into any coppices until the spring of the said coppices be of eight years' growth'. They were also told that they should 'suffer no deer to come into coppices whereby the spring may be hurt or hindered'. Each compartment was protected by a bank topped with a fence to guard the tender shoots from the depredations of livestock and deer. The aim was to have the spring protected 'with the least expense of wood', this end being accomplished by 'entrenching and ditching the coppice and setting a hedge on top of the banks'.[11] Once the growing coppice reached a certain maturity the compartment could be opened up to admit deer and the animals of those with common grazing rights in the forest. The coppices were interlinked by a series of broad rides which provided grazing for both deer and commonable beasts. Rides were of sufficient importance to be maintained around an area of assarts within Hazelborough Walk, and between Hanger Walk and Shrob Walk, even though they were no longer required to provide routes through woodland. Morton observed that, in Whittlewood, fourteen towns were allowed a right of common for their horses and cows 'in the open coppices and ridings' on 'account of the injuries that may happen to be done to them [the husbandry of the towns] by the excursions of the deer'.[12]

The Whittlewood map also shows that, at this time, the forest contained three lawns: Wakefield Lawn, at 244 acres (Figure 3.4), Shrob Lawn, at 150 acres, and Sholebrook Lawn, at 100 acres. The lawns provided dedicated pasture for the deer and were, according to Morton, 'secluded by rails from the forrest cattel'.[13] The map depicts Wakefield Lawn as surrounded by a paled fence and Sholebrook as partly so surrounded (Sholebrook Lawn is called 'Sholebrook rayles' on the map). Shrob Lawn has an enclosing line, but not pales; this might imply that it was surrounded by a ditch and bank, as were the coppices (also indicated by an unbroken line). All three lawns had lodges situated on them. Although Hazelborough Walk did not have a lawn, it had Black Hedges Lodge and Wappenham Lodge at the far west of the forest. Similarly, Hanger Walk had Briary Lodge.

11. Articles of instruction for the chief regarders and preservators of the Queen's Majesty's woods in the forests of Rockingham, Salcey and Whittlewood, reproduced in Pettit, *Royal forests*, pp. 194–6.

12. Morton, *Natural history*, p. 11. J.M. Neeson described the importance of the provision of tethered grazing on the grass 'joynts' that ran across open fields: *Commoners: common right, enclosure and social change in England, 1700–1820* (1993; Cambridge, 1996), p. 95.

13. Morton, *Natural history*, p. 11.

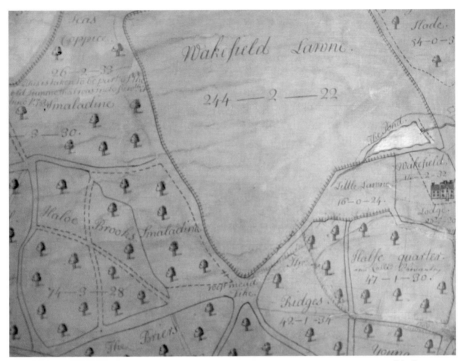

Figure 3.4 1608 Whittlewood map: detail of Wakefield Lawn (NRO, map 4210). By kind permission of the Grafton Estate.

Whittlewood was surveyed in the late eighteenth century and a new map of the forest appeared in 1787.[14] This map depicts the forest in yet more detail than its predecessor. It shows, for example, the amount of paling used not just around the lawns but around much of the outer perimeter of the wooded area of the forest. Gates are shown where roads enter into the confines of the forest. This suggests that, by the eighteenth century at least, Whittlewood did not conform to the open character described by Manwood as definitive of a forest.[15] The map was produced as part of a survey prepared for the commissioners appointed to look into the state of the nation's forests, and the subsequent report (presented to the House of Commons in 1792) confirmed these observations. The majority of Whittlewood Forest was surrounded by a 'ring mound' which was topped by a wooden fence maintained at the expense of the Crown. This had been regarded as the forest boundary 'beyond the memory of the oldest man'. The only exception was Hazelborough Walk, which was 'in places open' so that 'the deer and common cattle often stray into the village of Silstone [Silverstone], and other

14.   TNA, MR 1/359.
15.   Manwood, Treatise, p. 2.

adjacent places'.[16] Grafton estate records from the nineteenth century confirm the continued existence of a physical barrier on the forest perimeter. In trying to preserve the offices of the forest's 'page keepers' from potential Treasury cuts, the duke of Grafton explained that the long and narrow shape of the forest meant that it had a greater quantity of 'outward boundary' than if it had 'a more compact shape'. He went on to talk of the 'outward mound', which required constant vigilance to preserve it from the 'pilfering and other depredations' to which it was exposed. If the boundary was not maintained by the page keepers it would soon 'lay the forest open' (with the doubly deleterious results of farmers' cattle getting in and forest deer getting out).[17]

The 1787 map and subsequent report also identified the 'plains' in Whittlewood more clearly than had the 1608 map. Plains were open areas of rough grazing (in contrast to the enclosed lawns) and their depiction on the map is suggestive of wood pasture. Winter Hill in Hazelborough Walk is shown as enclosed coppice on the 1608 map, with the remark 'common of late'; by 1787 it was once again open and shown as wood pasture. The large plain called Holy Brook was previously coppice, according to the report, but had become a plain 'open at all times' to compensate the commoners for the land that the second duke of Grafton had enclosed as a pleasure ground known as the 'pheasantry'. Hanger Walk had a small plain called 'Hanger Hollows'. The survey that accompanied the 1787 map gave the acreage of each walk and subdivided the total by landscape type. In the case of all the walks, the acreage of coppices and their internal rides greatly predominated, as shown in Table 3.1.

Table 3.1 Land use within Whittlewood, 1787.

	Coppices and ridings within them	Plains and open ridings	Lawns and lodge yards	Inclosures to the lodges
Hazelborough	587	220	0.5	31
Hazelborough (Bathursts)	418	155	–	–
Sholebrook	1095	150	83	57
Wakefield	1083	313	245	172
Hanger	456	40	–	16
Shrob	252	7	–	35

16. *Commons Journal*, 47, p. 141.
17. NRO, Grafton archive: G4050/2.

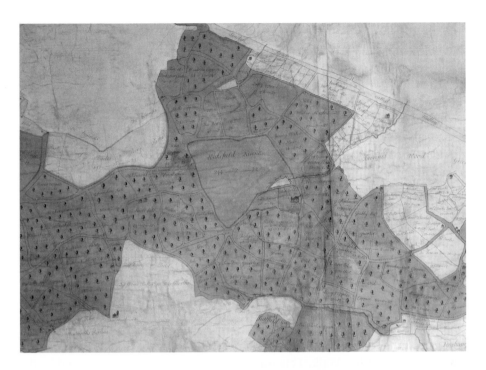

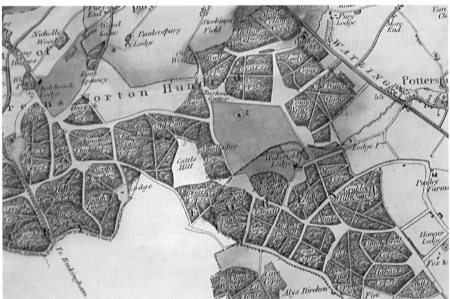

Figure 3.5 Comparison of Whittlewood map (1608) and Bryant's map of 1827. Whittlewood map (NRO, map 4210). By kind permission of the Grafton Estate.

A comparison of the 1787 and 1608 maps reveals a striking continuity in land use. One major change is the disappearance of Shrob Lawn, now indistinguishable from the surrounding farmland, although Shrob Lodge and the walk's coppices persisted into the late eighteenth century. In the remaining walks the coppices are identifiably the same. Priesthay Wood and Monks Wood have also disappeared from Hazelborough Walk, but consultation of later maps shows that these actually remained as woodland, although they were no longer part of the forest. Similarly, the tongue of forest protruding southwards from Wakefield Walk, although no longer appearing on the forest map, remained as woodland.

The later evidence is provided by Andrew Bryant's large-scale map of Northamptonshire, dating from 1827 (Figure 3.5).[18] It shows the county woodland in sufficient detail for us to assess how much of the Whittlewood depicted in the earlier maps survived. Bryant's map reveals very little reduction in the area of woodland across the two centuries. On the western side of the forest the woodland nearest to Syresham village has gone. But, besides this area, every coppice shown on the earlier maps is identifiable on the later one, although they have sometimes acquired new names along the way. A similar network of rides separating the coppice compartments is also evident. Wakefield Lawn and Sholebrook still appear as large enclosed areas. One major change relates to the detached portion of the forest, Handley Walk. This was not included on the 1608 map and by the time of Bryant's map had disappeared from the landscape. Bryant's map actually contained more woodland in some areas than either of the forest maps, but the forest maps were only concerned with depicting land that was part of the forest; woodlands in private hands, such as Bucknells Wood to the west of Silverstone village and Earls Wood to the south, were omitted altogether.

This series of maps shows that, as far as the distribution of woodland is concerned, there was a great deal of continuity in Whittlewood between 1608 and 1827. That is not to say that the forest did not change hands, however. At the time of the 1608 map the woodland was under the direct control of the Crown. In 1629 Handley Walk was granted to Simon Bennet for £6000, including the underwood, timber, soil and all rights, and the walk was disafforested. By 1635 the trees were felled and the land converted to arable. Even before the grant to Bennet, Handley had stood apart from the rest of the forest in ways additional to the purely spatial. It had previously been enclosed and common rights extinguished, and was often referred to as 'Handley Park' rather than Handley Walk. The other walks remained in Crown (or government) hands until 1665, when the underwood was granted, together with the Honor of Grafton, as part of Queen Catherine's jointure. In 1672 the underwood was granted in reversion to Henry, earl of Arlington. On Catherine's death in 1705 it was inherited by Charles, second duke of Grafton, the

18.   Andrew Bryant, Map of the county of Northampton from actual survey in the years 1824, 1825 and 1826 (1827).

grandson of Charles II and Arlington. The wardenship of Whittlewood was also settled on the duke of Grafton, and henceforth the history of much of Whittlewood became part of the history of the Grafton estate (although the Crown reserved the timber and the deer, and in the early eighteenth century granted the timber and underwood of seven coppices in Hazelborough Walk to the earl of Bathurst).[19]

The next significant event in the history of Whittlewood was disafforestation. This came earlier to Hazelborough Walk (1826) than to the rest of the forest, and enclosure followed hard on the heels of disafforestation. The enclosure award confirmed that the soil and the timber of Hazelborough Walk, together with 'herbage and feed' for the deer, belonged to the Crown. The largest allotment was therefore made to the king (some 517 acres), with the next largest (some 386 acres) going to the fourth duke of Grafton in compensation for his right to the underwood and his forest offices (Grafton had already bought the rights in Hazelborough previously granted to the earl of Bathurst). The enclosure document stated that the main aim of the enclosure was to enable improvement to the woodland such that the production of timber could be increased (the report to the Commons made 34 years previously had identified Hazelborough Walk as the poorest part of the forest in terms of timber production). The three remaining forest walks were disafforested and enclosed in 1856.[20] The fifth duke of Grafton benefited from this, receiving the freehold of Wakefield Lodge and park. The estate also made extensive purchases of land, both woodland and arable, in the eastern portion of Whittlewood.[21] This marks the point where the landscape of Whittlewood did begin to change. Examination of the six-inch OS maps for Whittlewood show that by the 1880s the woodland was considerably reduced, with the straight roads and field boundaries characteristic of nineteenth-century enclosure taking its place. When reminiscing about his foxhunting experiences with the Grafton, J.M.K. Elliott remarked that the forest in the 1850s was 'nearly double its present size' (the 'present' being the 1890s).[22]

The earliest map that can be found for Salcey Forest dates from 1787, when it was surveyed along with Whittlewood.[23] In 1712 Morton had the extent of Salcey as about a mile in breadth and almost a mile and a half in length. Its three walks

19. NRO, Grafton archive: G4104; *Commons Journal*, 47, pp. 142–3.
20. TNA, MR 1/1653.
21. *VCH Northamptonshire*, 5, pp. 18–37. The process of disafforestation can be traced in the various bills that were produced and the related correspondence that survives in the Grafton papers. An eighteenth-century memorandum cautioned about how complex such a process would be, and the various rights that had to be taken into consideration (including common rights of the in towns and out towns and the disposition of tithes connected to the underwood). The working out of these considerations can be viewed in this useful packet of papers. NRO, Grafton archive: G3999, G4000.
22. J.M.K. Elliott, *Fifty years' foxhunting with the Grafton and other packs of hounds* (London, 1900), p. 65.
23. TNA, MPE 1/938

were divided into 24 coppices, 'which are cut down each in their turn'.[24] This description accords well with the forest depicted on the late eighteenth-century map. The commissioners reported to the House of Commons on Salcey in 1790. When they reported on Whittlewood two years later they commented on how similar it was to its near neighbour. Salcey had one lawn, lying at the heart of the forest, with an accompanying lodge. There were four other lodges, occupied by the three keepers and the one page keeper, and each lodge had a certain amount of land with it. As with Whittlewood, the coppices were separated by rides. The forest map also shows several plains, again depicted as wood pasture; some of the rides are very broad and also appear as wood pasture. Salcey, too, was enclosed on its outer boundary, 'the greatest part of which is fenced by proprietors', while the 'residue' was fenced 'with post and rail' at the expense of the Crown. Earlier but less direct evidence of forest enclosure can be found in a series of accounts for Salcey. Itemised bills for labourers' work include payments for hedging and ditching around newly cut coppices. There were separate and distinct entries for lengths that comprised part of the 'forest hedge', presumably because the Crown or proprietors of the adjacent land were expected to pay for such lengths.[25] Comparison of the 1787 map of Salcey with Bryant's map shows even less change in the forest up to 1827 than can be seen at Whittlewood.

Like that of Whittlewood, the underwood of Salcey passed from the Crown first to Queen Catherine, and then to the dukes of Grafton. In 1660 the wardenship of the forest was granted in reversion to George Montagu and his male heirs forever.[26] Salcey was disafforested and enclosed in 1826, at the same time as Whittlewood's Hazelborough Walk.[27] As with Whittlewood, the main aim of the enclosure was stated to be the improvement of the woodland, and once more the largest allotment (1174 acres) went to the Crown, with a mere 152 acres going to the duke of Grafton. A comparison with the first edition six-inch OS maps from the late nineteenth century shows very little reduction in woodland and, in fact, Salcey Forest remains very much the same size and shape to this date. The only major change is that the extreme western portion of the forest is separated from the remainder by the M1 motorway.

Rockingham was far larger and more complex in its structure than either Whittlewood or Salcey. Map evidence must be pieced together from a broader range of sources, as maps survive from different dates for various portions of the forest. A seventeenth-century map covering the area between Northampton and Stamford shows the entire expanse of Rockingham Forest, but not in the same detail as the 1608 Whittlewood map.[28] Although the Rockingham map suggests

24. Morton, Natural history, p. 11.
25. NRO, Grafton archive: G2464.
26. Commons Journal, 46, p. 98–9.
27. TNA, MPEE 104.
28. TNA, MPE 459.

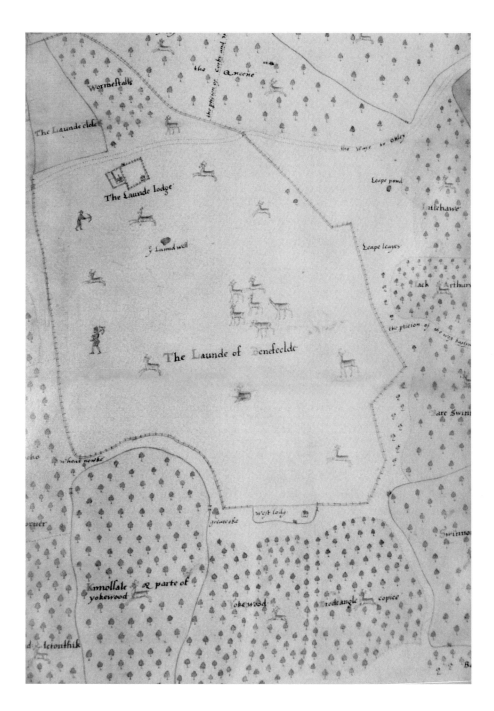

Figure 3.6 Benefield Lawn, from Hatton map (NRO, FH272). By kind permission of the
Northamptonshire Record Office.

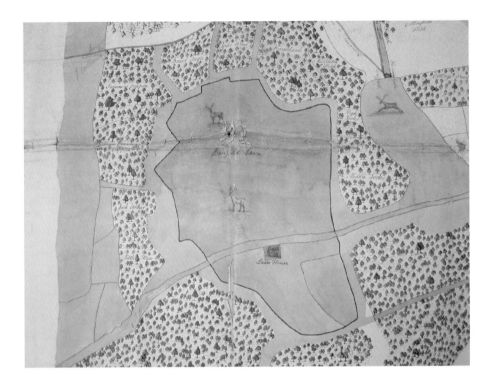

Figure 3.7 Benefield Lawn, from copy of seventeenth-century map (NRO, BRU Map 126). By kind permission of the Brudenell family.

that the woods were divided into coppiced compartments separated by rides it gives neither names nor acreages. For more details we must look to maps of the individual bailiwicks. An early, and very attractive, map was commissioned by Sir Christopher Hatton in the 1580s (Figure 3.6).[29] Intended to show his Northamptonshire estates, it covered in the process Rockingham Bailiwick. Benefield Lawn, later praised by Morton for being 'spacious and faire', was shown enclosed by paling with a further small close within it and a small area of woodland called 'Wormestalls'. A lodge lay at its heart. The lawn was depicted as being surrounded by woodland, with names suggesting coppices. Their depiction on the map suggests that some of the coppices were enclosed and some open. To the west, immediately beneath Rockingham Park, lay Rockinghamshire, a more open area containing some pockets of woodland. Further west still there were two small plains below the village of Gretton, but otherwise the area comprised woodland down to the open area of Kirby Pasture. A copy of a seventeenth-century map of the same area also survives (Figure 3.7).[30] This, usefully, has marked on it the forest boundary, indicating that Kirby Plain lay outside the forest. The depiction

29. NRO, Finch Hatton archive: FH272.
30. NRO, Brudenell archive: Bru Map 126.

of the woodland showed a mixture of small trees and large, which presumably signified coppiced and standard trees. A map of Cliffe Bailiwick, dating from the reign of James I, depicts coppices and rides in some detail, although it shows only the Crown's woods and omits the private woods and the purlieus.[31] For Brigstock Bailiwick, a later map (1810) of lands encompassing Geddington Chase reveals some interesting details regarding types of woodland.[32] The mapmaker showed the woodland in sufficient detail to allow us to distinguish thick tree covering from something appearing more akin to wood pasture, and there was also a large area of what looks to have been rough grazing, identified as Upley Hills. None of the maps show paling around sections of the forest, as Whittlewood and Salcey had. It is not possible to state whether the forest was of a more open character or whether such details were deemed unimportant by the mapmakers, but some of the maps do portray forest gates.

As the structure of Rockingham Forest was more complex and dispersed than its Northamptonshire companions, so too was its disposition. More of the forest fell into the hands of a greater range of people at an earlier date than was the case for either Whittlewood or Salcey. The large royal parks of Great and Little Brigstock were granted to Sir Robert Cecil in 1602. Later, as earl of Salisbury, he was successful in obtaining a licence to disafforest and enclose the parks for agriculture (causing considerable consternation among the villagers of Brigstock and Stanion, who lost their common rights in the park and were faced with the predation of the newly homeless deer). Elsewhere in Brigstock Bailiwick the soil and the underwood of Farming Woods were granted to John, Lord Mordaunt, in 1628. A few months later, and by then earl of Peterborough, he was granted the timber too. Peterborough's entire interest in Farming Woods was passed to a London merchant in 1650. The underwood and soil of Geddington Woods were granted to Edward, Lord Montagu, in 1628, to be joined by the timber later in the same year. Geddington Woods were disafforested in 1676 and became known as Geddington Chase, but the rights of common were maintained, along with the deer.[33]

Large sections of Rockingham Bailiwick were alienated even earlier. Corby Woods were granted away from the Crown, together with the manor, in 1553, eventually passing to the earls of Cardigan by the late seventeenth century. Cottingham Woods were granted to Sir Christopher Hatton in 1572, his rights including timber, underwood, soil and freedom from the Forest Law. In 1583 Gretton Woods, Little Weldon Woods and Benefield Lawn were added to Hatton's estates (to which we doubtless owe the happy event of his commissioning a fine

31. TNA, MR 1/314.
32. NRO, maps: Map 5965.
33. Pettit, Royal forests, pp. 189–91; Commons Journal, 47, p. 190.

set of maps in the 1580s), as were Pipewell Woods in 1629.[34]

In Cliffe Bailwick, Cliffe Park was granted to the earl of Essex in 1592, but by 1598 it was in the Cecils' hands. Henceforth it stayed with the earls of Exeter. Morehay and Westhay were granted on a lease to the earl of Berkshire during James's reign, but the underwood and keepership were granted to the earl of Westmoreland in 1628 (who also paid for the termination of the lease), to be joined later the same year by the timber. By 1700 Morehay had passed to Exeter. Sulehay and Shortwood went to the earls of Westmoreland, being granted first to their ancestor, Sir Walter Mildmay, in 1571.[35]

From this account we can see that much of the forest lands fell victim to Charles I's efforts to raise money in 1628. Where the other Northamptonshire forests came under the influence of the dukes of Grafton, more noble families were vying for the lands of Rockingham, with considerable rivalries often developing. The Hattons in particular caused contention with their exercise of the forest keepership. An entire notebook is filled with the results of Sir Richard de Capell Brooke's historical research into where the reality of the Hatton's rights might differ from the ones that they claimed.[36] The 1792 report to the House of Commons about Rockingham Forest reveals friction between the commissioners and the landholders too. Hatton and Westmoreland both refused to supply the commissioners with much of the requested information, and both families claimed greater rights over wood, timber, soil and deer than the commissioners thought they were entitled to. After the report some attempts were made to resolve the situation by selling the remaining Crown rights in sections of the forest, but the continuing disagreement as to the extent of these rights is demonstrated by the contentious correspondence between the surveyor general and the tenth earl of Westmoreland, which resulted in the obtaining of barristers' opinions.[37] Unfortunately for this study, no survey and map was made of Rockingham for the purposes of the report to the Commons because the commissioners considered that the Crown did not have enough interest left in the forest to justify it. Given the extent of alienation in Rockingham Forest it is surprising that a comparison of the early maps with Bryant's county map from 1827 shows levels of woodland survival similar to those in Whittlewood and Salcey.[38]

34. *Commons Journal*, 47, p. 189.
35. *Commons Journal*, 47, p. 191.
36. NRO, Brooke of Oakley archive: Brooke vol. 163.
37. NRO, Westmoreland of Abethorpe archive: W(A) box4/parcel VIII/no 1.
38. This picture is supported by the series of maps in *Rockingham Forest: an atlas of the medieval and early modern landscape*. The atlas provides equivalent medieval and early modern maps, produced using digital mapping tools and based on data from a range of sources. Reproductions of the Victorian six-inch OS maps are also provided. A comparison of the medieval and early modern maps reveals a considerable diminution in the amount of wood pasture but continuity in the amount of woodland. When we look at the six-inch OS maps from the 1880s, however, we

The reports to the Commons contained detailed information about the coppice rotations in the Northamptonshire forests. Whittlewood and Salcey were both cut every 21 years, while in Rockingham the cycle was 16 or 18 years depending on the bailiwick.[39] All of these were quite long rotations by commercial coppice standards,[40] but there is evidence that, in practice, the Northamptonshire coppice rotation could be longer still.[41] Coppice compartments were sometimes left for 50 years or more before cutting, and were then consigned entirely to nature so far as regeneration was concerned. Good management would have involved the selection and promotion of suitable species, such as oak and ash. Failure to select and thin led to much 'waste' in the form of thorns competing too successfully with more profitable species. This was not helped by the accepted system in which the purchasers of the coppice wood were responsible for cutting it and carting it away. According to the Elizabethan instructions the buyer must carry the wood out of the coppice by Midsummer Day, else the woodward could claim half the wood himself as a fee for carrying it 'outside the coppice gate'. It might be assumed that the purchaser of the wood might not take such care for the preservation of the coppice as the person responsible for it.[42] The standard trees fared little better, often being left too long before felling, so that they became 'dotards' – too old to be commercially useful. Mid sixteenth-century surveys of the wood and early seventeenth-century surveys of timber, both aimed at improving royal revenue from the forests, support a picture of neglect. For example, from a total of 2420 acres of coppiced woodland in Whittlewood (2025 forest acres), the 1564 survey had 955 acres as saleable and 500 acres as 'waste'. According to the 1608 timber survey, with a total of 120,000, Northamptonshire had more trees 'certified' than any other county save Hampshire (300,000). Of these, 10,000 were deemed available for sale (equal with Hampshire). In fact, only £1410 was realised from the 'extraordinary' sales of Northamptonshire timber in 1609.[43] Much later, the 1790s reports on the Northamptonshire forests blamed the unprofitability of both wood and timber partly on the continuing need to manage the forests for

find a considerable reduction in woodland. The medieval maps represent the landscape in the early fourteenth century. The early modern mapping shows the landscape as it was c.1750. G. Foard, D. Hall and T. Partida, *Rockingham Forest: an atlas of the medieval and early modern landscape* (Northampton, 2009), pp. 73–158.

39. Morton, *Natural history*, p. 11.
40. Rackham suggested that five, seven or fifteen years were more the norm. Rackham, *Trees and woodland*, pp. 63–4.
41. Pettit found the Crown woodlands in the Northamptonshire forests to be sadly wanting in terms of efficient management and economic exploitation in the Elizabethan and Jacobean periods. Pettit, *Royal forests*, pp. 98–101.
42. Pettit, *Royal forests*, p. 195.
43. Pettit, *Royal forests*, p. 100.

deer.[44] These conclusions were also repeated in Pitt's survey of the agriculture of the county, where he found in Whittlewood 'for a large tract together, a mere thicket of blackthorns' which would have been 'impenetrable were it not for the rides but by art'.[45] But 'neglected' coppices overrun with low woodland and thorn would provide both cover and browse for deer. We can therefore conclude that, at the beginning of the seventeenth century, the Northamptonshire forests were still providing a suitable environment for the preservation of deer.

It is worth investigating whether the alienation of the underwood made an appreciable difference to the management of the forest landscape in Northamptonshire. We get a picture of the importance of the woodland in estate management from the letters of Daniel Eaton, steward to the third earl of Cardigan from 1725 to 1732. The constant references to valuing coppices, arranging labour to cut them and collecting payment from the purchasers illustrate that the Brudenell woodland was far from neglected.[46] A similar level of concern with woodland management is evident in the Grafton estate records, in valuations of Salcey woodland from 1743 to 1762 and of sales of coppice wood from Whittlewood in the years 1798–1815.[47] The reports to parliament gave some detail as to coppice management in the 1780s and 1790s. The coppices were cut and then enclosed to deny access to deer and to the commoners' horses and cattle. In Salcey deer were admitted after seven years by means of 'creeps' and 'deer leaps', while horses and cows remained excluded for a further two years. In Whittlewood deer and common cattle were all admitted after nine years. In Rockingham, with its shorter cutting cycle of 16–18 years, deer were admitted after four years and common cattle after seven years.[48] Nineteenth-century records from the Grafton estate suggest that not that much had changed in the theory of coppice management by that date, even if the implementation had improved. Coppices were still being cut every 21 years, after which they were enclosed by a 'strong, black thorn hedge' to defend them from the deer and cattle for nine years.[49]

This survey of the royal forests of Northamptonshire has illustrated two major points, the first regarding the character of the landscape compared with other forests and the second concerning the survival of woodland within the forests. The landscape of Whittlewood, Salcey and Rockingham fitted entirely neither a seventeenth-century nor a twentieth-century description of an archetypal royal forest. Manwood repeatedly stressed the open nature of the forest ('the territory

44. *Commons Journal*, 47, pp. 104, 150; *Commons Journal*, 46, p. 195. Pettit later echoed their findings. Pettit, *Royal forests*, pp. 48–9.
45. W. Pitt, *General view of the agriculture of Northamptonshire* (Northampton, 1809), p. 148.
46. J. Wake and D. Champion-Webster (eds), *The letters of Daniel Eaton to the third earl of Cardigan 1725–1732* (Northampton, 1971).
47. NRO, Grafton archive: G2464–G2471, G4050/2.
48. NRO, Brooke of Oakley archive: B(O)327/27.
49. *Commons Journal*, 46, p. 98; *Commons Journal*, 47, pp. 142, 194.

itself doth lie open and not enclosed', 'a forest doth lie open, and not enclosed with hedge, ditch, pale, or stone-wall'), but our evidence suggests that, in the case of Whittlewood and Salcey at least, the forests were enclosed around their perimeters, as well as internally.[50] This is confirmed by estate records as well as the map evidence and parliamentary reports. Modern historians have characterised forest landscapes as comprising mainly wood pasture, with some enclosed coppice in 'compartmented' forests.[51] The Northamptonshire forests certainly had open plains and ridings, but they were dominated by coppices, enclosed and then opened in rotation. Our map evidence illustrates that this landscape survived largely intact over our period; there was no great diminution in the area of woodland in any of the three forests. The Northamptonshire forests provided as much potential deer habitat in 1800 as they did in 1600.

The forest and the deer

The traditional explanation for the hunting transition has been the decline of deer and the disappearance of their habitat.[52] So far our examination of the Northamptonshire forests has detected no great change in the wooded landscape over the period 1600 to 1850. Woodland within the forest was not much depleted across our period of study. Proving continuity in deer habitat is not the same as proving continuity in deer population, however. The traditional explanation asserts that the deer suffered depredations in the Civil Wars from which they never recovered. Is there evidence from Northamptonshire that would support this view? The surviving evidence is eclectic and tends towards the qualitative rather than the quantitative: there were few attempts to assess actual deer population.

Early writers on the county certainly commented on the deer as well as the woodland in the forest areas. According to Leland the 'fairest game of the forest was seen at Benefield Lawn', although he also asserted that there was 'no redde deere but fallow in Rockingham Forest'.[53] Norden, on the other hand, stated that 'Deere, Red and Fallowe, both in Parks, Forests and Chases are so plentiful as noe shire yieldeth like'.[54] The sixteenth-century maps commissioned by Sir Christopher Hatton included depictions of deer in the woods, lawns and parks which find echoes in the copy of the seventeenth-century map of Gretton Woods and the surrounding area.[55]

There is evidence of a long tradition of deer preservation in Northampton's royal forests. When James ascended the throne of England he made the state of the nation's deer one of his foremost concerns. He perceived that the deer

50. Manwood, *Treatise*, pp. 2, 3.
51. Rackham, *Trees and woodland*, pp. 164–83.
52. This account has most recently been repeated in Griffin, *Blood sport*.
53. J. Leland, *The itinerary of John Leland the antiquary*, 9 vols (Oxford, 1768–9), I, p. 21.
54. Norden, *Delineation*, p. 29.
55. NRO, Finch Hatton archive: FH272; NRO, Brudenell archive: Bru Map 126.

population had suffered in the last years of Elizabeth's reign, and took steps to ensure the preservation of the favoured royal quarry. Various warrants were issued to this end, and included Northamptonshire in their scope. In 1604 Thomas, Lord Burghley, in his role as warden of Rockingham Forest, was commanded to enforce a restraint on the killing of deer there for three years, and in 1609 Christopher Hatton, as keeper of Benefield Lawn, was instructed to enforce a restraint on the killing of deer at Benefield and in the woods of Gretton and Whedon for five years.[56] Stuart preoccupations with preserving deer find echoes in the state papers for the early years of the commonwealth. The papers confirm that deer had suffered in the 1640s: the 'great spoil committed by soldiers and others' is acknowledged. In Northamptonshire there was specific concern about 'divers disorderly and dangerous persons' within the counties of Northampton and Buckingham who had 'abused the officers of Whittlewood Forest and provoked others to do so' and had 'coursed, killed, and destroyed the deer'.[57]

The concern for the well-being of the nation's deer became more marked at the Restoration. Charles II's early years were punctuated with nationwide restraints on warrants for deer. In 1660 the earl of Exeter begged authority from the Crown to grant no warrants for deer under his charge in his walk in Rockingham, estimating that there were but 'twenty brace' left. Similarly Edward, Lord Rockingham, as keeper of Corby woods, requested a restraint on warrants, the deer being 'much decayed'.[58] The king wrote to Christopher Hatton in 1660 and commanded that Hatton 'forbiare the deere for the officers of the said forest or upon any other warrant until further orders'.[59] There is evidence, however, that the deer population in some parts of the Northamptonshire forests were healthier than in other areas of the kingdom. The earl of Exeter was annually granted a licence to hunt in Rockingham Forest in the summer months (the buck season),[60] and in October 1662 Sir John Robinson was granted a warrant to kill deer in Farming Woods (in Brigstock Bailiwick), 'provided he leave sufficient of the Royal disport'.[61] Various warrants were being granted for deer in the western bailiwicks of Rockingham, whilst elsewhere in the kingdom warrants were continually suspended.[62]

56. *CSPD James I, 1603–1610* (London, 1857), pp. 161, 518. This Christopher Hatton was a relative of the Elizabethan Lord Chancellor, and had inherited the Hatton estate in 1597.
57. *CSPD Interregnum, 1649–1650* (London, 1875), pp. 300, 367.
58. *CSPD Charles II, 1660–1661* (London, 1860), p. 187.
59. NRO, Finch Hatton archive: FH2858. This Christopher Hatton succeeded to the Hatton estate in 1619 and, a staunch Royalist, was created Baron Hatton in 1643.
60. For example, *CSPD Charles II, 1661–1662* (London, 1861), p. 627.
61. *CSPD Charles II, 1661–1662*, p. 530.
62. For example, in July 1664 instructions were issued to the rangers of Rockingham Forest to serve warrants for fee deer, while in June another three-year restraint on the killing of deer had been

A deposition of a keeper in Rockingham Bailiwick estimated in 1674 that there were around 400 deer in the six walks combined.[63] This does illustrate some lasting deterioration in the population, but numbers were still considered sufficiently sustainable for the keepers to serve a brace of bucks and does to the crown annually from each of the walks (and presumably other venison was being taken from this portion of the forest too).

By the beginning of the eighteenth century Morton was able to talk in glowing terms of the deer population of the Northamptonshire forests. He claimed that Wakefield Lawn 'shews sometimes seven or eight hundred deer, generally three or four hundred in any fine day'.[64] In 1711 the earl of Westmoreland asked for some restraint in the killing of deer in his part of Cliffe Bailiwick because a hard winter some three or four years previously had had a bad effect on the population, especially the males. Then he estimated that they killed no fewer than 100 deer per year, not including the venison used in his house or disposed of among neighbouring gentlemen, or killed in the purlieus of Blatherwick and Bedford. The deer population evidently regained its strength, because a 1714 account of deer that could be 'safely killed' amounted to some 172 bucks and does plus 20 brace for the queen and the forest officers' fee deer.[65] The 1714 warrant for deer for George I's table from the Board of the Green Cloth expected 13 brace from Rockingham, which was the largest number taken from all the royal forests (next came the New Forest and Windsor Great Park at eight brace each; Whittlewood was expected to serve four brace and Salcey two).[66]

Daniel Eaton's letters to his master, the third earl of Cardigan, made frequent reference to the state of the deer on the Cardigan estates. Eaton was mostly concerned with the welfare of the deer in Deene Park, but his interest did extend to deer at large in the woods (especially where they were causing damage to the coppice). In May 1725 he reported looking at woods in the charge of Thomas Bell and finding 'a great number of deer in all of them'; there were in fact 'a great many fine deer' in all the woods that he rode through.[67] Thirty years later Daniel Eaton's son, also called Daniel and steward to the fourth earl of Cardigan, kept a series of records of the bucks killed each summer in Deene Park and in the woods he calls 'the Purlieus'. Although the number taken in the park constantly exceeded the number taken in the woods by quite some margin (for example, 83 in the park against 12 in the woods in the summer of 1763), these figures do demonstrate that there was a sustainable deer population still living in Rockingham Forest at this time.[68]

issued in Waltham Forest. *CSPD Charles II, 1663–1664* (London, 1862), pp. 654, 623.
63. *Commons Journal*, 47, p. 205.
64. Morton, *Natural history*, p. 11.
65. NRO, Westmoreland of Abethorpe archive: W(A) VI 2/25; W(A)VI 2/23.
66. NRO, Westmoreland of Abethorpe archive: W(A) VI 2/26.
67. Wake and Champion-Webster, *Letters of Daniel Eaton*, p. 20.
68. NRO, Brudenell archive: Bru.I.xiii.2, 3, 4a, 4b, 5b, 5c and 17.

The parliamentary reports of the 1790s made some attempt at estimating the strength of the deer population. In Whittlewood there were calculated to be some 1800 deer 'of all sorts' in the forest. In Salcey the figure was given as 1000. There was no attempt to assess the population of Rockingham, mostly owing to the lack of cooperation from the landholders and the keepers there. The report does remark on the fact that the Hattons never entirely removed the deer from Benefield Lawn, despite having enclosed it for pasture, and that the earls of Westmoreland similarly maintained the deer in their woods although they had been granted permission to remove them.[69] There are records of the deer killed in the Hatton portion of Rockingham Forest in 1789–90, amounting to 37 bucks and 31 does in Over Walk, and 32 bucks and 24 does in Gretton Walk.[70] George Finch Hatton was anxious to preserve the deer in his charge, and in 1819 posted a notice in an attempt to prevent the gathering of nuts in the forest because it disturbed the deer.[71] In 1828 the duke of Grafton estimated the total number of deer in Whittlewood at 1500, of which 230 were killed annually. A list of the duties of the lieutenant of Whittlewood, made in 1832, admitted that the number of deer in Sholebrook Walk, for which the lieutenant was directly responsible, 'cannot well be ascertained', but estimated them to be around 350 head, of which 11 brace of bucks and eight brace of does were killed annually.[72]

This investigation of the deer population in the Northamptonshire forests has revealed some decline in numbers in the mid-seventeenth century, but equally striking is the effort made to preserve and promote the deer. This runs in parallel to the continuity of woodland already noted in the forests in this period. Even where the interests in the forest now lay in private hands, and the Crown's involvement was limited to receiving a few brace of bucks and does every year, steps were being taken to preserve the deer in the forests as well as in the parks. It is also noticeable that contemporaries were only too well aware of the potential conflict between the preservation of the deer and the profitable exploitation of the wood and timber. Daniel Eaton could remark in the same letter both how the deer damaged the underwood in his master's purlieus and how well the deer looked,[73] while the reports to parliament made in the 1790s all recommended that the forest be improved either by containing the deer within a limited part or by removing them altogether. But it was not until disafforestation in the mid-nineteenth century that such action was

69. *Commons Journal*, 47, pp. 189, 193.
70. NRO, Finch Hatton archive: FH2457.
71. NRO, Brooke of Oakley archive: B(O)313/21. In response, the de Capell Brookes apparently encouraged their tenants to gather nuts: R. Moore-Colyer, 'Woods and woodland management: the bailiwick of Rockingham, Northamptonshire c.1700–1849', *Northamptonshire Past and Present*, 9/3 (1996–7), p. 254.
72. NRO, Grafton archive: G3982, G3999/3.
73. Wake and Champion-Webster, *Letters of Daniel Eaton*, p. 20.

finally taken. The draft bills for the disafforestation of Whittlewood contained clauses pledging that the Crown would remove the deer from the forest within two years of the passing of the act.[74] J.E. Linnell's book *Old Oak*, containing memories of nineteenth-century Silverstone, suggested that the enclosure of the forest and the removal of the deer was a far from universally popular move: 'it was a dark day for Silson when the forest passed into the hands of private individuals', when 'the deer were all caught up to be killed, or sent away to stock private demenses'.[75]

Northamptonshire deer parks

In an examination of the history of deer hunting in Northamptonshire the role of the county's deer parks cannot be overlooked. These were enclosed at different times and in different circumstances, and possibly to meet different ends. Some of the parks were medieval creations that had survived to the early modern period, others were created in the sixteenth or seventeenth centuries. With the eighteenth century came the era of the 'landscape park' and in Northamptonshire, a county with so many noble seats, this fashion was embraced enthusiastically. Some of the landscape parks were carved from agricultural land, but many were adapted from existing deer parks. Just as many parks were created or transformed in this period, however, so many disappeared; they were disparked and their acres absorbed into the agricultural landscape, often leaving their mark in the form of field and farm names.[76]

Writing in 1712, Morton had no doubt that Northamptonshire was exceptionally well-endowed with deer parks: ''tis observed that there are more in Northamptonshire, than in any other county in England, than in all Europe besides'.[77] Over a century later, Surtees remarked that 'there are more deer parks

74. NRO, Grafton archive: G3999.
75. J.E. Linnell, *Old Oak: the story of a forest village* (London, 1932), p. 13.
76. As regards the chronology of deer parks, in Northamptonshire Steane had 'a sprinkling' of medieval deer parks through the county, belonging to magnates and the Crown. He was also in no doubt that 'parks were on the increase in the Tudor and early Stuart period'. Speaking more generally of England as a whole, Rackham had the 'heyday' of the deer park as 1300, with a decline in the later Middle Ages, although he also detected a 'Tudor revival'. Williamson agreed with Rackham's chronology but pointed out that, despite a sixteenth-century revival, deer parks did not recover to 'anything approaching medieval levels'. For comparison, recent work on Suffolk parks clearly indicated two peaks of park creation in that county: one in the decades around 1300 and another in the decades leading up to 1600. J.M. Steane, *The making of the English landscape: the Northamptonshire landscape* (London, 1974), pp. 208–9; Rackham, *Trees and woodland*, pp. 152, 158; T. Williamson, *Polite landscapes: gardens and society in eighteenth-century England* (Stroud, 1995), p. 23; R. Hoppitt, 'Hunting Suffolk's parks; towards a reliable chronology of imparkment', in R. Liddiard (ed.), *The medieval park: new perspectives* (Macclesfield, 2007), p. 147.
77. Morton, *Natural history*, p. 12.

Figure 3.8 Distribution of deer parks: Saxton map.

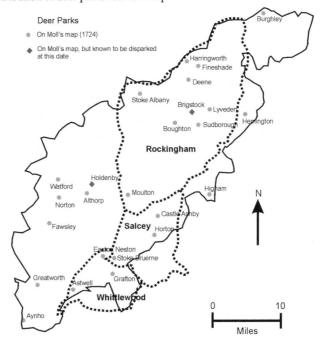

Figure 3.9 Distribution of deer parks: Herman Moll map of 1724 from *A New Description of England and Wales*.

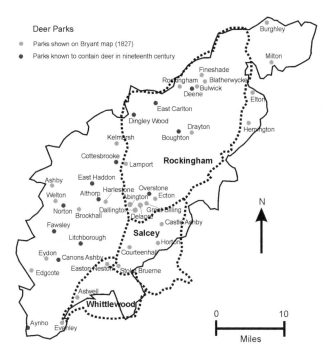

Figure 3.10 Distribution of deer parks: Bryant map.

in Northamptonshire, than in any other county of equal extent'.[78] In the sixteenth
century Norden went to the trouble of listing the deer parks in the county,
classifying them by whether they belonged to the queen, to her nobles, to knights
or to esquires. He named a total of 24 parks.[79] Saxton's sixteenth-century maps of
Northamptonshire were the first to depict the parks in the county and make some
attempt to portray their size and shape as well as their location. Later map makers
followed his example, and it is possible to use these maps to trace the development
of parks in the county (the maps should not be taken as definitive sources,
however; Saxton omits the Brudenell's park at Deene, for example, although we
know from other sources that it was in existence at the time he made his map).
Figures 3.8–3.10 plot the parks on Saxton's and subsequent maps and show the
distribution of parks at the beginning, middle and end of our study period. The
dashed lines represent the bounds of the forests at their greatest extent.

There is discussion among historians about the relationship of parks with
the principal residences with which they were associated. Medieval parks are

78. 'The Pytchley (1833–1834)', in R.S. Surtees, in *Town and country papers* (R.S. Surtees Society, 1993).
    p. 90.
79. Norden, *Delineation*, p. 29.

generally thought to have been distant from their residences, while early modern parks were likely to be adjacent to them.[80] Where the location of medieval deer parks has been traced in Northamptonshire, there is a tendency for them to be located on or near to parish boundaries. The county contains two sets of adjacent parks (Brigstock Great and Little parks and Drayton Park, and Grafton, Pury and Plum parks) which meet each other at the parish boundaries and there are several other examples of parks abutting the boundaries, tending to confirm the view that parks were created away from manor houses, which usually lay at the centre of the village. Where parks were associated with castles they often lay at some remove too. Moulton Park was some three miles from Northampton Castle, and Higham Park was also three miles distant from the castle with which it was associated. In Northamptonshire, at least, it seems that medieval parks were more likely to be distant from the residences with which they were associated.

When we consider the location of the later deer parks, enclosed in the sixteenth and seventeenth centuries, there does seem to be significant change. Some parks, such as Holdenby, were made at the same time as a new great house was built on the site of an old manor. Others, such as Deene, were added to over a period of time as the house was enlarged, improved or rebuilt. Morton certainly had no doubt as to the changing location of the county's parks. All of the parks he described as existing at his time lay 'at a convenient distance' from the houses of their owners, while the older ones, by his time disparked, were remote.[81] (This observation is supported by the fact that, as we shall see, few of Northamptonshire's medieval deer parks went on to form the basis of landscape parks in the eighteenth century, while many of the early modern deer parks did exactly that.)

In addition to the location of Northamptonshire parks, we must also consider their structure. If we accept that the main purpose of a deer park was the preservation of deer, then the types of habitat provided by parks are important. To a large extent parks needed to be forests-in-miniature. An ideal layout would provide open grazing, trees for browsing and thicker tree plantations to furnish

80. Shirley, the nineteenth-century historian of deer parks, suggested that early parks were distant from the house because they were 'carved from waste and wilderness'. This view was echoed by Williamson, nearly a century and a half later, who maintained that most medieval parks lay in remote locations, far from the home of the owner. Williamson had changes in the location of parks starting in the late Middle Ages, with more and more being established 'immediately adjacent to a gentleman's residence'. Liddiard has more recently suggested that we have underestimated the extent to which medieval parks were valued for their aesthetic qualities and viewed as adornments to large residences. Mileson acknowledged this decorative role of parks, but asserted that these considerations could be discerned in a minority, rather than a majority, of cases. Shirley, *Deer parks* (London, 1867), p. 50; Williamson, *Polite landscapes*, pp. 22, 24; R. Liddiard, 'Medieval designed landscapes: problems and possibilities', in M. Gardiner and S. Rippon (eds), *Landscape history after Hoskins: medieval landscapes* (Macclesfield, 2007), pp. 201–2; S.A. Mileson, *Parks in medieval England* (Oxford, 2009), pp. 96–7.

81. Morton, *Natural history*, p. 12.

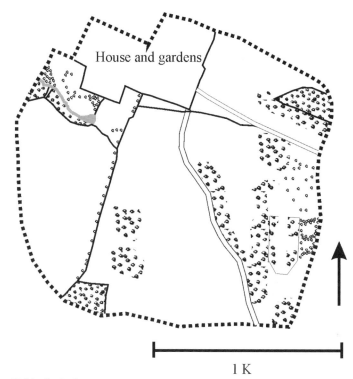

House and gardens

1 K

Figure 3.11 Holdenby Park.

the cover that the deer desired to rest in, the whole being surrounded by a fence or wall that needed to be some seven to eight foot high in order to prevent the deer from leaving. As Markham put it when advising on how to make a park in the early seventeenth century: 'Nor ought the parke to consist of one kinde of ground only – but of divers, as part high wood, part grasse or champion, and part coppice or under-wood, or thicke spring.'[82] Parks were required to fulfil other needs too, however; for example, sixteenth-century statutes required the owners of parks to undertake the breeding of horses within them.[83] This was part of a drive to improve the quality of horses in England and to ensure that there would be sufficient mounts in the event of a war. The deer might also find themselves sharing their grazing with cows or sheep. The wood cover was likely to be managed as coppice, and, as in the forests we have been examining, sections of it would be closed off when newly cut to protect the regrowth from the effects of overenthusiastic grazing. Wood was thus another potential product of a deer park.

82. Gervase Markham's *The countrey farme*, cited in Shirley, *Deer parks*, pp. 234–5. Shirley points out that the *Countrey farme* was translated from a French source, but the edition claimed that it was 'reconciled' with English practices by Markham.

83. J. Thirsk, *Horses in early modern England, for service, for pleasure, for power* (Reading, 1978).

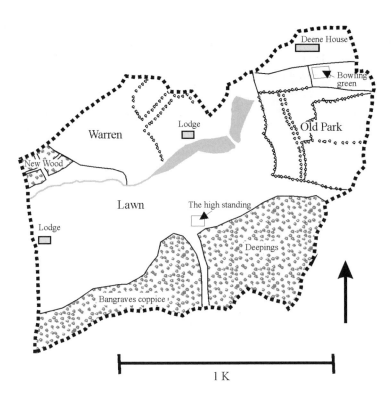

Figure 3.12 Deene Park.

Markham also had advice on the compartmentation of the park: 'nor must these several grounds lie open – they must be separated one from the other by a strong rale, through which deere or shepe (but no greate cattell) may passe'.[84]

Evidence exists of the internal structure of the Northamptonshire parks. The set of maps that Christopher Hatton commissioned in the 1580s includes two that cover the formation of his park at Holdenby (subsequently a royal park when Hatton died without issue and his nephew sold it to James I). The 1580 map shows the manor before the making of the park and the 1587 map shows the park in place and railed.[85] Maps of Deene Park in the seventeenth century similarly show the internal configuration of the park, and are also embellished with pictorial representations of the animals that inhabited it.[86] Figure 3.11 shows Holdenby Park in the 1580s, while Figure 3.12 shows Deene Park in 1630. The eighteenth-century commissioners' reports talked of the lawns of the forest as being 'in the nature of parks', and Wakefield Lawn and Benefield Lawn on the seventeenth-

84. Gervase Markham's *The countrey farme*, cited in Shirley, *Deer parks*, pp. 234.
85. NRO, Finch Hatton archive: FH272.
86. NRO, maps: Map 4093, Map 4096.

century maps show many of the same features as the cartographic depictions of the parks: the enclosing rails, the pasture for grazing and the trees for browsing. Both parks and lawns were fulfilling the same function: providing a protective environment for the keeping of deer.

It has been suggested that the structure of the park in the early modern period was different from that of its medieval precursor, and that this was connected to the change in location already observed. As deer parks were becoming 'essential adjuncts' to the great house, rather than distant deer farms, so the density of trees within the park was reduced while the wide areas of pasture became more prominent. This was not for the benefit of the deer, but rather so that the owners and their guests could enjoy extensive prospects and appreciate the full size of the park. In this period the 'wild irregularity' of the park provided a 'pleasing contrast' with the geometric order of the formal gardens immediately surrounding the house.[87] This argument serves to emphasise the role of the deer park as the precursor to the eighteenth-century landscape park. Northamptonshire provides some notable examples – such as Althorp and Boughton – of deer parks that went on to be incorporated into what is now regarded as a 'landscape park'. Deene was also rearranged, enlarged and improved to fit in with newer ideals; indeed, the enthusiasm for sculpting the landscape extended beyond the bounds of the park, and surviving records show the planting and felling of trees being planned to enhance 'the vista'.[88] Forest lawns, as well as parks, became the underpinning of designed landscapes intended to show off a prestigious house; thus, Wakefield Lawn effectively became the park to the Northamptonshire seat of the dukes of Grafton. One of the Whittlewood coppices became a 'pheasantry' (the pleasure grounds to the great house) and the holders of common rights in the forest had to be granted year-round access to other coppices in exchange for this. In the late 1700s the third duke was trying to reach a similar accommodation so that common animals could be excluded from the approach to his residence and the way would not be so dirty.[89] There seem to have been only a few landscape parks created directly from medieval deer parks in Northamptonshire, such as Rockingham and, possibly, Blatherwycke; for the most part parks were required to be adjacent to the great house, and so medieval parks were not suitable.[90] For our purposes, however, the most important point about the landscape parks in Northamptonshire is that they continued to be places where deer were kept. Deene

87. Williamson, *Polite landscapes*, p. 24.
88. NRO, Brudenell archive: Bru.I.xiii.24a
89. NRO, Grafton archive: G3980.
90. In their survey of Rockingham Forest, Foard *et al.* classified parks made from the sixteenth century onwards as 'landscape parks', rather than as deer parks. G. Foard, D. Hall and T. Britnell, *The historic landscape of Rockingham Forest* (2003), <http://www.rockingham-forest-trust.org.uk/RF%20pdfs/Rockingham%20Forest%20Project%20final%20report.pdf>. Accessed 13 December 2012, p. 52.

Park may have had canals, avenues and waterfalls added, but Daniel Eaton's letters in the 1720s continually reflected concern and interest in the park's deer.[91] In the middle of the century his son drew up detailed plans on the best way to manage the park to support deer. This included the number of does and bucks to be kept, as well as the number of sheep and horses thought to complement the keeping of the deer (through the different grazing habits of each animal).[92] When listing the Northamptonshire parks still in existence in the nineteenth century, Shirley also included the number and type of deer that the park supported.[93]

With renewed interest in the subject of deer parks – one of the 'thorny issues' still causing debate among historians – some fundamental questions have been asked about their actual purpose.[94] There is no doubt that deer were pursued within the park pales, and killed, but could this be considered as a sport, or just as a way of harvesting venison? It has been argued that medieval parks were venison farms more than hunting arenas.[95] Others have conceded that bow and stable hunts were staged in parks, but considered them to have been too small to have hosted *par force* hunts, and even queried whether bow and stable hunting could be really considered as hunting, as it comprised the destruction of contained animals and did not meet the criteria to identify hunting set out by anthropologists such as Cartmill.[96] Some, however, have had quite a different view of the medieval park, seeing it as 'the ideal aristocratic hunting ground – bounded, controllable, secure and visible'. What the park lacked in space it made up for in controllability.[97] A recent study of medieval parks devoted considerable space to the debate about the primary purpose of the deer park and, while acknowledging that parks did have other practical and pleasurable uses, it was unequivocal in the assertion that the main function of the park was as a hunting reserve for deer.[98] Many of the more sceptical views of park hunting have been informed by the belief that parks were just not physically large enough to hunt in,[99] but such views are predicated on

91. Wake and Champion-Webster, *Letters of Daniel Eaton*.
92. NRO, Brudenell archive: Bru.I.xiii.1.
93. Shirley, *Deer parks*, pp. 147–53.
94. Liddiard, *Medieval park*, p. 4.
95. Birrell contended that the harvesting of the venison was mostly carried out by servants and could therefore not be regarded as 'hunting'. Rackham similarly discounted the roles of parks as hunting reserves, putting their economic importance above their recreational worth. Fletcher admitted that he initially agreed with Birrell and Rackham, but then modified his views and concluded that parks were far more than venison farms. J. Birrell, 'Deer and deer farming in medieval England', *Agricultural History Review*, 40/2 (1992), pp. 112–26; Rackham, *Trees and woodland*, p. 153; J. Fletcher, *Gardens of earthly delight: the history of deer parks* (Oxford, 2011), p. 105.
96. N. Sykes, 'Animal bones and animal parks', in Liddiard (ed.), *Medieval park*, p. 51.
97. A. Pluskowski, 'The social construction of medieval park ecosystems: an interdisciplinary persepective', in Liddiard (ed.), *Medieval park*, p. 63.
98. Mileson, *Parks in medieval England*, pp. 16–44.
99. Historians and archaeologists have recovered information about the size of early deer parks

modern notions of what a hunt is. The slower speed of both horses and hounds and the greater emphasis on the quality of the pursued animal and the skill of following its scent would require less acreage by far than a modern foxhunt. It was also not unknown for the pursued deer to jump the pale and for the hunt to continue at large. When alternative hunting methods, such as coursing deer with greyhounds and driving deer past stands, are considered there were plenty of ways in which 'sport' could be arranged within the confines of a deer park.[100]

The subject of the park as hunting arena is of sufficient importance to this work to merit a more detailed examination. Having established that there was a continuum of park creation and destruction in the county, with an early modern revival in park-making and an enthusiastic embracing of the fashion for the landscape park, we need to address the issue of how far deer continued to be hunted in these parks. This is also a good point to ask the parallel question, postponed from our earlier examination of the forest landscape: how far did the hunting of deer persist in the open forest? In the case of both forest and park there were still deer to hunt, but at what point did hunting as entertainment give way to hunting as venison harvesting? When were the servants left to dispatch the deer while their masters were elsewhere hunting the fox?

Hunting deer in Northamptonshire parks and forests

Northamptonshire seems to have lost its appeal as a royal hunting ground after the death of Henry VIII. Having created the Honor of Grafton and enlarged the parks that abutted each other on the border of Whittlewood Forest, Henry visited Grafton every August for a few weeks' hunting.[101] James I visited Grafton once or

from attempts to trace their boundaries in modern landscapes and from the survival of licences to empark. Unsurprisingly, the largest were the royal parks, while some other parks were very small indeed. Grafton, at its peak, covered over 1000 acres. At the other end of the scale, the park at Ashley covered 12 acres when it was emparked in the 1280s; Blatherwycke also covered 12 acres. Eastwood covered a mere 7 acres 3 roods when emparked in 1267. VCH Northamptonshire, 5, p. 20; J. Steane, 'The medieval parks of Northamptonshire', *Northamptonshire Past and Present*, 5/3 (1975), p. 219.

100. The controversy about the use of deer parks extends to the early modern park. Cantor and Squires described Tudor and Stuart parks as 'amenity parks' in which hunting was of 'secondary importance' to their primary aim of enhancing a dwelling. Rackham, who, as we observed, denied that the medieval park was really a hunting reserve, suggested that Henry VIII introduced a 'new function' for parks as places for 'ceremonial hunts'. Our earlier accounts of hunting methods have touched upon the lavish spectacles that the Tudor monarchs staged in their parks and had provided for them by their loyal park-owning subjects. L. Cantor and A. Squires, *The historic parks and gardens of Leicestershire and Rutland* (Newton Linford, 1997), p. 48. O. Rackham, *An illustrated history of the countryside* (London, 1994), p. 61.

101. Hall describes a process of 'vigorous emparking and enclosing' which resulted in an unbroken tract of forest, park and enclosures that ran for 13 miles from Whittlewood to Salcey, and which was available for hunting 'without any interruption by open fields'. D. Hall, 'The woodland

twice, and similarly hunted in Rockingham on a few occasions, but his favoured hunting locations lay along a corridor from London to East Anglia and included the park at Theobalds, and Royston, Newmarket and Thetford. As we have seen, most of Rockingham Forest was alienated under the Stuart monarchs, while Grafton was granted first to Queen Catherine and then to the dukes of Grafton, along with many of the rights in Whittlewood Forest. The dukes of Grafton subsequently abandoned Grafton itself and made Wakefield Lodge their Northamptonshire seat. The post-Restoration state papers refer to the Forest of Whittlewood as being 'not fit for his Majesty's hunting'.[102]

Northamptonshire was famously well endowed with nobility, and there is evidence that they continued to hunt in the county's forests.[103] We have already referred to the 1623 warrant permitting John, Lord Mordaunt, to hunt deer in the forests of Rockingham, Whittlewood and Salcey and the parks of Grafton and Ampthill.[104] The fourth earl of Exeter was granted annual warrants after the Restoration, and a Hatton family letter from 1670 confirmed that he took advantage of them (mentioning in passing that 'my lord of Exeter is hunting in the Forest').[105] The right to hunt deer in the forest continued to be subject to regulation. As late as 1711 the third earl of Cardigan was granted the right to hawk and hunt in Rockingham Forest with 'his company and servants', but red and fallow deer were explicitly excluded. The Brudenells suffered no such limitation in their own woods; a 1683 letter from a servant to Lord Hatton describes the hunting of deer in Hatton's woods, but also mentions that 'Lord Cardigan has hunted his purlieus very much this season'.[106] Accounts surviving from the 1680s confirm that the Hattons still employed a huntsman. Between August 1681 and May 1682 he received payments for dog food and for travelling expenses; another item covered oats for the huntsman's horse and for the deer and fawns. Money was also received for work that the huntsman had done with hounds belonging to a Mr Pulkins.[107]

There is also plenty of evidence from the seventeenth century that deer were being taken illegally from the Northamptonshire forests. In 1643 Thomas Spenser, a shepherd, was in trouble for being found carrying a dead buck away from Gretton Woods on a horse in the company of a Michael Brewer. In his defence, Spenser claimed that they had found the buck already dead.[108] In 1672 a gentleman named

landscapes of southern Northamptonshire', *Northamptonshire Past and Present*, 54 (2001), p. 44.

102. *CSPD Charles II, 1663–1664*, p. 393.
103. Norden referred to Northamptonshire as the 'Heralds garden' because of its preponderance of aristocrats. Norden, *Delineation*, p. 2.
104. *CSPD James I, 1623–1625* (London, 1859), p. 11.
105. NRO, Finch Hatton archive: FH1433.
106. NRO, Finch Hatton archive: FH2954.
107. NRO, Finch Hatton archive: FH2646.
108. NRO, Finch Hatton archive: FH3141.

William Good instructed two men (a labourer and a mason) to enter the Hatton's woods called Bangrave to shoot a buck. With the assistance of Good and his servant, they then carried the buck to Good's house. William Good claimed that he had Hatton's consent to 'hunt, kill and carry away' any deer as a consequence of a lease that he had. As the deer was killed on a Sunday and carried to Good's house at 9pm there must be some doubt as to the veracity of his claims.[109] Fifteen years later Robert Lichfield, a Brigstock carpenter, claimed that Mr Thomas Barton asked him to fetch a buck from a coppice in Farming Woods that Barton had killed the day before, Lichfield receiving a share of the animal for his trouble.[110] In 1701 William Gleatherer of Oakley Magna saw a gentleman course and kill a deer with a greyhound near Pipewell Woods. This Mr Smith was in the company of a grazier, a clerk, a labourer and another gentleman. In his defence, the grazier, Daniel Hull, claimed that he did not know that the closes in which they were coursing were within the bounds of the forest.[111] It is worth noting that nearly all these incidents involved a group of men of mixed social status, including one or more gentlemen, echoing our earlier description of the poaching of deer.

There is little or no information in our local sources about exactly how deer were being hunted, legally or otherwise, and whether their pursuers followed the organisation and ceremony set out by books such as Markham's and Blome's. The nearest we come is a seventeenth-century record of the eighteen different calls that 'the huntsman shall blow', formally recorded and preserved in the Hatton papers.[112] As we enter the eighteenth century the records regarding deer become more concerned with how many deer were taken and how venison was distributed. We also learn that, while dutiful servants were tending the deer and killing them as required, their masters might be otherwise occupied. Among the principal concerns of the letters from Daniel Eaton to his master, the third earl of Cardigan, in the 1720s are deer, woodland, horses and hounds. But it is also clear from the letters that the hounds are kept for hunting foxes, not deer. When Cardigan was absent from Deene, Eaton kept him informed of the training of the hounds, which included teaching them not to chase sheep or deer, and described runs after foxes that the hounds had had. Cardigan's huntsman was Jack Kingston, but when deer were taken they were killed by the park keeper, John Peak.[113]

Davis's 1787 survey of Whittlewood, made in preparation for the report to the parliamentary commissioners, described the forest purlieus, whose proprietors could hunt deer from sunrise to sunset, and the free hays, where the proprietors could hunt day or night, but remarked that 'neither of the above customs are now

109. NRO, Finch Hatton archive: FH3842, FH3843.
110. NRO, Finch Hatton archive: FH2056.
111. NRO, Finch Hatton archive: FH2829.
112. NRO, Finch Hatton archive: FH4248.
113. Wake and Champion-Webster, *Letters of Daniel Eaton*, pp. 9, 13, 32, 38.

exercised, there being annual tributes of venison paid in lieu of such rights'.[114] The attention of the forest rangers, the dukes of Grafton, had already turned to foxhunting. The second duke was one of the subscribers to the Charlton hunt in 1738 (the Charlton was based in Sussex and claims are made that it was the first 'modern' fox hunt).[115] He also had his own pack of hounds, which was originally kept at Croydon[116] and later moved between Wakefield Lawn and Euston Park, in Suffolk, before eventually settling down to become a Northamptonshire pack.[117] One man's reminiscences of hunting with the Grafton hounds provides a rare insight into the mechanics of controlling the forest deer. In recounting an incident in the 1830s when the foxhounds ran riot among the forest deer at Wakefield Lawn and Lady Coppice, the author introduced us to Clarke, the royal keeper, who had 'a pack of bloodhounds with which to hunt the deer'.[118]

Conclusion

This survey of the forests and parks of Northamptonshire tells us that Northamptonshire was still well provided with deer habitat in the period of the hunting transition. The earls of Cardigan and dukes of Grafton had ample deer to hunt, if the fancy so took them. The traditional explanation for the transfer of hunting ambition from the deer to the fox, that of lack of habitat and shortage of prey, clearly does not hold water for Northamptonshire, at least. If there was not a negative reason for the hunting transition, perhaps there was a positive one. If it was not so difficult to hunt deer, possibly the change came because it was much more desirable to hunt the fox.

114. NRO, Survey of Whittlewood Forest by Richard Davis of Lewknor: NPL3044.

115. S. Rees, The Charlton hunt: a history (Chichester, 1998).

116. B. Falk, The royal Fitzroys: dukes of Grafton through four centuries (London, 1950), p. 97.

117. NRO, Charles King Chace Book, 1800–1808: YZ2586.

118. Elliott, Fifty years' foxhunting, p. 11.

4

Modern foxhunting

The origins of foxhunting in its modern form lie in the second half of the eighteenth century. The new sport did not emerge in its finished form overnight, however. Although its birth is generally traced to the 1750s, its gestation occupied the first half of that century and it reached maturity in the nineteenth century. Foxhunting in the early eighteenth century occurred across England, but by the early nineteenth century its focus was Leicestershire, Northamptonshire and Rutland. These counties were known to foxhunters as 'the shires', and their principal hunts, the Quorn, the Belvoir, the Cottesmore and the Pytchley, were the 'shire packs'.

Northamptonshire boasted some enthusiastic aristocratic proponents of the sport in the eighteenth century. As we have seen, Charles Fitzroy, second duke of Grafton, was an early adherent of the sport. He had his own pack of foxhounds (started some time between 1710 and 1715) that he moved between his Northamptonshire and Suffolk estates and Croydon. He also hunted fox with the Charlton, being one of the initial subscribers, and kept a hunting box in Richmond, from where he could hunt with the Royal Buckhounds and Robert Walpole's beagles. This interest was maintained by succeeding dukes. The political career of the third duke, Augustus, was reputedly destined to failure because it took second place to his passion for hunting and horseracing (and for his mistress, Nancy Parsons, who he scandalously installed at Wakefield Lawn).[1] The third duke kept up the practice of moving hounds between Wakefield Lawn and Euston Park, but Croydon had, by then, been given up as a bad job. The mastership of the Grafton continued in the Fitzroy family, including various dukes and the third Baron Southampton (who resided at Whittlebury), until 1882, when the pack was presented to the country.[2] The Grafton hunt was never counted as a 'shire' pack, but it did figure among the second rank of hunts when the sport was at the height of its popularity.

The Spencers were another of Northamptonshire's noble families who showed an early enthusiasm for foxhunting. Charles, fifth earl Sunderland and

1. Falk, Royal Fitzroys, pp. 75, 97–8, 112, 121.
2. Falk, Royal Fitzroys, pp. 227–35; Elliott, Fifty years' foxhunting, pp. 1–8, 21–37.

later third duke of Marlborough, was in possession of Althorp for only four years before inheriting his dukedom and Blenheim Palace. In this brief period he made his impact on Althorp by building the magnificent neo-Palladian stables to house his hunters in 1732–3 and by commissioning John Wootton in 1733 to paint two gigantic hunting pictures, in addition to life-size portraits of horses and hounds.[3] It was Charles's nephew, John, Earl Spencer, who bought new hounds around 1765, moved them to kennels at Pytchley and took over the already-established Pytchley hunt. Between September and November the hunt was based at Pytchley and chased foxes over the land to the east of the Northampton–Market Harborough road. The hounds were then moved to Althorp, where they hunted the land to the west of the road. In the new year they moved back to Pytchley again. Up until the end of the eighteenth century the Althorp country contained a large portion of what later became the Grafton hunt country, and they hunted as far south as Whittlewood Forest. Earl Spencer continued to hunt until the year before his death in 1783. Although the second earl was more famous for his passion for books than for hunting, he nevertheless kept the mastership of the Pytchley until 1797, when he handed it over to John Warde. This was not the end of the Spencer family's involvement with the Pytchley, however, as the earl's son, Viscount Althorp, took the pack from 1808 and hunted them until he retired at the end of the 1818 season, having suffered a bad fall the previous November.[4] The hunt ceased once more to be the private property of the Spencer family and adopted the organisation typical of 'modern' fox hunts. The Pytchley came to enjoy a high reputation as one of the venerated 'shire' packs.

In the east of the county the Fitzwilliam hunt was founded at Milton. The Fitzwilliams came later to foxhunting than the Fitzroys or Spencers, a pack being established in 1769 by the fourth earl, who was succeeded as master in 1833 by his son, the fifth earl. The pack stayed under the control of the Fitzwilliam family for the rest of the nineteenth century. The Fitzwilliam country encompassed parts of Huntingdonshire and Cambridgeshire as well as Northamptonshire.[5]

There were other hound packs hunting fox in Northamptonshire in the early stages of the sport's development. Justinian Isham's diary, covering the first decades of the eighteenth century, made several references to hunting fox with 'Mr. Andrews'.[6] A letter dated 1783, written to Lord Craven and passed to the Spencers, talked of Lumley Arnold of Ashby Lodge, whose pack of hounds was interfering with the Pytchley sport.[7] These packs did not belong to a great

3.   G. Worsley, The British stable (New Haven, CT, and London, 2004), p. 137; G. Paget, The history of the Althorp and Pytchley hunt 1634–1920 (London, 1937), p. 36.
4.   Paget, Althorp and Pytchley hunt, pp. 37, 41; H.O. Nethercote, The Pytchley hunt past and present (London, 1888), pp. 10–13, 30; C. Spencer, The Spencer family (London, 1999), pp. 50–184.
5.   VCH Northamptonshire, 2, pp. 373–5.
6.   NRO, Isham archive: IL2686.
7.   Cited in Paget, Althorp and Pytchley hunt, p. 37.

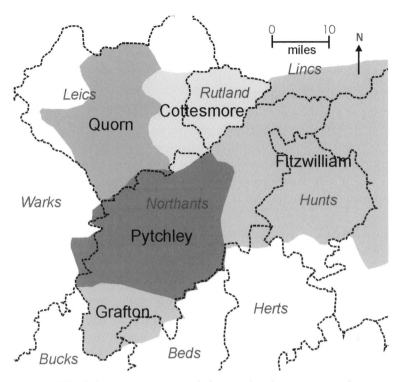

Figure 4.1 East Midlands hunt countries around 1850 (modern hunt names used).

family and were not the foundation of a famous nineteenth-century hunt, and so have disappeared from the record. In 1730 the third earl of Cardigan formed his hunting confederacy with the noblemen with whom he habitually hunted. Under the terms of this agreement the expenses of horses and hounds were met jointly by the members (the third duke of Rutland, the earl of Cardigan, the fourth earl of Gainsborough, John, Lord Gower, and Emanuel, Lord Howe). The experienced hounds were to be kept at Croxton Park (midway between Melton and Grantham) for October and November, Cottesmore in Rutland for December and January and Thrawson (Thrapston?) for February and March.[8] The letters that survive from Cardigan's steward, Daniel Eaton, betray a constant concern with the hounds, and Justinian Isham's diary describes a visit to Deene in 1710 to inspect the kennels.[9] But Cardigan's confederacy did not survive to form the basis of a later hunt.

By the time that modern foxhunting had arrived at its finished form in the nineteenth century, Northamptonshire as a hunting country was divided between the Pytchley in the centre, the Grafton underneath the Pytchley, and the Fitzwilliam to the east (Figure 4.1). Of these, only the Pytchley was counted as a

8.   Wake and Champion-Webster, *Letters of Daniel Eaton*, p. 153.
9.   NRO, Isham archive: IL2686.

shire pack and not all of its territory was equally valued by the hunt followers: it was only the area bordering Leicestershire and Warwickshire that was considered to be 'shire' country.

The development of foxhunting

Foxhunting as practised in the eighteenth century had not yet reached its modern form, but nevertheless its methods and status already marked a significant departure from the sport's traditional position in the hierarchy of the chase. Foxes had long been treated as quarry, and they figured in the hunting sources that we used in our investigation of deer hunting. There is a contrast, however, in the estimated worth of the fox in the eyes of earlier and later hunters. Medieval sources gave little space to the fox and did not have a very high opinion of the sport provided by it. They expected its hunting to be accomplished on foot with the aid of nets and hays (Surtees found evidence that the royal fox hunt of Edward I used a horse only to carry this equipment).[10] Most sixteenth- and seventeenth-century writers gave it scarcely more credit. Sir Thomas Elyot, in giving advice on pastimes suitable for young gentlemen, did not 'dispraise' the hunting of foxes with running hounds but observed that 'it is not to be compared to the other hunting in commodotie of exercise'. He recommended that it be 'used in the deepe wynter when the other game is unseasonable'.[11] Markham, writing in the early seventeenth century, covered foxhunting together with badger hunting and maintained that these provided chases of 'a great deal less use or cunning' than those afforded in the hunting of stag, buck or hare. He rated the scent of fox and badger as being too 'hot' to be attractive and suggested that few dogs would hunt them 'with all egernesse'.[12]

Foxes were vermin, and in the early modern period the parish often gave a reward for their destruction.[13] Although included among the 'beasts of the chase' by early hunting writers they received no legal protection from either the Forest Laws or the Game Laws. Hunting the fox seems to have been viewed more as an occupation suitable for the lower sections of society. There is evidence, however, that some were beginning to see the fox as a good and entertaining quarry for the gentleman. At the end of the sixteenth century Cockaine's *A short treatise of hunting* contained more advice on hunting the fox than any other prey. He was full of praise for the potential excitement of the sport: 'and this tast I will give you of the flying

---

10. Surtees, *Town and country papers*, p. 216; Edward of Norwich, *Master of game*, pp. 64–7; Phoebus, *Livre de chase*, pp. 60–61.
11. T. Elyot, *The book named the Governor* (London, 1531), f. 72.
12. Markham, *Countrey contentments* (1615; New York, 1973), p. 33.
13. This practice apparently persisted into the eighteenth century. The last payments for dead foxes occur in the parish constable accounts as follows: 1786 (Old), 1769 (Marston Trussel), 1777 (Boddington, Crick and Wicken), 1782 (Stanion). Wake and Champion-Webster, *Letters of Daniel Eaton*, p. xlvi.

of this chase, that the author hereof hath killed a Foxe distant from the covert where hee was found, fourteene miles aloft the ground with hounds'.[14] The virtues of foxhunting were also described by Blome towards the end of the seventeenth century. He recommended the hunting of the fox, alongside the hunting of stag or buck, as providing entertainment for horseman of a 'warlike nature'. Blome gave an historic account of how foxhunting was carried out by 'country people'. They would join together with dogs of all kinds and try to beat the fox out of woods and coverts, where it would be coursed by the dogs and taken by nets. But, in Blome's judgement, 'the knowledge of foxhunting had lately achieved much greater perfection', and foxhunting had become a 'very healthful' recreation.[15]

James, duke of York, was an early enthusiast of the sport. Writing from Newmarket in March 1684, he reported that he had 'been twice a fox hunting and had very good sport both times', and there are more references to James's foxhunting in the *Calendar of state papers*.[16] The foundation of the Charlton hunt, which is regarded as one of the harbingers of modern foxhunting, has been attributed to Charles II's illegitimate son, the duke of Monmouth.[17] Thus, writing in a 1714 hunting manual, Stringer was able to assert that the sport of foxhunting was 'much used by Kings, Princes, Noblemen, and Gentlemen'.[18]

Initially foxhunting derived many of its methods from deer hunting. For example, hounds were deployed in relays rather than by the modern method of using the whole pack to draw for, and put up, the fox. Cox advised his readers to send only the 'sure Finders' to draw, and then add more hounds to the chase as 'you dare trust them'. He warned against casting too many hounds at once because 'Woods and Coverts are full of sundry Chases, and so you may engage them in too many at one time.'[19]

The birth of modern foxhunting

Although foxhunting had significant early adherents in Northamptonshire, and an area of the county came to be part of the fashionable 'shires', the modern form of foxhunting is commonly judged to have started with the foundation of the Quorn hunt in Leicestershire. Hugo Meynell moved to Quorndon Hall near Loughborough in 1753 and commenced the hunting of foxes and the breeding of foxhounds possessed of increased speed and stamina. Meynell was a man of fashion and reputation, and his involvement with the sport was reckoned to have

14. Cockaine, *Short treatise*, opposite B. 3.
15. Blome, *Gentleman's recreation*, pp. 86–7.
16. J.P. Hore, *The history of Newmarket and the annals of the turf*, 3 vols (London, 1886), 1, p. 48. *CSPD Charles II, 1683: January–June* (London, 1933), pp. 87–150. <http://www.british-history.ac.uk/report.aspx?compid=57440>. Accessed 13 January 2013.
17. Rees, *Charlton hunt*, p. 2.
18. A. Stringer, *The experience'd huntsman* (Belfast, 1714), p. 159.
19. Cox, *Gentleman's recreation*, p. 111.

counteracted some of the negative stereotypes of the 'country bumpkin squire' that became common among the elite earlier in the eighteenth century.[20] It has been countered that many other individuals were breeding improved hounds at this time, but two factors set Meynell apart: the country he hunted and the time of the day he started his hunts. The eastern part of the hunt's territory took in an increasing area of Leicestershire laid down to pasture, the area that was to become the prime shires hunting country in the nineteenth century. Meynell commenced his sport at 11am, in contrast to other huntsmen, who would commence at dawn. His rationale was that the fox would run faster after being given time to digest its night's meal and recover from the associated exertions.[21]

Many of the methods that Meynell laid down became the distinguishing features of modern foxhunting, the major one of these being the speed at which the sport was conducted. As we have seen, the hunting of foxes from horseback was well established by the mid-eighteenth century, but it originally involved rising before dawn and picking up the fox's scent as it returned to its lair after a night's hunting. Once hounds scented a fox, they would follow it relentlessly, albeit slowly, and the pursuit of a single fox could last all day. A phrase used to describe this was 'walking the fox to death'.[22] A modern fox hunt met at 11am or 12 noon, when the fox was more likely to make a run for it and provide those following the hounds with the opportunity of a good, fast gallop. It was a feature of modern foxhunting in the shires, and an essential argument of this work, that most of the followers were more interested in the riding than the hunting.

The modern fox hunt followed a well-defined procedure. It started with an 'earth stopper' blocking fox holes in the designated coverts the night before the hunt visited in order to prevent the fox going to earth when it returned from its night's hunting and force it to lay up in the undergrowth. The next morning, the hunt would assemble at a pre-arranged venue. The meet itself was a social occasion, typically taking place in a town square or the front lawn of some local large house. The master was in charge of the hunt, and usually owned the pack, but he would usually employ a huntsman actually to hunt the hounds. To help keep the pack in order there would be two 'whippers-in'. Everyone else on horseback was collectively known as 'the field'.

When the field was assembled, and had taken some time to socialise at the meet, the hunt would move off to the covert where the earths had been stopped. The huntsman would then draw the covert, which involved sending the hounds into the undergrowth in the attempt to put up a fox. This could be a lengthy

20. See Chapter 5 for a discussion of fashion and hunting. Meynell was a friend of Johnson, and Boswell's *Life* contains an apposite quote of Meynell's: 'The chief advantage of London (said he,) is, that a man is always *so near his burrow*'. J. Boswell, *Life of Johnson* (1791; Oxford, 1998), p. 1014. Meynell was also a friend of the third duke of Grafton; Falk, *Royal Fitzroys*, p. 157.

21. C.D.B. Ellis, *Leicestershire and the Quorn hunt* (Leicester, 1951), p. 10.

22. 'The Druid' (H.H. Dixon), *Silk and scarlet* (London, 1859), p. 243.

procedure, and so gave the field more opportunities for conversation (known as 'coffee-housing'). The aim was to have a fox off and running before the hounds could get it. To 'chop' a fox – kill it in covert – was considered a great disaster. Once the fox had 'broken cover' the hounds and the hunt would set off in pursuit; the faster the fox ran, the better. The chase then continued until the fox was caught and killed, or until it got completely away (although there might be a 'check' where the hounds temporarily lost the scent, and a 'cast' to direct them in finding it again). The hunt would then proceed to another covert and repeat the process.

This was the form of hunting that came to grip the country in the nineteenth century. Meynell continued to hunt the parts of Leicestershire both to the east and west of the river Soar, but it was to the east that the popular country lay. By the beginning of the nineteenth century keen foxhunters were basing themselves in Melton Mowbray, from where they could also reach the meets of the Cottesmore and Belvoir hunts and gallop across the favoured Leicestershire grasslands for six days a week. The shire counties came to be the winter playground of the country's elite, whose antics were widely reported in press and in pictures. Many aspired to join the 'fast set' in the shires, while others contented themselves with following the same sport in the 'provinces'.

The change in pace in the pursuit of hounds was an innovation that occurred under Meynell, and gave rise to 'hard riding' as an integral part of the sport, but such horsemanship was not at Meynell's instigation. It was a Mr Childe of Kinlet Hall in Shropshire who was credited with setting the trend as he followed Meynell's hounds, a trend that was enthusiastically adopted by other hunt followers.[23] In contrast, Dick Christian described Meynell himself as being like a 'regular little apple dumpling on horseback'.[24] Meynell apparently had his work cut out in restraining the more enthusiastic of his followers and preventing them from 'ruining' the sport by riding into the hounds. As one follower of Meynell reported to Cook, 'his indignation in the field was sometimes excessive'.[25]

A key feature of the developing sport was the ever-growing size of the field, particularly in the fashionable shire hunt countries. As modern foxhunting developed it became increasingly a 'public' rather than a private sport and, in the case of the shires, people travelled from other regions of the country to take part. In the early decades of the nineteenth century meets came to be fixed and regular, and their locations were published in advance. Many of the hunt costs were met by subscribers. This public face both reflected the burgeoning popularity of the sport and fed it, and the fields of mounted followers grew ever larger. It came to matter

23. Nimrod (C. Apperley), *The chace, the road and the turf* (1837; London, 1927), p. 21. Nimrod lists another dozen or so men in his footnotes whom he considers to be among the first followers of this new fashion.
24. Druid, *Silk and scarlet*, p. 358.
25. Colonel John Cook, *Observations on fox hunting* (1826; London, 1922), p. 128.

less and less what the personal preferences of the masters of foxhounds might be, because they perceived that they had to satisfy their followers.

In 1781 Beckford had voiced concern about the role of the field. His opinion was that the 'greater number' of those that rode after hounds were not sportsmen and had little knowledge of how to help, rather than hinder, the huntsman in his work. Beckford also observed that the 'steam of many horses', when carried by the wind, could seriously interfere with the scent that the hounds were following.[26] The early Althorp Chace books listed the followers of the hunt at each meet. It is not clear if the intention was to list the entire field or just those of sufficient status who were known to the author, but the lists are quite short. For example, on Saturday 16 October 1773 Lord Spencer, Mr Bouverie, Mr Bryant and Mr Samwell were listed. On 3 November the book noted seven regulars and added that 'some other gentlemen' attended. By 1774 the phrase 'and several others from Northampton' began to appear, but this would still tend to indicate that the fields were small compared with what was to come.[27] By the 1830s Surtees could describe a meet of the Beaufort hunt that had a field of 400 or more mounted followers. He also talked of sitting on his horse on a Northamptonshire hill and observing 'a tail of riders of at least two miles, scattered in all directions, and increasing in every instant'.[28] This can be contrasted with accounts of earlier hunts, where much smaller groups would follow the hounds. Stringer, writing in 1714, worried about the damaging effect that competitive horsemen riding 'upon the very heels of the hounds' had in forcing the hounds to overshoot the scent. But he talked of 20 or 30 horses being in the way when the hounds were cast back, clearly a very much smaller field than could be expected in the next century.[29] One of the witnesses who reported to the select committee of the House of Lords on horses in 1873 commented that you could, by then, see some 300 to 500 riders in a hunting field.[30]

Another distinguishing feature of modern foxhunting was that people travelled to take part. This tendency developed slowly towards the end of the eighteenth century and reached full expression in the nineteenth. Surtees reckoned that in 'Beckford's time' (the 1780s) people did not leave home to hunt 'except for Leicestershire and, perhaps, Northamptonshire'. The situation was more one where 'either gentlemen kept hounds at their own expense, or a few friends joined, and kept a pack among them'.[31] Improvements in road travel facilitated travelling for recreation, however, and in the eighteenth century this probably

26. Peter Beckford, *Thoughts on hunting in a series of familiar letters to a friend* (1781; Lanham, MD, 2000), pp. 118, 140.
27. NRO, Althorp Chace Books: ML4428.
28. Surtees, *Town and country papers*, pp. 82, 98.
29. Stringer, *Experience'd huntsman*, pp. 27–8.
30. Parliamentary Papers, BCPP, 1873, XIV, p. 252.
31. Surtees, *Town and country papers*, pp. 145–6.

had its greatest impact in the movement to London for the 'season' and the growing popularity of the spa resorts. Towards the end of the century, foxhunting began to be popular enough to travel for. Dick Christian talks of the 'company' staying at Loughborough in 'Mr. Meynell's time', but then moving to Melton Mowbray so they could hunt several days a week with the Quorn, the Belvoir and the Cottesmore.[32] This was the beginning of Melton's position as a fashionable winter resort.

Private coach travel had begun to become popular in the sixteenth century and public coaches had become well established since the seventeenth.[33] A sharp increase in the effectiveness of road travel in the 1750s and 1760s has been detected, following a long period of relatively little change. This is attributed to the combination of turnpike roads and steel springs, allowing greater speed without increased cost.[34] The final quarter of the eighteenth century witnessed further decreases in travel times and a 'huge increase' in the number of coach services, including routes between provincial towns as well as from London to the provinces.[35] The early nineteenth century saw yet another dramatic improvement in coach travel associated with Macadam's and Telford's innovations in road surfaces. Nimrod illustrated the dramatic increase in speed and safety with a fanciful account of a 1740s traveller taking an 1830s journey. According to Nimrod 'coach travelling is no longer a disgusting and tedious labour, but has long since been converted into comparative ease, and really approaches something like luxury'.[36]

The roads of both Northamptonshire and Leicestershire had been execrable, as might be expected of heavy clay countries. Celia Fiennes described the road from Uppingham to Leicester as 'the most tiresome, being full of sloughs'.[37] Near Crick, Watling Street was 'deep heavy ground as in all these rich countrys'.[38] Defoe reckoned the Northampton–Market Harborough road 'in the midst of the deep dismal roads, the dirtiest and worst in all that part of the country'.[39] By the time Meynell was hunting his hounds from Quorndon there was a turnpike road connecting London to Leicester and Leicester to Loughborough, meaning

32. Druid, Silk and scarlet, p. 67.
33. J. Crofts, Packhorse, waggon and post: land carriage and communications under the Tudors and Stuarts (London, 1967), pp. 109–32.
34. D. Gerhold, Carriers and coachmasters: trade and travel before the turnpikes (Chichester, 2005), p. 171. Steane included a map showing the network of turnpike roads that criss-crossed Northamptonshire in the eighteenth and nineteenth centuries. He also identified Northampton's importance as a place where major east–west and north–south stage coach routes intersected. Steane connected this fact with the pre-eminence of the town's horse fairs for the trading of carriage and coach horses. Steane, Northamptonshire Landscape, pp. 252–7.
35. T. Barker and D. Gerhold, The rise and rise of road transport, 1700–1990 (Basingstoke, 1993), p. 54.
36. Nimrod, Chace, p. 49.
37. C. Fiennes, The journeys of Celia Fiennes (London, 1983), p. 191.
38. C. Fiennes, The illustrated journeys of Celia Fiennes, ed. C. Morris (London, 1982), p. 228.
39. D. Defoe, A tour through England and Wales, 2 vols (London, 1928), 1, p. 87.

his followers could at least reach the hunting grounds with comparative ease. The appearance of more turnpikes over the second half of the eighteenth century then made the meets of the other shire packs accessible. In Monk's judgement the turnpikes of Leicestershire were 'tolerably good', although he felt that they suffered from the passage of 'heavy narrow-wheeled waggons' used for carrying coal and lime.[40] He hoped for improvement when canals removed the need to haul heavy freight by road. These hopes seem to have been fulfilled: in 1835 Nimrod observed that 'the roads about Melton are uncommonly good, particularly that to Leicester'.[41] Northamptonshire may not have been so lucky. In his *General view of the agriculture of the county*, Donaldson devoted a none-too-complimentary section to the state of the county's roads. Although all the great roads that led through the county were turnpiked, Donaldson complained that these 'show no great ingenuity, either in the engineer who planned, or in the undertakers or overseers who executed the work'. The private or parish roads that ran between the turnpikes were even worse. In many places these were in 'a very ruinous situation' and, in general, so narrow as to 'admit of only one track'.[42] The traveller John Byng was, however, in no doubt that the road situation had improved immeasurably over the preceding few decades. Writing in 1790, at the age of 48, he commented that he was 'just old enough to remember turnpike roads few, and those bad; and when travelling was slow, difficult and, in carriages, somewhat dangerous'. In contrast, he now found 'quick and easy communication of travell'.[43] Such improvements were particularly important for foxhunting, because it was a winter sport.

The coming of the railways added further to the popularity of hunting. Initially the foxhunting fraternity had been appalled at the prospect of railways being built across their hunting grounds, thinking that foxes, horses and hounds would not dare to cross the lines. In 1834 Surtees predicted that the railways would render hunting 'a matter of history'.[44] The actual effect of the railway was quite different, however. Railway travel effectively opened foxhunting in general, and foxhunting in the shires in particular, to a much wider group of participants, and the foxhunting writers eventually came to recognise that the new transport network was a blessing to the sport. In the 1870s Brooksby published *Hunting countries*, a 'where to hunt' guide aimed explicitly at the rail traveller. His advice on where to go and where to stay was made with reference to the railway routes and the railway timetable.[45]

40. J. Monk, *General view of the agriculture of the county of Leicester* (London, 1794), p. 53.
41. Nimrod (C. Apperley), *Nimrod's hunting tours* (1835; London, 1926), p. 133.
42. J. Donaldson, *General view of the agriculture of the county of Northampton, with observations on the means of its improvement* (Edinburgh, 1794), pp. 48–9.
43. C. Bruyn Andrews (ed.), *The Torrington diaries*, 4 vols (London, 1934–8), 2, p. 149.
44. D. Itzkowitz, *Peculiar privilege: a social history of foxhunting, 1753–1885* (Hassocks, 1977), p. 51.
45. Brooksby (E. Pennell-Elmhirst), *The hunting countries of England, their facilities, character and requirements*, 2 vols (London, 1878).

The railways brought greater mobility to foxhunters in several ways. Those unable to relocate themselves for an entire winter season could stable hunters in their favoured country and travel to them as often as required. Eventually they could even catch a morning train from St Pancras or Euston and join a shire meet that same day (similarly, foxhunters could travel from the industrial cities of the Midlands or the North). For those who did base themselves in the shires, the cessation of hunting owing to bad weather no longer meant enforced idleness; they could simply return by train to London until the weather cleared. Foxhunters could also take advantage of railway travel to reach a far greater variety of meets. Special trains were laid on to transport horses, men and even the hounds themselves. Brooksby described a meet in north Warwickshire where 'hounds came by train; so did the master; so did a strong proportion of the field – from Leamington, Coventry, Birmingham and elsewhere'.[46] Rugby in particular benefited from its situation on a railway junction, and became a popular hunting base. Although Rugby was 'far from every kennel' a foxhunter based there could travel to a variety of meets by rail, taking himself and his horses as far as Aylesbury Vale if he so desired.[47]

Conclusion

This account of the emergence of 'modern' foxhunting and description of its methods has stressed the importance of the Midland 'shires'. It was this specific area that supplanted forest and park as the archetypal hunting landscape. The transport developments of road, coach and, later, rail, meant that people could, and did, travel to the favoured hunting grounds of the Midlands, making towns such as Melton Mowbray and Market Harborough into hunting resorts. The next chapter looks at the landscape of the Northamptonshire portion of the 'shires' country in some detail and assesses its agency in the hunting transition.

---

46. Brooksby (E. Pennell-Elmhirst), *The cream of Leicestershire: eleven seasons' skimmings, notable runs and incidents of the chase* (London, 1883), p. 220.
47. Brooksby, *Cream*, p. 132.

5

The landscape of foxhunting

Our examination of Northampton's deer-hunting country drew on an eclectic range of sources. There is no such difficulty in establishing the popularity of foxhunting in the late eighteenth and, particularly, the nineteenth centuries, however. Because foxhunting was so popular there were many who wrote about it both in published sources and in private diaries. Whereas many of the sources available for early deer hunting apply to the forests and parks of the whole country, foxhunting sources are more often about Northamptonshire and Leicestershire, because it was the interaction between foxhunting and this specific landscape that shaped the modern sport that the rest of the country tried to emulate.

As we have already observed, Northamptonshire as a county was most noted for its open tracts of champion land. Morton acknowledged that the 'fielden' portion of the county was larger in area than his other divisions of 'woodland', 'fen' and 'heath' combined.[1] But only a portion of the Northamptonshire champion grounds were part of the famous shires, the quintessential foxhunting terrain: an area roughly contained between Rugby to the west, Northampton to the south and Market Harborough to the north-east, and sometimes identified as 'High Northamptonshire'. This was part of the hunt country of the Pytchley.

In the earlier description of the landscape of the traditional deer hunt we talked of a landscape of the 'find'. By contrast, the landscape required of modern foxhunting was very much one of the 'chase'. The essential element of the fox hunt by the nineteenth century was the short, fast and furious chase. We have previously observed that killing the fox in covert, without a chance of a gallop after it, was considered one of the worst things that could happen. An early nineteenth-century sporting anecdote tells of a French visitor mistakenly congratulating a master on such an occasion on the speedy dispatch of a fox, an extreme *faux-pas* in the face of a severely disappointed field.[2] While many hunts might boast of the length of

---

1. Morton, *Natural history*, p. 13.
2. Cook, *Observations*, p. 119. This very mistake was repeated two centuries later, when a modern anthropologist suggested to members of the hunt that the 'chopping' of a fox he had just witnessed was a 'good result'. He got much the same reaction. G. Marvin, 'A passionate pursuit:

a particular pursuit, the most desirable run was short and sharp. Speed had been increasing in the eighteenth century: Beckford recommended a good pursuit lasting between one and two hours, but J. Ortho Paget, commenting on the text a hundred years later, remarked that 'now that horses and hounds are faster than in Beckford's time, we might say not less that thirty five minutes or more than one hour forty minutes, at least, in a grass country'.[3] By contrast with deer hunting, it was not considered a total disaster to change foxes during a pursuit. Ideally the hounds would stick to the same one until the death, but if they changed prey in a covert at least the field would still get their gallop. The main disadvantage was that the new fox would be fresh and it might lead to a longer and faster pursuit than was ideal. Cook commented that all long runs where the fox got away were the result of the pack changing foxes.[4]

This contrast between traditional deer hunting and modern foxhunting is probably one of degree rather than an absolute. The chase was an important part of the experience of a deer hunt, but not the overridingly important part. The horseback pursuit became ever more significant as foxhunting developed, however. Scarth Dixon, attempting a history of early hunting in 1912, could not conceive that priorities could ever have been any different; his often speculative accounts of medieval or early modern hunting practice were predicated on the belief that its participants would always be looking for a gallop.[5] However misguided this opinion might have been on earlier forms of hunting, it clearly reflected the priorities of the modern form. The change in emphasis in the *modus operandi* of hunting was both cause and effect in the continued swelling of the size of the field of followers. When Meynell was developing his 'science' in Leicestershire he had a preference for the west and north sides of his Quorn hunt country. The mixture of rocky outcrop and woodland that he found in Charnwood provided the type of challenge to hounds that a man more interested in hunting than in riding would enjoy, but his growing band of followers much preferred the grassland to the east of the river Soar, and they pressured Meynell to take his hounds to the grasslands on more days of the week.[6]

The land use most suited for a large number of horses galloping at speed was grass. This is the key to rise of the 'shires' of Leicestershire, Northamptonshire and Rutland as the focus of the new sport in the nineteenth century. The area that

foxhunting as performance', *The Sociological Review*, 51 (2003), p. 55.

3.   Beckford, *Thoughts on Hunting*, p. 125.
4.   Cook, *Observations*, p. 102.
5.   For example, he says of George Villiers, second duke of Buckingham: 'Hard riding doubtless appealed to him. One cannot imagine him dropping into the "regulation canter" which represented pace to James I.' Scarth Dixon, *Hunting*, p. 74.
6.   Ellis, reconstructing the early hunt fixtures from Thomas Jones's diary, had Meynell hunting in the Melton area only two or three times a month, and only once a month on the Harborough side. Ellis, *Leicestershire and the Quorn*, p. 17.

became the prime hunting grounds of Northamptonshire had many ancient grass enclosures and was undergoing a process whereby new enclosure involved the conversion of arable to pasture. Morton, writing of Northamptonshire in 1712, observed that 'of our Fielden or Tillage ground a considerable part is now enclosed, and converted into pasture'. In some places there were 'four or five lordships lying together enclosed'. One of the largest and richest 'knot of pastures' began in the angle where Northamptonshire, Leicestershire and Warwickshire meet: precisely the area that formed part of England's most favoured foxhunting landscape.[7]

Enclosure in Northamptonshire nearly always led to conversion to pasture. Although the county is often regarded as one of the archetypal regions of Midland open-field agriculture, from the fifteenth century onwards it experienced an accelerating conversion from arable to livestock farming. Some parishes were enclosed early, by unity of possession, some later, by agreement; some parishes enclosed one of their three open fields.[8] In his survey of Northamptonshire Pitt suggested that as much as a quarter of the county (not counting the forest and woodland areas) were 'antient enclosures', given over to feeding sheep and oxen.[9] The open-field parishes that escaped early enclosure were all subject to parliamentary enclosure during the eighteenth and early nineteenth centuries. Pitt had another quarter of the county occupied by these 'modern enclosures'. In addition to the enclosed lands, Northamptonshire also boasted what Pitt described as 'natural grass lands' (he added these to parks, paddocks and plantation to account for a further quarter of the county's total land).[10]

The portion of the county that concerns us, High Northamptonshire, shared features in common with the Leicestershire Wolds and High Leicestershire, the other areas of 'the shires', in having a significant number of deserted villages. Historians have taken this as being indicative of the earliest form of enclosure, whereby people moved, or were removed, and were replaced by sheep. There was some very old pasture indeed in this area.[11] Figure 5.1 shows the correlation between the area we have identified as the prime shire hunting country and the high ground of the Leicestershire Wolds, High Leicestershire and High

---

7. Morton, *Natural history*, pp. 14–15.
8. D. Hall, 'Enclosure in Northamptonshire', *Northamptonshire Past and Present*, 9/4 (1997–98), p. 352. Neeson has much of the west and south-west of the county enclosed in the sixteenth and seventeenth centuries, with the rest of the county undergoing parliamentary enclosure in a movement spreading from the south-west in the 1750s. This surge bypassed the southern forests and moved through the scarp along the western side of the county and into the central parishes between Northampton and Kettering in the 1760s and 1770s, reaching the Nene Valley, Rockingham Forest and the fens in the 1790s and 1800s. Neeson, *Commoners*, pp. 58, 224.
9. Pitt, *General view, Northamptonshire*, pp. 36, 111.
10. Pitt, *General View, Northamptonshire*, p. 111.
11. For a discussion of early enclosure in south-east Leicestershire, see J.A. Yelling, *Common field and enclosure 1450–1850* (London, 1977), pp. 46–58.

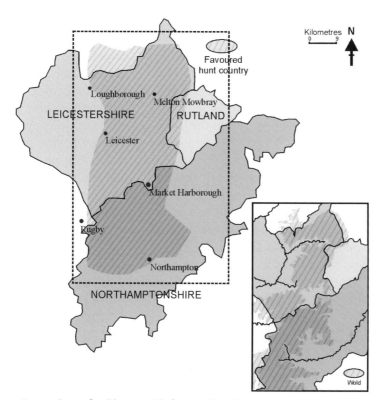

Figure 5.1 Comparison of wold areas with favoured hunting country.

Northamptonshire.[12] Historians have advanced a number of theories about the forces driving the conversion to pasture in this area. It has been suggested that the unattractiveness of arable farming in a region of intractable clay soils after the fourteenth-century population decline and the resultant depression of cereal prices was a major influence, a situation not helped by the scarcity of manure in open-field parishes, where arable could reach right up to the parish boundary, leaving nothing but fallow to support the livestock. Enclosure and conversion to pasture was easier, and even more attractive, in the marginal and less populous parishes in the upland regions we identified in Figure 5.1 (and it mattered far less if livestock farms were remote from the markets, as the produce could walk there).[13]

12. For a description of forces shaping the Wolds, High Leicestershire and High Northamptonshire, see H.S.A. Fox, 'The people of the wolds in English settlement history', in M. Aston, D. Austin and C. Dyer (eds), *The rural settlements of medieval England: studies dedicated to M.W. Beresford and J.G. Hurst* (Oxford, 1989), pp. 77–101.
13. Roberts and Wrathmell, *Region and Place*; T. Williamson, *The transformation of rural England: farming and the landscape 1700–1870* (Exeter, 2002), pp. 29–51.

Foxhunters were to benefit from more and more of the county being put down to grass as the common fields were enclosed: from 'old enclosures', where there was already grass, through the large-scale parliamentary enclosures that occurred in the later eighteenth century, to the late enclosures of the early nineteenth century.[14] Grassland not only provided good going and good scent, but also fitted in well with the seasonality of foxhunting; there was little winter wheat to be trampled, and in the cattle-fattening areas there was hardly any stock in the fields.[15] Enclosure and conversion to grass have often been explained in purely financial terms, but as Thomas said of English landowners, 'for centuries they had self-consciously designed a rural landscape which would provide for both profit and recreation'.[16] Perhaps landowners' growing appetite for foxhunting is worth considering as a motive behind the surge of the 'green tide'. But, whatever the reasons, these developments in the Northamptonshire landscape undoubtedly met the requirements of the modern foxhunter. Writing in the 1830s, Surtees remarked that if he wanted to show a foreigner 'the very cream' of hunting country he would take him to the Pytchley Hunt's Waterloo Gorse (below Market Harborough) and present him with a view of 'grass, grass, grass – nothing but grass for miles and miles'.[17] Cecil seems to have agreed with Surtees as to the worth of Northamptonshire: while acknowledging the fame of Leicestershire, he informed his readers that 'next in superiority the Pytchley Hunt was by many ranked; but with all the advantages which Leicestershire presents, it is doubtful whether Northamptonshire is not equally deserving of fame'. As proof, Cecil quoted the opinion of a man who was in turn master of both the Quorn and the Pytchley: 'no one can be more capable of judging on this point than Mr Osbaldeston, as he hunted both countries, and has been known to declare his opinion in favour of the Pytchley'.[18]

Old enclosure was usually associated with large field sizes, parliamentary enclosure with small fields.[19] Northamptonshire's early enclosures were characterised by fields of 50 acres or more. Smaller fields, more suitable for mixed

---

14. For example, a letter in the Grafton records mentions the duke paying for the grass seed for a twenty-acre field after the Paulerspury enclosure in 1820. NRO, Grafton archive: G3951/23.

15. According to Moscrop, graziers bought in cattle from March to May and sold them between July and November, but kept some over until a general clearance in January. W.J. Moscrop, 'A report on the farming of Leicestershire', *Journal of the Royal Agricultural Society of England*, 2nd ser., 2 (1866), p. 292; For the seasonality of cattle keeping see R.J. Colyer, 'Some aspects of cattle production in Northamptonshire and Leicestershire during the nineteenth century', *Northamptonshire Past and Present*, 5 (1973), pp. 45–54.

16. K. Thomas, *Man and the natural world: changing attitudes in England 1500–1800* (1983; London, 1984), p. 13.

17. Surtees, *Town and country papers*, p. 90.

18. Cecil (C. Tongue), *Records of the chase* (1854; London, 1922), p. 104.

19. W.G. Hoskins, *Leicestershire: an illustrated essay on the history of the landscape* (London, 1957), p. 93.

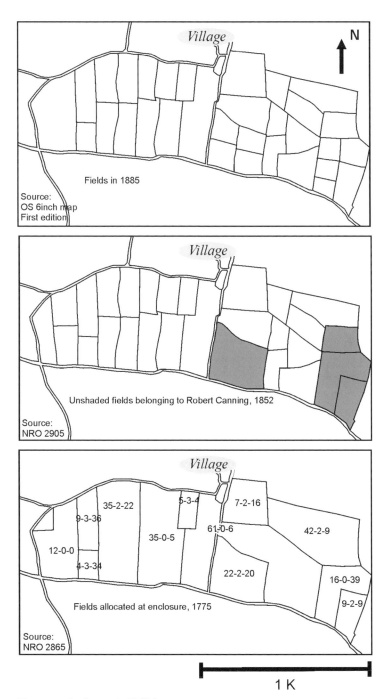

Figure 5.2 Enclosure in Hellidon.

farming, were associated with the period 1750–1850.[20] It is wrong, however, to assume that small enclosures arrived with the surveyor. Some landowners received very large allotments, and while enclosure awards required the new landowners to ring fence these allotments their internal subdivision was up to each individual. This tended to wait upon money, convenience and the results of the land deals that followed enclosure. Figure 5.2 shows how a portion of the parish of Hellidon, on the south-west corner of the Pytchley country, was divided after enclosure in 1775. Initially all the fields shown were allocated to separate individuals. The largest single allocation in this group was 61 acres, but the Hellidon award also contained other large allocations of up to 133 acres in a single parcel. By 1852, most had been consolidated into the hands of Robert Cannings. The OS six-inch map of 1885 also shows the subdivision of the fields not belonging to Cannings. This pattern was repeated across the grazing lands of the foxhunting shires.

As the livestock industry of the region gravitated towards cattle rather than sheep, the large grazing grounds of the old enclosures tended to be subdivided too. It was recognised that rotating stock among smaller fields was a better way to utilise grass. Monk commented that Bakewell, the famous livestock improver, was 'certain that fifty acres of pasture ground divided in five enclosures will go as far in grazing cattle as sixty acres all in one piece'.[21] In 1866 Moscrop quoted a 'first-class' grazier from the Market Harborough district recommending a field size of 24 acres for cattle.[22]

The hunting sources confirm this picture of the fieldscape. First-hand hunting sources from the eighteenth century are rare, but some do exist, in the form of the Althorp Chace books: records kept of the Pytchley hounds between the years 1773 and 1808. The earliest of these books concentrated on the area that was hunted from Althorp, which largely coincided with the country that became part of the venerated shires. These accounts give a vivid picture of crossing the Northamptonshire countryside during the formative years of the sport. Reports of each day's sport were full of references to crossing 'great grass grounds', 'old inclosures', 'new inclosures' and the 'open fields' belonging to one or other of the villages.[23] Nearer to Whittlewood, Surtees was told that the enclosures around Fawsley had been 200 acres when Charles Knightley came into possession of the estate early in the nineteenth century. In Surtees's day the boundaries 'could still be traced among the newly planted hedges with which they were divided'.[24]

As the landscape continued to develop so the nature of the sport of foxhunting was further refined. Enclosure led to the erection of fences and if hunters wanted to keep with the hounds they had to jump them. Jumping had never figured largely

20. Hall, 'Enclosure in Northamptonshire', p. 352.
21. Monk, General View, Leicester, p. 45.
22. Moscrop, 'Report', p. 198.
23. NRO, Althorp Chace Books: ML4428.
24. Surtees, Town and country papers, p. 102.

in early modern hunting; forests, by their very nature, were supposed to be open. When necessary, riders would jump from the trot or even from the standstill: as late as 1839 Delmé Radcliffe reminded his readers that 'there is no doubt that all quadrupeds can jump height as well standing as with a run at it'.[25] The 'flying leap', performed at speed, was an innovation of the modern sport, and became ever more an integral part of it. There is evidence that the hunters were not always pleased with these changes, however. The Althorp Chace books contain more than one reference to the horsemen missing the best of the action because they were held up by the 'new inclosures' and their 'post and rails'. Charles King, huntsman with the Grafton at the end of the eighteenth century and the Pytchley at the beginning of the nineteenth, 'would rather get his horse's hind legs to a fence and make him creep through than jump it'.[26] Other followers would seek alternatives to jumping at all; Nethercote reported that the Pytchley had 'not been without some remarkable examples of members troubled with jumpaphobia'.[27] Elliott tells us that Lord Southampton managed to keep up well with his hounds while hardly jumping anything.[28] It was, however, central to foxhunting mythology that riders were fearless and tackled awesome fences with insouciance. The horsemen (and sometimes women) who were lauded above all were those who rode straight across country, taking each fence as it came. Thomas Assheton Smith, who was famous for his riding and was master of the Quorn in the early nineteenth century, apparently claimed that 'there is no place you cannot get over, with a fall'.[29] The Buckinghamshire hard rider, Mr Peyton, would deliberately aim a tired horse at timber, because he reckoned that at least he would fall on the 'right side' (that is, where the hounds were).[30] The fearsome fences of the shires were part and parcel of their reputation, and the fences of the 'prime' portion of Northamptonshire's hunting grounds were generally deemed to be more severe than those of Leicestershire or Rutland. In the district around Lilbourne Surtees claimed that 'there are some of the stiffest, highest fences, with some of the widest drains in the whole of Northamptonshire, or perhaps in the whole of England'.[31]

The method of fencing enclosure allotments usually comprised a quickset hedge protected by rails with a ditch on one side.[32] This pattern extended to the internal division of allotments and forms the landscape of parliamentary enclosure

25. F.P. Delmé Radcliffe, *The noble science* (London, 1839), p. 116.
26. Nethercote, *The Pytchley hunt*, p. 8.
27. Nethercote, *The Pytchley hunt*, pp. 154, 206.
28. Elliott, *Fifty years' foxhunting*, p. 63.
29. Nimrod, *Hunting tours*, p. 5.
30. Delmé Radcliffe, *Noble science*, p. 126.
31. Surtees, *Town and country papers*, p. 92.
32. This was sometimes prescribed in enclosure agreements: for example, the Potterspury and Yardley Gobion enclosure award stipulated quickset hedges with post and three rails on one side and post and two rails on the other. Steane, *Northamptonshire landscape*, p. 232.

Figure 5.3 A young quickset. *In and Out Clever* by Sir Robert Frankland, 1811.

that we have inherited. In the formative years of foxhunting, however, these hedges would have offered no greater obstacle than a few rows of seedlings 'of such tender growth as required protection by a low rail on each side' (Figure 5.3).[33] It was awkward to jump, but nowhere near as dangerous as what came later.

A hawthorn hedge generally needs to be 10 to 20 years old before it can be cut and laid, but many of the hedges of the shires seem to have been left far longer. In the first half of the nineteenth century Nimrod reckoned that the 'bullfinch' was the most common obstacle. This was 'a quickset hedge of perhaps fifty years growth, with a ditch on one side or the other, and so high and strong that horses cannot clear it'.[34] Foxhunters tackled such an obstacle by jumping *through* the hedge (Figure 5.4). Nimrod claimed that their transit left no more sign 'than if a bird had hopped through'.[35] The bullfinch seems to have been a particular feature of Leicestershire and Northamptonshire. Some of the annual tenancy agreements expressly forbade tenants from cutting the hedges except for repair.[36] There was disagreement among agricultural writers as to whether this represented neglect or good husbandry. Both Monk and Moscrop, writing about Leicestershire some 72 years apart, recommended that hedges were trimmed annually, as elsewhere (for a neat appearance as much as anything).[37] On the other hand, Pitt, writing about

33. G.J. Whyte-Melville, *Riding recollections* (1875; London, 1985), p. 17.
34. Nimrod, *Chace*, p. 17.
35. Nimrod, *Chace*, p. 17.
36. LRO, Hartopp papers: 8D39/7377, 8D39/7382.
37. Monk, *General View, Leicester*, p. 44; Moscrop, 'Report', p. 294.

Figure 5.4 A bullfinch. Detail from an illustration by John Sturgess in Brooksby (E. Pennell-Elmhirst), *The Cream of Leicestershire: Eleven Seasons' Skimmings* (London, 1883).

Figure 5.5 Approaching an oxer over ridge-and-furrow. *The Horse for Leicestershire* by John Sturgess in Brooksby (E. Pennell-Elmhirst), *The Cream of Leicestershire: Eleven Seasons' Skimmings* (London, 1883).

Northamptonshire, quoted Young's observation that the 'only secure way' to fence cattle was to leave 'very strong rows of white thorn uncut; and when so old as to want renewing, to cut them off and keep cattle out till grown out again'.[38]

The situation became increasingly hazardous for foxhunters as the shire districts began to concentrate more on the fattening of cattle after 1830, leading to the introduction of 'oxers' (Figure 5.5). These fences were 'rendered necessary by the difficulty of keeping fattening cattle within their pastures' and comprised 'a wide ditch, then a sturdy blackthorn hedge, and at least two yards beyond that a strong rail about four feet high'.[39] The intention was that the single rail would stop bullocks running into, and through, the hedge. Foxhunters had to attempt to clear such an obstacle in a single leap. In some cases the fences would be 'double oxers', with rails on each side.

As the nineteenth century progressed, so cut-and-laid hedges became more common. Brooksby observed in the 1870s that 'vast numbers of venerable tangled bullfinches have been transformed into smart stake-and-bounds'.[40] Stake-and-bound fences were constructed by weaving the cut hedge between vertical stakes and securing it at the top with a binder (principally plaited bramble at this time). There were local variations in hedge-laying techniques and, in an attempt to contain unruly bullocks, Northamptonshire had the 'rasper', described by Nimrod as an obstacle where 'a considerable portion of the blackthorn, left uncut, leans outwards from the fence, somewhat about breast high'.[41]

When bullfinch, oxer or rasper proved unnegotiable, the hard rider could always resort to timber. This came in the form of stiles or gates or plain post-and-rail fencing. Nimrod recommended that, if all else failed, a hunter 'makes his way to one corner of the field, where he finds a flight of very high and strong rails, but without a ditch'.[42] Elliott reports a run with the Grafton where they were 'obliged to jump timber' because the hedges were so large.[43] Timber was the most feared obstacle of all, however, because, where it did not break easily, a horse could be somersaulted and land on his rider. Nethercote reports two fatal accidents at the same stretch of post-and-rail fence beneath Winwick Warren in the 1840s.[44]

Foxhunters often destroyed the farmers' fences in their efforts to cross the country. It was considered good manners to break down fences when jumping them to make it easier for the following riders. Such destructiveness was present from the earliest days of modern foxhunting. In a letter dated 23 March 1778 Charles Dormer humorously entreated his friend to leave off hunting with the

---

38. Pitt, *General View, Northamptonshire*, p. 56.
39. Nimrod, *Chace*, p. 17.
40. Brooksby, *Cream*, p. 3.
41. Nimrod, *Chace*, p. 39.
42. Nimrod (C. Apperley), *The horse and the hound* (Edinburgh, 1843), p. 247.
43. Elliott, *Fifty years' foxhunting*, p. 40.
44. Nethercote, *The Pytchley hunt*, p. 131.

Quorn in order to visit him in Oxfordshire. He begged him to consider that 'the honest farmer ... is already busy in repairing his mounds and fences but you cruel foxhunters render all his labour in vain'.[45] Northampton's fearsome reputation for fences seemed to result in more fence breaking. Nimrod quoted Thomas Assheton Smith saying 'that he goes *over* Leicestershire, but *through* Northamptonshire'.[46] Nethercote described the young hunters of the Pytchley being 'not too proud' to wait until an old Guardsman, Colonel Allix, had 'made a hole in the big place through which he might find a way into the field beyond'.[47] One innovation of the farmers that did cause much consternation was wire, but this did not appear until the 1860s and took hold only in the 1880s (and so falls outside our period of study).[48]

The nineteenth-century drive to improve enclosed pastureland by drainage also played a role in the evolution of the sport. The progress of a horse was considerably slowed by wet and boggy ground, and this could also lead to accidents and injuries to both horse and rider. The draining of the fields led to drier going in the winter hunting season, which in turn encouraged the ever-increasing pace of the chase. Whyte-Melville attributed easier riding in earlier times to undrained pastures, a 'few furlongs' of which 'could bring the hardest puller back when he goes in over his fetlocks every stride'.[49] The pasture that these fences divided may have accounted for the popularity of the shires, but, as we would have been wrong to envisage a landscape of small neat hedges, we would be equally mistaken to picture smooth, even grass fields. There was much ridge-and-furrow in these pastures, which itself bore witness to the conversion to grazing after enclosure. In the eighteenth century the fields were largely undrained, and in Leicestershire Monk reported that the furrows were full of 'rushes and other trumpery'.[50] Nimrod talked of 'high ridges with deep, holding furrows between each'.[51] Riders needed to stay on the ridges in order to attain the firmer going, and even this was soft by today's standards. Heavy going was detested because it slowed horses down and caused tendon injuries (involving a long lay-off). The Althorp Chace books frequently reported deep and heavy going, and 60 years later Henry Dryden's Northamptonshire hunting diaries carefully recorded the going he encountered during the chase with phrases such as 'country very deep', 'tremendously deep' and 'stiffish'.[52]

45. LRO, Letter, Charles Dormer to Fortescue Turville: DG39/1099.
46. Nimrod, *Hunting tours*, p. 191.
47. Nethercote, *The Pytchley hunt*, p. 23.
48. Itzkowitz, *Peculiar privilege*, p. 155.
49. Whyte-Melville, *Riding recollections*, p. 37 (the fetlock is the lowest major joint on a horse's leg).
50. Monk, *General View, Leicester*, p. 59.
51. Nimrod, *Chace*, p. 38.
52. NRO, Althorp Chace Books: ML4428, ML4429, ML4430; Henry Dryden's diary 1839–1842: ZA477.

The process of enclosing fields, where ditches were cut along every hedgeline, improved matters to some degree, but the eighteenth century saw the introduction of underdraining techniques, which gathered momentum in the nineteenth century. Early efforts involved the digging of shallow trenches that were backfilled with wood or stones, through which water could flow; spring tapping and turf drains were also popular. Technical innovation brought the tile drain and later the drainage pipe. Leicestershire and Northamptonshire had a large proportion of clayey and loamy soils with impeded drainage,[53] and both Monk and Pitt cited further drainage as one of the main improvements that could be made to Leicestershire.[54] Modern research using records of the take-up of government grants has shown that these drainage techniques were not as widely adopted in Leicestershire and Northamptonshire as in more arable counties, but they still made an impact.[55] Foxhunters held these improvements as being partly responsible for the ever-increasing pace of the hunt.[56]

Farmers were recommended by contemporary agricultural writers to take additional steps to improve their pasture. During the early days of the Pytchley the hunt looked for foxes in small patches of gorse that seemed to inhabit both the new enclosures and the older 'grounds'.[57] Pitt's recommendations for improving the pastures included 'extirpating bushes, furze, and weeds', and he also reported that in some of Northamptonshire's grazing grounds the ant hills were so abundant that 'it is possible to walk over many acres, step by step, from one ant hill to another, without ever coming upon the level ground'.[58] In 1852 the pasture of Northamptonshire was 'too frequently overrun with thistles, nettles, and hassocks'.[59] But Moscrop had detected improvement in Leicestershire at least, talking of graziers who kept their pastures as 'smooth as a cricket ground'.[60]

To summarise the development of the foxhunting fieldscape: the eighteenth century brought conversion to grass, which ultimately gave rise to foxhunting at the gallop. The improvements of the nineteenth century made it possible to go even faster. The fearsome fences constructed by the farmers made jumping from a

53. Leicestershire 77.5% of 1873 county area, Northamptonshire 64.8%; this ranks them first and third in the country. A.D.M. Phillips, *The underdraining of farmland in England during the nineteenth century* (Cambridge, 1989), p. 39.

54. Monk, *General View, Leicester*, p. 59; W. Pitt, *General view of the agriculture of the county of Leicester* (London, 1809), p. 59.

55. Leicestershire and Northamptonshire appear in the mid-range of total loan expenditure on draining. Phillips, *Underdraining*, p. 77.

56. Whyte-Melville, *Riding recollections*, p. 37.

57. NRO, Althorp Chase Books: ML4428, ML4429, ML4430.

58. Pitt, *General View, Northamptonshire*, pp. 136, 139.

59. W. Bearn, 'On the farming of Northamptonshire', *Journal of the Royal Agricultural Society of England*, 13 (1852), p. 80.

60. Moscrop, 'Report', p. 296.

gallop a central part of the chase (at least for the braver riders). All came together to produce the short, sharp bursts that characterised foxhunting in the shires in its 'golden age', and contrasted with the slower, more drawn-out character of earlier hunting. These factors helped to shape foxhunting in its modern form, and it was this modern form that caught the attention of a group of men looking for winter entertainment. It went on to catch the imagination of a far wider public who, while not necessarily participating themselves, came to see the sport as a somehow quintessential part of English life.

Our account has stressed the role that enclosure, both old and new, and the conversion to pasture played in the formation of foxhunting. The modern sport found its highest expression in the form practised in the East Midlands, including part of our Northamptonshire study area: the hallowed 'shires' of foxhunting history. This is very much the view of earlier historians, such as Ellis, Hoskins and Carr.[61] But this interpretation has recently been challenged by Jane Bevan, who has questioned the relationship between enclosure and the rise of foxhunting.[62] Bevan used eighteenth-century hunting diaries to counter that many early owners of foxhound packs in fact avoided newly enclosed lands, preferring instead the remaining open fields, driven as much as anything by the desire to avoid jumping. There are three strands that need to be considered in assessing this new interpretation of the evidence: the prevalence of grassland in the favoured hunting areas, the chronology of the rise of foxhunting and the pre-eminence of the shires, and the difference in motives between those who hunted the hounds and those who followed them on horseback.

Enclosure and conversion to pasture tended to go together in this area of Northamptonshire at this time. This was true of both the older enclosures and those accomplished by parliamentary statute in the eighteenth and early nineteenth centuries. But it was possible to have a wide conversion to grassland without enclosure. Morton not only told us about the 'considerable part' of the county bordering Leicestershire and Warwickshire enclosed and converted to pasture but also described an alternative arrangement whereby 'many of the lordships, and especially of the larger ones, have a common, or unenclosed pasture for their cattle in the outskirts of the field'.[63] This was the situation in Naseby. In 1733 the village came to an arrangement whereby the extremities of the three open fields were given over to grazing. By the time that the Naseby incumbent, John Mastin, produced his history of the parish in 1792, fully two-thirds of the open fields were down to pasture. The same writer recommended Naseby to foxhunters, 'being within reach of the foxhounds of Althorpe and Pytchley, and those of Mr Meynell

---

61. Ellis, *Leicestershire and the Quorn*, p. 29; W.G. Hoskins, *The making of the English landscape* (1955; London, 1985), p. 196; Carr, *English foxhunting*, p. 68.
62. J. Bevan, 'Agricultural change and the development of foxhunting in the eighteenth century', *Agricultural History Review*, 58/1 (2010), pp. 49–75.
63. Morton, *Natural history*, pp. 14–15.

often hunt in the neighbourhood'.[64] Naseby was also the site of one of the earliest purpose-designed fox coverts, planted by the Ashby family in 1789.[65] If certain masters of foxhounds were showing a preference for open-field areas, therefore, this did not necessarily preclude a preference for grass.

Most writers on foxhunting, from the early nineteenth century to the present day, have acknowledged that the eighteenth-century form of the sport was still a 'work in progress' and very different from its finished form. Nimrod, for example, was all too conscious of the transformation that foxhunting had undergone. The eighteenth-century beginnings of the sport he described as slow, but a treat to a 'real sportsman' (that is, someone more interested in the working of the hounds).[66] In 1826 Cook talked about the method of riding to hounds being 'so much altered' within the 'last few years'.[67] Writing in 1912, Scarth Dixon observed that foxhunting 'did not occupy the first place till the eighteenth century was well advanced' then 'it grew and increased in popularity with a rapidity that was unprecedented, and when the nineteenth century opened it claimed place as the national winter sport'.[68] Later historians of foxhunting and landscape have observed this chronology themselves. Hoskins had foxhunting developing in Leicestershire in the 1770s 'in time to enjoy the exhilaration of galloping over miles of unfenced country'. He acknowledged, however, that enclosure 'made things more difficult' or at least 'necessitated new and exciting skills'.[69] Eighteenth-century foxhunters seemed to have been equally, or even more, happy to hunt across open fields than enclosed pasture. But foxhunting did not become a truly 'popular' sport (in the sense that many people participated) until the early nineteenth century and by that time the East Midlands landscape produced by both ancient and parliamentary enclosure, and still being refined by subdivision, drainage and other improvements, was a vital part of the sport.

This chronology of the development of foxhunting intertwines with the differing motives of the hunt participants. Our earlier account of enclosure and agricultural improvement, and the consequent increase in the amount of jumping required to cross a hunting country, has shown that jumping was far from universally popular with hunt followers. But this was not necessarily an overriding feature in deciding where to hunt. The eighteenth-century masters and huntsmen, including Meynell, the Spencers and the Graftons, were still far more interested in the hunting than the riding. They were driven by where to find foxes and where the best scent was to be had. This is not incompatible with the

---

64. J. Mastin, *The history and antiquities of Naseby* (Cambridge, 1792), pp. 15, 21, 49.

65. Paget, *Althorp and Pytchley hunt*, p. 19.

66. Nimrod, *Chace*, pp. 4–8.

67. Cook, *Observations*, p. 7.

68. Scarth Dixon, *Hunting*, p. 332.

69. Hoskins, *Making of the English landscape*, p. 196.

greater speed of pursuit that was a feature of later eighteenth-century foxhunting, but should not be interpreted as using the hunt as the means to ride a horse fast. These masters were fascinated with the breeding of a faster foxhound and pushing the limits of what the hounds could achieve.[70] John, Viscount Spencer, master of the Pytchley from 1808 to 1818, claimed that his 'leading passion' in life had been to 'see sporting-dogs hunt'.[71] The fact that these men were using better and faster horses to keep up with the action was growing in significance, but was not their driving force.[72] It did, however, become the driving force for the ever-growing number of mounted followers, and particularly the 'hard riders'. Their influence began to shape the hunt and dictate the ground that the hunt covered, and they voted overwhelmingly for the grassland of the shires. As the country became ever-more subdivided they made a virtue out of a necessity as far as jumping was concerned and found that they had the horses, the skills and the appetite to tackle these obstacles.

The landscape of fox preservation

As we have seen, explanations of the development of modern foxhunting have attributed its birth to a shortage of deer. But, ironically, foxhunting sources displayed a continual worry about a shortage of foxes. By 1781 Beckford was already talking about actions to take when faced with a depletion of the fox population. He strongly advised against buying in foxes because that would cause thefts from neighbouring hunt countries.[73] Some hunts had to resort to hunting 'bag men' – foxes that were caught earlier and released into the covert just before being hunted. The seventeenth-century diary of Thomas Isham contained incidents of capturing foxes in order to hunt them later.[74] In November 1773 the Althorp Chace book recorded the hunting of a 'bag' fox and in November 1776 reported their whipper-in rescuing a fox from a drain and releasing it 'before the

70. Beckford, although very much a hound man (and starting his hunt at dawn rather than mid-morning), still stressed the speed of the foxhunt, contrasting the old aim 'to walk down a fox' with the new one of keeping close at him, and killing him 'as soon as you can'. Beckford, *Thoughts on hunting*, p. 180.
71. Paget, *Althorp and Pytchley hunt*, p. 34.
72. Bevan also rather overplays the third duke of Grafton's preference for hunting from Euston Park. By her own calculations the hounds spend longer in Northamptonshire than in Suffolk (four months *versus* three months). Wakefield Lodge was rebuilt as a hunting box for the second duke, complete with new stables. Worsley suggests that the apartments above the stables were intended for Grafton's hunting guests. This does not suggest that Northamptonshire hunting was considered 'second best'. (It is unfortunate for our purposes that the third duke's Suffolk hunting diary alone survives; there is no Northamptonshire equivalent, so no direct comparisons are possible.) Worsley, *British stable*, p. 204.
73. Beckford, *Thoughts on hunting*, p. 201.
74. N. Marlow (trans.), *The diary of Thomas Isham of Lamport, 1671–73* (Farnborough, 1971), pp. 105, 159.

country people could put him into the sack that they had got for him' (selling a captured fox could be profitable).[75] In 1833 the duke of Grafton was paying a man ten shillings for watching fox coverts, presumably to thwart fox-nappers.[76] But hunting bagged foxes was seen increasingly as a disreputable practice and one unlikely to supply good sport. A good run depended on the fox determinedly breaking cover and making a fast dash towards another known place of safety. Bagged foxes were unfamiliar with the district, so did not know where to run. Dryden reported a disappointing run with the Grafton in 1841, when a fox killed within one field was 'supposed to be a bag man'.[77] A trade in captured foxes carried on from Leadenhall in London led bagged or imported foxes to be known as 'Leadenhallers', a term of some disparagement.[78]

Hunts therefore took steps to preserve and boost the population of the foxes that they had. Some masters imported foxes from Scotland or France to increase local numbers and 'improve the breed'. When Lord Alford took the Pytchley mastership he attempted to improve local foxes by releasing 'six brace of the largest Scotch ones he could procure' at Cottesbroke.[79] The Grafton hunt's Sholebrooke Kennel accounts record frequent payments to people who rescued fox cubs and even raised them by hand.[80] Foxes, like deer, required cover and would by choice make their home in woodland, but the very thing that made the shires such popular hunting county was the open grassland; Charnwood in Leicestershire and the royal forests of Northamptonshire were considered decidedly 'second rate' areas in comparison. To maintain the fox population hunts had to take steps to provide habitat in the form of planted fox coverts.

Fox coverts provided both a habitat in which the fox could thrive and an essential focus for the start of a hunt. In some areas existing woodland could be managed to preserve foxes; in others coverts had to be planted to make up for a shortage of natural habitat. Planted coverts usually comprised gorse; it was only with time that such areas themselves developed into woodland, with trees either growing up naturally or being planted for ornamental effect. It was the undergrowth associated with most woodland, rather than woodland *per se*, that the fox required. But not all patches of woodland or scrub would serve the hunt's purpose. First, the covert needed to be of a certain size: an acre at minimum, but preferably more. Second, an agreement needed to be made with the owner of the

75. NRO, Althorp Chace Books: ML4428.
76. NRO, Grafton archive: G2017.
77. NRO, Henry Dryden's diary 1839–1842: ZA477.
78. For Cook, the disgust at hunting a 'bagman' extended to the hounds themselves. He maintained that if the pack were in 'sport and in blood' (that is, had hunted and killed recently) they would refuse to eat a bagman after catching him. Cook, *Observations*, p. 105. Dixon reckoned about a thousand imported foxes went through Leadenhall market in a year. Druid, *Scarlet and silk*, p. 362.
79. Nethercote, *The Pytchley hunt*, p. 152.
80. NRO, Grafton archive: G3867.

covert such that he, or his tenant, would preserve the foxes that bred there and allow the hunt access. Hunts very often paid 'covert rent' to such landowners.

Large woodlands would not necessarily provide ideal habitat so far as modern foxhunting was concerned. As Cook explained, such an environment would be one where foxes 'commonly hang, and seldom go away'.[81] Large expanses of woodland were, however, popular when it came to 'cub hunting': the early autumn activity that was primarily aimed at training young hounds. The intention then was to hunt the fox within the covert, and to disperse other foxes that were not being hunted. Cub hunting, like earlier forms of the sport, was primarily about the hound, not the horse, and large woods provided the ideal environment for such an undertaking.[82]

For Cook, the covert most likely to provide satisfaction to the modern foxhunter was the medium-sized gorse covert (unfortunately, the writer does not specify what size constitutes 'medium', but a survey of Northamptonshire coverts would put this figure at about 10 to 30 acres). But Cook also warned the reader that the successful construction of such a covert was no small undertaking. The ground had to be thoroughly prepared and only the best seed used. The covert then required thorough weeding as soon as the first shoots appeared. Cook also had advice on constructing the earths that would encourage foxes to take up residence. He favoured introducing badgers to perform the dirty work over the construction of earths by men with spades.[83] Nimrod estimated that a well-planted gorse covert would hold foxes in its second year.[84] Figure 5.6 shows hounds drawing a gorse covert: an area of low, dense ground cover as it would appear early in its life. Over time ungrazed gorse would get 'leggy' and expire altogether if overshadowed by trees, when the covert would be described as 'hollow' and would cease to hold foxes; management and maintenance of coverts was therefore required. Squire Bouverie of Delapre, near Northampton, wrote to Sir William Langham in 1800 requesting that he arrange for his tenant to carry out maintenance work on the fox covert Bouverie was renting. This involved cutting the gorse (or 'furze') where necessary and 'such parts where the furze does not grow well ploughed and some more sown'.[85] Gorse was often gradually replaced by blackthorn or hawthorn, which provided a denser and more permanent cover. Many fox coverts bore the name 'Gorse' long after they had ceased to comprise gorse bushes. (Waterloo Gorse in the 1870s was 'the blackthorn, except for old denomination'.)[86]

81. Cook, *Observations*, p. 48.
82. Meynell spent two months in the autumn hunting his entire pack in the woodlands. In November he divided the hounds into an old pack and a young pack. The young hounds were under two years old and were hunted twice a week, as much in the woodlands as possible. J. Hawkes, *The Meynellian science or fox-hunting upon system* (1808; Leicester, 1932), pp. 41–2.
83. Cook, *Observations*, pp. 43–9. See below, p. 90, for a survey of Northamptonshire coverts.
84. Nimrod, *Hunting tours*, p. 139.
85. NRO, Langham archive: L(C)1082.
86. Brooksby, *Cream*, p. 274.

Figure 5.6 A gorse covert. Detail from *Heading the Fox* after Sir Robert Frankland (London, 1814) © Trustees of the British Museum.

Northamptonshire provided many examples of purpose-made coverts, and we can see the process of their development gathering momentum. The earliest of the Althorp Chace books rarely refer to what can now be identified as dedicated fox coverts. In the 1770s the chases most often included locations such as Badby Wood, Daventry Wood and Weedon Wood. In 1781 the books included references to 'Elkington New Cover', suggesting that covers were beginning to be deliberately planted.[87] Elsewhere we learn that the Royal Horse Guards (the 'Blues') planted a covert known as 'Blue covert' in Droughton parish in 1779 and that Naseby Covert was planted in 1789 by George Ashby.[88] The 1805–8 Althorp Chace books include references to previously unmentioned coverts such as Nethercote's and Isted's, names that are well known from the list of 'the company' at each meet.[89] Waterloo

87. NRO, Althorp Chace Books: ML4428, ML4429.
88. Paget, *Althorp and Pytchley hunt*, pp. 11, 19.
89. NRO, Althorp Chace Books: ML4428, ML4429.

Gorse was originally planted in 1812 and then subsequently renamed in honour of the battle.[90] In 1849 Lord Alford, then master of the Pytchley, leased an 11-acre close in Clipston for 24 years at the rent of £20 per annum for the purposes of 'making a covert for the breed and protection of foxes'[91] which became known as Alfords Thorns. Earl Spencer established a new covert near Church Brampton in 1853 which he attempted to call 'Balaclava'. The name did not take and it became known as 'Sandar's Gorse' (after the farmer on whose land it stood, and who maintained it).[92] Not all of the coverts founded were guaranteed of success, however, and where they were frequently found to be devoid of foxes (known as 'drawing a blank') they might be grubbed up and returned to agricultural use. Sandar's Gorse was planted because it was believed that the 'picturesque and popular' Cank had 'seen its best days and was losing its attraction for foxes'. It was not long then until Cank was 'improved from off the face of covertland'.[93]

In some areas there was natural woodland that could serve as fox coverts. The Pytchley hunt took advantage of the forest woodlands in the east of its territory and also of detached parcels of woodland such as Sywell Wood and Harlestone Heath. Where existing woodland was used as cover, or where a covert developed into woodland over the years, the hunt would have rides cut and maintained to keep the woods accessible. As we have seen, the coppices in the forests of Rockingham, Whittlewood and Salcey were already criss-crossed by rides. Woodland rides could be thick mud in the winter; Surtees described the rides in Sywell Wood as being 'more like a quagmire than anything else'.[94] This was yet another reason why woodland-based hunts were not popular with riders.

Coverts could also be claimed from the 'wild'. Land, if neglected and left to its own devices, would generally develop in a way almost suitable as a fox covert; the Pytchley covert Cock-a-roost was founded by 'enclosing the patches of gorse growing naturally on the hillside'.[95] Quite a few Pytchley coverts took advantage of the patches of woodland on steep slopes that Fox notes as a characteristic feature of the wolds (for example, the Hemplow Hills and Laughton Hills coverts).[96] The early Althorp Chace books, covering the 1770s, make reference to drawing 'small patches of furze' found in enclosures near Yelvertoft, and near Guilsborough, suggesting some agricultural neglect.[97] Whether reclaimed from the wild or purpose-made, coverts needed, as noted, to be a fairly good size. When the Althorp hounds found a fox in a 'little furze cover' near Winwick Warren in December

90. Paget, *Althorp and Pytchley hunt*, p. 9.
91. NRO, Clipston parish records: 206p/247.
92. Nethercote, *The Pytchley hunt*, p. 41.
93. Nethercote, *The Pytchley hunt*, pp. 41–2 (Cank was subsequently re-established).
94. Surtees, *Town and country papers*, p. 110.
95. Nethercote, *The Pytchley hunt*, p. 234.
96. Fox, 'The people of the wolds', p. 82.
97. NRO, Althorp Chace Books: ML4428.

1775 'there was a great danger of his being killed in cover it being so small'.[98] Many coverts were around 20 acres but some were as large as 100 or even more: Waterloo Gorse and Crick Covert were both about 10 acres, Loatland Wood was 40 acres, Naseby Covert was 50 acres and Nobottle Wood was some 160 acres.[99] The Pytchley's coverts tended to be smaller and more sparse in the north-west of their country, but large and numerous in the east. The names of the coverts often seem to be significant in describing their size and nature: 'spinney' indicated a small covert, usually under 10 acres, while 'Gorse' or 'Covert' was applied most often to medium-size plantations of 10 to 30 acres. All of these tended to be purpose-made for holding foxes. 'Woods' were the largest coverts of all and their existence was likely to pre-date, and not depend on, their fox-keeping function.

The place of a covert in the hierarchy depended on its size and position, its reliability at yielding foxes and the country to which it was adjacent. The location – whether it was near well-drained grassland (popular) or holding ploughland (not so welcome) – could affect the 'enjoyability' of the chase. Indeed, coverts might be purposely located in a particular place to attempt to encourage foxes to run a certain line of country (a late example of this has Major Paget 'experimenting with a little spinney at Wheler Lodge' to encourage the Sulby foxes to run the Hemplow Hills).[100] The west of the country was most popular with hunt followers because the sparse coverts encouraged the foxes to take long runs over the ancient pastures of that area; as Brooksby expressed it when describing this area, 'the Pytchley field generally – prefer the small gorse coverts and the grass to the deep woods and the plough of the Northampton country'.[101]

No one was expected to take a sizeable plot of land out of production without recompense, and one way or another rent was paid for the coverts. Who paid it varied according to the covert, the hunt and the date. Sometimes hunt expenses were met by the master. This was often the case when the pack was run by a great magnate (the Belvoir and the dukes of Rutland, the Pytchley and the Spencers and the Grafton and the Fitzroys at various times), or even, occasionally, when the hunts were run by less exalted masters (for example, the Quorn and Sir Harry Goodricke). When the first Earl Spencer took the Pytchley country in 1765 he paid for the hounds, but the cost of the covert rents was paid by the hunt club members.[102] At other times masters took subscriptions from hunt supporters to meet at least some of the expenses. Arrangements tended to become more formal as time went on. In early days individuals might pay for a certain covert as their contribution to the hunt. Squire Bouverie paid for a Pytchley covert, as evidenced by the letter quoted above, this in spite of the fact that Bouverie himself

98. NRO, Althorp Chace Books: ML4428.
99. Paget, *Althorp and Pytchley hunt*, pp. 9, 19, 25, 29.
100. Paget, *Althorp and Pytchley hunt*, p. 20.
101. Brooksby, *Hunting countries of England*, p. 135.
102. Paget, *Althorp and Pytchley hunt*, p. 72.

was 'never an enthusiastic sportsman or much of a performer in the field'.[103] In the late nineteenth century surviving Pytchley accounts show a list of covert-fund subscribers separate from the main list (unfortunately the accounts do not list the coverts being paid for).[104] However it was organised, the outlay on fox coverts was quite considerable; Dick Christian reckoned Goodricke's outlay on coverts alone to be £600 per season.[105] Nimrod put the Quorn covert bill even higher, at £1000 (a figure confirmed by a begging letter sent out by the Quorn hunt committee in 1860 seeking help with this expense).[106]

These arrangements illustrate the tripartite relationship between the hunt, the landlord and the tenant that underlay the organisation of foxhunting. Sometimes this could lead to misunderstandings. In 1807 the Quorn master, Thomas Assheton Smith, wrote a letter to Sir Justinian Isham of Lamport regarding a fox covert at Shangton Holt. Apparently Isham had offered to get his tenant to maintain it as a covert, but the tenant, on not receiving confirmation from the hunt, proceeded to plough up 'the greatest part of one quarter' of it. As Assheton Smith considered the 'main excellence' of the covert to derive from its size, he requested to be allowed to rent the whole of it.[107]

It was likely to be the least favoured parcels of land that were given over to form coverts. The famous Pytchley covert Blueberries was enclosed in 1576 at the north-western edge of the parish of Lamport. Sir Gyles Isham suggested that the name – it was originally called 'Blewbarrows' – was derived from its situation on an exposed hill.[108] There is some suggestion, too, that the hunts rented parish land that had been allocated at enclosure to provide common grazing or to support the poor. Glapthorne Cow Pasture in the Woodland Pytchley country became a fox covert, while 'Old Poor Gorse' in Old parish was the portion of the common reserved under the enclosure act for the poor to collect firewood. It was rented by the hunt from the overseers of the parish, who apparently used the money to buy coal for the poor.[109]

The protection of foxes was something that went hand-in-hand with allowing the hunt to use land for a fox covert. When Herbert Hay Langham took over as master of the Pytchley in 1878 he wrote to all the covert owners in his country seeking permission to continue to draw coverts (and, presumably, to continue paying rent for them). Many of the replies detailed the state of the foxes in the coverts and contained remarks such as 'the preservation of foxes will be carefully attended to', 'I will do my best to preserve foxes' and 'You may feel quite certain

103. Nethercote, *The Pytchley hunt*, p. 23.
104. NRO, Langham archive: L(C)32–35
105. Druid, *Silk and scarlet*, p. 66.
106. Nimrod, *Chace*, p. 16; LRO, Letter, Mr Clowes to Charles William Packe: DE5047/113/1.
107. NRO, Isham archive: IL3115.
108. Marlow, *The diary of Thomas Isham*, Sir Gyles Isham's notes, p. 68.
109. Paget, *Althorp and Pytchley hunt*, p. 15.

Table 5.1 Northamptonshire fox coverts.

Code	Name	Exists today?	Earliest source
P1	Laughton Hills	Yes	Shared with South Quorn. Jones diary (1791)
P2	Dingley Warren	Yes	Langham diary (1866)
P3	Dingley Wood	Yes	King diary II (1817)
P4	Bosworth Gorse	Yes	Langham diary (1865)
P5	Kilworth Sticks	Yes	King diary II (1817)
P6	Misterton Gorse		Langham diary (1865)
P7	Kilworth Hall	Yes	
P8	Shawell Wood		Langham diary (1865)
P9	Marston Wood	Yes	King diary I (1805)
P10	Alfords Thorns	Yes (larger today)	Leased by Alford 1849
P11	Waterloo Gorse	No	Planted 1812 and later renamed (according to Paget)
P12	Loatland Wood	No	King diary I (1805)
P13	Sulby Covert	Yes	King diary II (1817)
P14	Stanford Hall	Yes	Langham diary (1865)
P15	Swinford Covert		Langham diary (1871)
P16	Hemplow Hills	Yes (shrunken)	Langham diary (1865)
P17	Naseby Covert	Yes	Pytchley club accounts (1798)
P18	Tally Ho	Yes	King diary I (1805)
P19	Kelmarsh Spinney		Pytchley club accounts (1798)
P20	Sunderland Wood	Yes	King diary I (1805)
P21	Blue Covert	Yes	King diary II (1817)
P22	Faxton Covert	Yes	Pytchley club accounts (1798)
P23	Scotland Wood	Yes	King diary I (1805)
P24	Bullocks Pen Spinney	Yes (shrunken)	Langham diary (1865)
P25	Cransley Wood	Yes	Pytchley club accounts (1798)
P26	Mawsley Wood	Yes	King diary I (1805)
P27	Short Wood	Yes	King diary I (1805)
P28	Maidwell Dales	Yes	Langham diary (1865)
P29	Pursers Hills	Yes	King diary I (1805)
P30	Berrydale	Yes	King diary I (1805)
P31	Yelvertoft Fieldside Covert	Yes	King diary I (1805)
P32	Firetail	Yes (shrunken)	Langham diary (1866)
P33	Callander	Yes	Langham diary (1866)
P34	Blueberries	No	Isham diary (1671)
P35	Old Poors Gorse	Yes	King diary II (1817)
P36	Pytchley Spinnies		King diary I (1805)
P37	Gib Wood		King diary II (1817)
P38	Clint Hill	Yes	Langham diary (1865)
P39	Creaton Wood	Yes	Langham diary (1866)
P40	Winwick Warren	Yes (larger today)	King diary I (1805)
P41	Crick Gorse	Yes	King diary II (1817)
P42	Badsaddle Wood	Yes	
P43	Watford Covert	Yes	King diary II (1817)
P44	Foxhill	Yes	
P45	Brixworth Covert		Pytchley club accounts (1798)
P46	Withmale Park		King diary I (1805)
P47	Hardwick Wood	Yes	Pytchley club accounts (1798)
P48	Blackberry Covert		Pytchley club accounts (1798)
P49	Viviens Covert		Langham diary (1866)
P50	Sywell Wood	Yes	King diary I (1805)
P51	Buckby Folly	Yes	King diary I (1805)
P52	Vanderplanks	Yes	Langham diary (1865)
P53	Haddon Spinney	Yes	King diary I (1805)
P54	Cank	Yes	King diary I (1805)
P55	Bragborough Hall	Yes	Langham diary (1866)
P56	Holdenby	Yes (slightly altered)	King diary II (1817)

P57	Sandars Gorse	Yes	Langham diary (1865)
P58	Overstone Park		King diary II (1817)
P59	Blackthorn Spinney	Yes	King diary II (1817)
P60	Althorp Park	Yes	
P61	Dallington Wood	Yes	King diary I (1805)
P62	Harlestone Heath	Yes	King diary II (1817)
P63	Billing Arbour	Yes	
P64	Nobottle Wood	Yes	King diary I (1805)
P65	Whilton Osier Beds	Yes (larger today)	Langham diary (1871)
P66	Brockhall	Yes	King diary II (1817)
P67	Dodford Holt	Yes	King diary II (1817)
P68	Harpole Covert	Yes (shrunken)	King diary II (1817)
P69	Delapre	Yes (shrunken)	King diary II (1817)
P70	Stowe Wood	Yes (shrunken)	King diary II (1817)
P71	Everdon Stubbs	Yes	King diary II (1817)

Diary sources:

Isham diary: N. Marlow (trans.), *The diary of Thomas Isham of Lamport, 1671–73* (Farnborough, 1971)
Jones diary: *Thomas Jones' diary* (Derby, 1816)
King diary I: Charles King Chace Book, 1800–1808, NRO, YZ2586
King diary II: Charles King Chace Book, 1817–1819, NRO, YZ2588
Langham diary: H.H. Langham Hunting Journal, 1865–1875, NRO, Langham archive: L(C)646

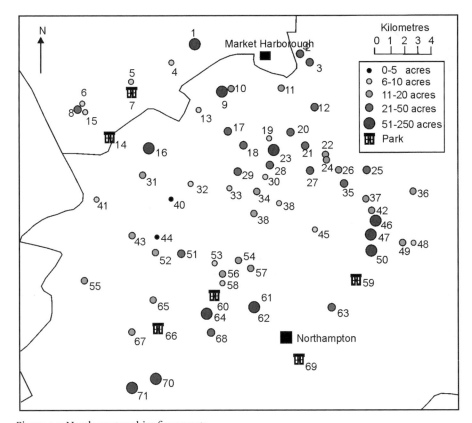

Figure 5.7 Northamptonshire fox coverts.

of my doing everything I can to preserve foxes.'[110] The amount of cooperation
the hunt could expect in the provision and maintenance of fox coverts and the
preservation of foxes is somewhat surprising, as by no means all the covert
owners were hunting men or women, as is clear from the Langham letters. An
added complication was that there were also coverts intended for the preservation
of game to cater for the increasingly popular sport of shooting. Game coverts
would not necessarily be intended to double as fox coverts, but no one told the
foxes that, and depredations on the gamebird population naturally followed. A
gamekeeper's instinct might be to shoot foxes, but 'vulpicide' was frowned upon
by society, and so there was generally a truce between the hunting and shooting
factions.[111] When making arrangements for cub hunting in 1889, Langham's
huntsman, Goodall, reported that 'Edwards the Selby keeper came to see me
yesterday he is anxious for us to do there he says there are a brace of foxes in the
covert and they want moving.'[112]

A large number of the coverts identified survive to the present day, the majority
being the same size and shape as they were in the 1880s. While it is true that some
coverts mentioned in the earlier hunting sources cannot be identified on the late
nineteenth-century OS maps, because they were either renamed or lost, those that
appear on these maps tend also to appear on modern maps. It is probable that the
modern landscape would have far less woodland were it not for the fox coverts.
Table 5.1 and Figure 5.7 show the fox coverts used by the Pytchley hunt in their
favoured shire country up to the 1880s (identified on the six-inch OS maps from
that decade).

Hunt countries

Fox coverts were closely connected to the concept of a hunt's 'country'. Nimrod
defined this as 'such portion of a county as is hunted by any one pack of hounds'.[113]
But the country was not so much the territory that the hounds could run across as
the coverts in which they could draw for foxes. Cook had some strong opinions
on the importance of honouring a hunt's country in regard to coverts: 'We all
know, by law the owners of coverts can allow whom they please to hunt them; if,
therefore, the boundary of a country is not held sacred, it is impossible to know
what will be the consequence, or how it will end.'[114] The acknowledged boundaries
of a hunt country evolved with the sport itself. Meynell's country was ill-defined

110. NRO, Langham archive: L(C)688, L(C)693, L(C)697.
111. Sporting magazines would publish the names of known vulpicides. Itzkowitz, *Peculiar privilege*, p. 150.
112. NRO, Langham archive: L(C)681.
113. Nimrod, *Chace*, p. 16. Hunt countries were a legacy of nineteenth century that have persisted to the present day, see G. Marvin, 'English foxhunting: a prohibited practice', *International Journal of Cultural Property*, 1/4 (2007), p. 349.
114. Cook, *Observations*, p. 51.

when he started, but as the neighbouring shire packs were close behind in terms of development he had to negotiate with great landlords and humbler landowners alike to secure rights for his hunt. Meynell needed to extract written agreements about the drawing of coverts and hunt boundaries not only with the owners of the coverts but with the masters of the 'rival' hunts. Dale quotes at length from an agreement between Meynell and Noel (master of what became the Cottesmore hunt) by which the coverts were divided:

> Owston, Laund, Skeffington, Loddington, Tugby, Allexton and Stockaston Woods, Easton Park, and the woods near Holt to be neutral coverts. The coverts on the Langton side of those above named to be drawn by Lord Gainsborough. Ashby Pasture not to be drawn by Lord Gainsborough. Billesdon Coplow to be neutral. No coverts on the Quorn side of Billesdon Coplow to be drawn by Lord Gainsborough. All earths in both hunts to be stopped in common.
>
> On these conditions Mr Meynell will engage to draw no coverts except those above mentioned, which he understands to be claimed by Lord Gainsborough as belonging to Mr Noel's hunt.[115]

Once established by such agreements, the country came to define the hunt. After Meynell the Quorn had a bewildering succession of masters, sometimes bringing new hounds, new staff and even new hunt premises. Initially most hunts took their names from the master, who often owned the hounds. For example, the Quorn was known by a series of names: hunting appointments cards published weekly by a Leicester firm list the hunt as 'Sir R. Sutton's' and then 'the Earl of Stamford's'; it is not until the 1860s that it is called 'the Quorn'.[116] The Pytchley had a similarly varied history, notwithstanding its early close association with the Spencer family. Although originally based at Pytchley, the hunt kennels moved to Althorp, Boughton, Brigstock and Brixworth under various masters. What was really handed on, and gave the hunts their identity and continuity, was the hunt country. The hunt countries have recently been described as 'a cultural geography' that 'overlies, transgresses and textures the more familiar spatialities of farms, estates and parishes'.[117] The hunt countries became formalised to such an extent that maps were published depicting them.[118] The hunts also became regulated so

---

115. T.F. Dale, *The history of the Belvoir hunt* (London, 1899), p. 34. Unfortunately, Dale gives no date for this agreement, but elsewhere Clayton gives the date as 1766. M. Clayton, *Foxhunting in paradise* (London, 1993), p. 209.
116. LRO, hunting appointment cards, DG9/2802.
117. Finch, 'Wider famed countries', p. 57.
118. For example, the hunting map of Leicestershire and Northamptonshire, published by A.H. Swiss in 1893, colour-codes the hunting countries and marks the location of the meets, with details printed in an accompanying booklet. The whole folds down into a pocket-sized package. LRO, Swiss No. 7 Hunting Map: DE2055/1.

that they would hunt certain parts of their country on certain days of the week, and different areas would be known as 'the Monday country', 'the Saturday country' and so on. In the early days the owners of the hounds would arrange meets and even move the hounds entirely to suit themselves: thus the Grafton hounds spent part of the season in Suffolk and part in Northamptonshire, and the meets of the Spencers' hounds as listed in the Althorp Chace books did not happen on regular days of the week.[119] But as the nineteenth century progressed hunts were deemed to have a duty to their followers, and to the farmers over whose lands they hunted, to be more regular in their habits.[120]

Conclusion

The eighteenth-century origins of English foxhunting were geographically widespread, with packs hunting a variety of terrains.[121] But while these various hunts seem to have shared many interests, improving their hounds and increasing the pace of pursuit, the sport had not then caught the popular imagination and gained large fields of mounted followers. Scarth Dixon quoted a 1736 letter in which a Yorkshire huntsman described a particularly exciting run; the company comprised eight men, with five in at the kill – a very different enterprise to what was to come. Early foxhunters were looking for a landscape to chase across, rather than a landscape in which to find prey, so the drive was from the forests to grassland and to open fields. Early packs were converting to fox from both deer and hare, and many continued to hunt whatever 'jumped up' in front of them.[122] Foxhunting might have remained a fairly marginal sport were it not for developments in the East Midlands in the second half of the eighteenth century.

The landscape changes we have traced in Northamptonshire – enclosure and conversion to grass – were not by themselves sufficient to shape modern foxhunting. It was their coinciding with Meynell's 'new science', based on starting the hunt in the late morning, with the widespread breeding of faster hounds and, above all, with the breeding of the thoroughbred horse, that produced foxhunting in its iconic form. The speed and the dash attracted ever-growing

---

119. NRO, Charles King Chace Book 1800–1808, YZ2586; Althorp Chace Books: ML4428, ML4429.
120. Cook, *Observations*, p. 34.
121. Scarth Dixon used the hound list of the Charlton hunt from the 1730s, as well as other sources, to trace the existence of foxhound packs in most areas of England (drafts of hounds from other packs appear in these lists). He paid particular attention to his native Yorkshire, finding evidence of numerous packs from the duke of Buckingham's late seventeenth-century pack (in Clevedon and Helmsley) through to those belonging to a variety of county squires. He also attempted to demonstrate that a similar state of affairs existed for Nottinghamshire, Lincolnshire and Hampshire (although with less evidence and more conjecture). A great swathe of land from Gloucestershire eastwards to London was hunted by the Berkeley and the Beaufort hunts, which converted from deer and hare to fox in the eighteenth century. Scarth Dixon, *Hunting*.
122. Cecil, *Records of the chase*, p. 21.

fields of followers, who mounted themselves on quality horses and went along for the ride. As the sport developed, jumping enclosure hedges became an essential part of the experience. It was these horse riders that paid the subscriptions as the hunt became an increasingly 'public' sport.[123] They expressed an overwhelming preference for the grassland of the Midland shires, and were prepared to travel to enjoy it.

123. The transformation in the organisation of hunting is examined in more detail in Chapter 8.

6

Old hunting in new conditions

The previous two chapters have charted the rise of foxhunting and its favoured landscape to a position of dominance by the nineteenth century. But we must also investigate what became of the pursuit of the deer once it had lost its role as the iconic form of hunting, and establish whether the forests of Northamptonshire retained any of their role as a hunting reserve.

Later deer hunting

The sport of hunting deer did not fade altogether with the ascendancy of foxhunting. Historians have, in fact, used the changing nature of the sport as evidence to support the argument that the pursuit of the fox supplanted the pursuit of the deer because the former were plentiful and the latter were scarce.[1] It is true that the nature of deer hunting was transformed in the eighteenth century, just as foxhunting was acquiring its modern form and growing in popularity. The most significant development was the growth of the practice of hunting the carted deer. This involved loading a captured animal into a cart and transporting it to the appointed place of the meet. The deer was then set loose and given a small head start before the hounds were released, *en masse*, to start the pursuit. Initially the deer would be killed once caught, but by the nineteenth century the practice was to recapture the deer and transport it home once more, when, after sufficient rest and recuperation, it could be hunted again.

The later sources are quiet on the subject of deer hunting when compared with the coverage given to the burgeoning sport of foxhunting. One place where the changing nature of deer hunting can be traced, however, is in the records of the Royal Buckhounds. The kings and queens of England continued to ride to hounds, albeit with varying degrees of enthusiasm. In the eighteenth century, however, they eschewed the royal forests in favour of locations such as the Windsor parks, Richmond Park and Bushey Park. Meetings of the Royal Buckhounds became part of court life. Sometimes a stag would be 'roused' from its resting place and then pursued by the hunt, sometimes it would be transported to the place of the meet

---

1. Carr, *English foxhunting*, p. 24; Griffin, *Blood sport*, pp. 106–7.

and then 'uncarted'.[2] Initially, carted deer would be killed at the end of the hunt, just like deer that were roused. There are some examples of a particularly notable animal being spared, either to hunt another day or to be free from pursuit forever (the latter being signified by the placing of a silver collar around the neck of the fortunate animal).[3] The meetings of the Royal Buckhounds could be extremely popular, although this seems to have been more for the opportunity of viewing members of the royal family at leisure rather than for the sheer pleasure of the chase. Such could be the press of people at Richmond that it rendered the riding troublesome and dangerous, and so Queen Caroline introduced a ticket system for hunting in New Park. No person was admitted to the park without a hunting ticket bearing the day's date and the seal of the ranger.[4]

By the time George IV was hunting with the buckhounds, it had become normal practice to recapture the carted deer and take it home. Such deer could obtain a celebrity status. 'Marlow Tom' was so named because he jumped a seven-foot wall with a fifteen-foot drop in that town and lived to run another day. High Flyer, Moonshine and the Popham Lane Deer were other examples of famous deer associated with the Royal Buckhounds in this period. *The Sporting Magazine* talked of High Flyer and Moonshine having 'blood and bottom', using the type of language typically employed to describe racehorses.[5]

The hunting of deer elsewhere in the country followed the pattern that we have seen for the royal hunt. G.K. Whitehead's book includes a gazetteer of known packs of stag hounds in the eighteenth, nineteenth and twentieth centuries,[6] while Figure 6.1 plots the whereabouts of packs that were in existence in the eighteenth and first half of the nineteenth century. The map shows a concentration of activity within reach of London and in East Anglia. Few packs of deer hounds are recorded as existing within the venerable foxhunting country of the shires. Neither do the packs generally coincide with the existence of royal forests (with the notable exception of Exmoor). The hunting by the duke and duchess of Grafton of a carted deer in 1760 was such an unusual occurrence that it was recorded in the newspaper:

> Tuesday their graces the Duke and Duchess of Grafton took the diversion of stag hunting in Northamptonshire. A stag was turned out on Whittlebury Forest which led them a chace to within half a mile of Northampton, and back again to the forest, where it was killed. The corn being cut down, and mostly carried in, the

2. For examples of hunts where deer were roused see Hore, *Royal Buckhounds*, pp. 275, 287. For example of hunts where deer were uncarted, see pp. 283, 287, 296, 304.
3. Hore, *Royal Buckhounds*, pp. 275, 319.
4. Hore, *Royal Buckhounds*, p. 306.
5. 'Sabretache', *Monarchy and the chase*, p. 116; *The Sporting Magazine*, November 1803.
6. G.K.Whitehead, *Hunting and stalking deer in Britain through the ages* (London, 1980), pp. 206–52.

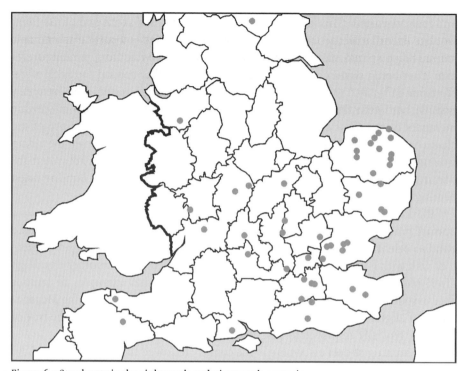

Figure 6.1 Stag hunts in the eighteenth and nineteenth centuries.

company met with no restriction in that fine champaign country, and her Grace being an excellent horsewoman was in at the death.[7]

The seventh earl of Cardigan, apparently disappointed in his ambitions to secure the mastership of the Pytchley in 1840, started a pack of bloodhounds with which to hunt the carted deer, but they were not a success.[8] In the nineteenth century the Royal Buckhounds were taken to hunt elsewhere than Windsor and Richmond, including regular two-week stays in the New Forest (where they would attempt to capture wild deer to take back to the Swinley deer paddocks, with limited success), but such expeditions do not seem to have stretched as far as the royal forests of Northamptonshire.[9]

The great majority of the stag hunts still extant in the first half of the nineteenth century were hunting the carted deer (with the notable exception of the North Devon hunt). It was generally regarded as being a somewhat inferior sport to foxhunting. Nethercote talks of William Angerstein, a late resident

7.   NRO, Wilson's diary: ZA8011.
8.   Paget, Althorp and Pytchley hunt, p. 262.
9.   Lord Ribblesdale, The queen's hounds and stag-hunting recollections (London, 1897), p. 68.

of Northamptonshire and follower of the Pytchley, establishing a pack of stag hounds when he moved to Norfolk on the basis that 'half a loaf' was 'better than no bread'. But Nethercote reported that Angerstein was not long in discovering that 'the pursuit of the deer in an essentially non-hunting country, and that of the fox over the big pastures in the neighbourhood of Crick or Market Harborough are enjoyments as distinct in their character as light from darkness'.[10]

In his account of the development of hounds in the eighteenth and nineteenth centuries Nimrod informs us that the traditional stag hound was, in fact, extinct. By the time he was writing the Royal Buckhounds and 'the few other packs that follow this game' consisted of foxhounds 'of the highest blood that can be procured'. Nimrod approved of this development because although the English stag hound 'was a noble animal of his kind' he was 'not sufficiently speedy'. As hunting developed, so did the taste for following on horseback. At the end of the eighteenth century both the royal hunt and the North Devon hunt were using large, slow hounds. In 1813, the duke of Richmond presented the Goodwood pack of foxhounds to George IV to replace the old-style hounds. In line with the new arrangements the 'yeomen prickers' of the Royal Buckhounds were pensioned off and replaced with three whippers-in.[11] The North Devon stag hounds were sold in 1825 and replaced in 1827 with a pack made up of drafts from various foxhound packs.[12]

The hunting of the carted deer even came to imitate foxhunting in its seasonality. The traditional pursuit of the deer had involved chasing stags or bucks in summer and hinds or does in the winter, and stag and hind seasons continued to be observed by the North Devon hunt. According to Palk Collyns, the stag season on Exmoor in the nineteenth century ran from 12 August to 8 October. This was then followed by a two- or three-week break until the hind season commenced, which continued up until Christmas. There was then another break until hind hunting recommenced 'as soon after lady day as weather permits' (lady day being 25 March) and carried on until 10 May. This had already pushed the start of the stag season somewhat later, because it had traditionally started around midsummer. *The Sporting Magazine* recorded the season of the Royal Buckhounds as commencing in September.[13] The carted deer packs seem to have followed foxhunting's calendar rather than that of the traditional sport. In Nimrod's opinion, the difference in seasonality was one of the reasons that the hunting of the wild red deer did not survive as an English sport: 'from the circumstance of the stag being, by his nature, unfit to be hunted during some of the months

10. Nethercote, *The Pytchley hunt*, p. 255. According to Whitehead's gazetteer, Angerstein's pack was founded in Rugby around 1870 and moved to Norfolk in 1872.
11. Nimrod, *The horse and the hound*, pp. 360, 428.
12. C. Palk Collyns, *Notes on the chase of the wild red deer in the counties of Devon and Somerset* (1862; London, 1902), pp. 111, 116.
13. *The Sporting Magazine*, November 1803.

that sportsmen like to be in the field'.[14] Nineteenth-century hunts often seem to have hunted castrated deer, known as 'haviers'. This was apparently because they were less temperamental than stags, and because a stag that had been to rut was deemed no good for hunting until well into December.[15] Depending on when a stag was castrated he would not regrow his antlers if they had already been cast. Stags, and haviers that had retained their antlers, often had these adornments sawn off to facilitate both their transport in a deer cart and their recapture at the conclusion of the chase.

The main virtues of hunting the carted deer seem to have lain in the certainty of the sport and its comparatively short duration. The hunting of the wild red deer as practised in the West Country continued to involve the harbouring of the deer: that is, the locating of the lair of an animal of the required sex and of suitable age and stature to ensure a good chase. The hounds were taken to the nearest farm, where the majority of the pack would be confined in a barn or similar. Then two or four of the most trusted would be taken to the site of the harbouring to act as 'tufters'. They would rouse the chosen quarry and set it running, at which point word would be sent back to where the rest of the pack were waiting, and they were brought forward and laid on the scent of the escaping deer. Clearly this could be a time-consuming and unreliable process, which might be viewed as part and parcel of the sport by enthusiasts but was unacceptable to anyone who had only a few hours to spare. As Palk Collyns commented, 'It must not be assumed that a deer can always be harboured for the day's sport.'[16] Turning a deer out of a cart to hunt would certainly provide more of a sure thing. Sometimes a carted deer would not be successfully recaptured at the end of the chase and the hunt would have to use more traditional techniques to harbour the 'outlier' in the next week or two to take it and return it to the safety of the deer paddock, but most of the meets would be fairly certain to show some sport.

Nimrod gave an assessment of the place of stag hunting in the sporting world of the early nineteenth century: although it could 'never be again reckoned amongst the popular diversions in England', the modern invention did have its uses. He observed that 'turning out deer before fox-hounds in the neighbourhood of the metropolis' had the 'advantage of affording a certainty of something in the shape of a run' which was most useful to 'persons whose time is precious'. No one seemed to have expected the sport to match the excitement offered by a fox hunt. Cecil acknowledged the same advantages enumerated by Nimrod, but also remarked that 'compared with fox-hunting there is a lameness about it – an artificial character not quite in accordance with the true spirit of a sportsman'.[17]

14. Nimrod, *Horse and hound*, p. 414.
15. Whitehead, *Hunting and stalking deer*, p. 123.
16. Palk Collyns, *Wild red deer*, p. 106.
17. Cecil, *Records of the chase*, p. 217.

Even advocates of hunting the wild deer on Exmoor acknowledged that their sport would only satisfy 'a first-flight Melton Man' if 'he is not merely a rider, but a sportsman to boot'.[18]

In the nineteenth century all pursuit of deer was covered by the term 'stag hunting', regardless of the sex of the animal pursued. It does, however, seem that the red deer was carted in preference to the fallow deer (which, as we have already seen, was the favoured quarry of earlier park-based hunting). There are some mentions of fallow deer in the records of nineteenth-century hunting: when Charles Davis was huntsman of the Royal Buckhounds he apparently entered his young hounds to the fallow deer in Windsor Park; a Mr T. Nevill of Chilland carted a fallow deer that had been presented to him by the earl of Portsmouth; and a Mr Mellish hunted wild fallow deer in Epping Forest up until 1805.[19] In the main, however, red deer stags, hinds and haviers were the favoured prey of the deer packs. It is a curiosity of the sport that the hunted animal became in many senses the star of the whole proceedings. Ribblesdale was in no doubt that successful stag hunting depended above all on 'the condition and the humour' of the deer that was hunted. If the animal was unfit or was not in the mood to run then the enterprise was doomed to failure. The same author expressed great satisfaction, at the end of a successful day's hunting, 'to be able to bid good-night to your good deer comfortably housed in the best loose box about the place, up to his knees in long wheat straw'.[20]

Historians have viewed the ascendancy of carted-deer hunting in the nineteenth century as evidence supporting the traditional explanation of the hunting transition. The switch to hunting the carted deer was made because the traditional haunts of deer had disappeared and it was no longer possible to pursue the wild animal. Carr summed it up thus: 'fewer forests and fewer deer parks meant fewer wild deer. The hunting of carted deer ... was one answer'.[21] I would argue, rather, that the practice of hunting carted deer was intended to bring, and largely succeeded in bringing, the new style of hunting to a population who might otherwise not be able to enjoy it on so regular a basis. This accounted for the prevalence of stag hunts in the south-east of England, within reach of London, and in Norfolk (where the pre-eminence of the shooting interests precluded widespread foxhunting). Those who enjoyed following these hunts valued fast runs and good-quality horses, just as foxhunters did. The deer were pursued by fast and fleet foxhounds, not by the slower and more ponderous stag hounds of previous centuries. When the royal hunt had days in Windsor Forest and the New Forest they found themselves with far fewer followers, with the majority preferring

18. Palk Collyns, *Wild red deer*, p. 171.
19. Ribblesdale, *Queen's hounds*, pp. 74, 98, 122.
20. Ribblesdale, *Queen's hounds*, pp. 92–3.
21. Carr, *English foxhunting*, p. 24. Griffin expresses a similar opinion on the significance of hunting the carted deer: Griffin, *Blood sport*, pp. 106–7.

the faster runs that could be had over a grass country. Carr suggested that hunting the carted deer was 'a tame substitute for the real thing', but, for enthusiasts of the fast horseback pursuit, the reverse seems to have been true. It was generally expected that the wild deer in the West Country would run slower and not as far as their pampered, well-fed relatives further east.[22] For the most part, nineteenth-century stag hunters were not 'making do' with some pale imitation of an ancient and noble sport; rather, they were making the best of a rather 'watered down' version of foxhunting.

Foxhunting in the Northamptonshire forests

We have previously concentrated on Northamptonshire's 'prime' foxhunting territory: the part of the county that constituted part of the hallowed 'shires'. But foxhunting also became a thriving sport in the remainder of the county, and it is interesting to consider how the 'new' sport fared in the landscape of the 'old' sport. We have described the archetypal grassland landscape over which it was good to gallop, and which led to horse riding becoming the key part of the sport; but contemporaries were well aware of the difference between those who hunted in order to ride and those who rode in order to hunt, and this difference finds expression in the hunting landscapes favoured by these different protagonists.

Two hunts counted the royal forests as part of their foxhunting country: the Pytchley hunted Rockingham and the Grafton hunted Whittlewood and Salcey. In both cases the forests were only a portion of their territory, but it is the woodland territories of these hunts that are of most interest at this point, and specifically how the old landscape of the chase was used for the purpose of the 'new' sport. Writers such as Brooksby had no doubt that woodland offered several advantages over hunting across an open landscape. Woodland foxes had the reputation of running straight and true, and hounds got a better scent without having to contend with the interruptions of roads, fallow fields, sheep and cows and their manure, not to mention the 'foot folk'. In this way woodland provided a necessary 'school for young hounds'. But Brooksby admitted that following such a hunt was a minority sport compared to hunting in the shires. There was a 'strong section' of woodland hunters who adored such sport, but it remained 'inexplicable' to others. The field of the Woodland Pytchley hunt remained a 'small and almost purely local one'.[23]

The later of the Althorp Chace books contain some accounts of hunting in the forest. In August 1808 the hounds were cub hunting around Geddington Chace, Boughton Woods, Farming Woods and Rockingham. The meets were not 'advertised', started much earlier in the morning and were not expected to be widely attended. In November the full foxhunting season began and the hounds

22. Palk Collyns, *Wild red deer*, p. 122.
23. Brooksby, *Hunting countries of England*, 1, pp. 147–9.

were hunting back on their prime grassland grounds to the south-west of the county, although some of their runs took them through Salcey Forest.[24]

Elliott's reminiscences of hunting with the Grafton in the nineteenth century included some vivid accounts of woodland runs through Whittlewood and Salcey. As with the Pytchley, the autumn cub hunting was accomplished in the woodland: in Whittlewood and Salcey Forests and other woods in the Grafton country (East Horn, Haversham, Gayhurst and Stoke Park woods). The author records one (to him) surprisingly good chase through Salcey Forest in the 1840s, but observed 'I do not suppose a fox will ever run like that again, and his running the ridings must have been caused by the state of alarm he was in' (a fox would normally be expected to take advantage of the cover provided by the coppices, which would not make for so fast a pursuit).[25] The author of these memoirs was a local man, not at all a 'shires' hunter, but he did prefer the grassland to the woodland. It may be an indication of the gap between 'hunters' and 'riders' that when Colonel Anstruther Thomson took over the Pytchley with the intention of hunting the hounds himself he retained the services of the huntsman for a season, but the colonel hunted the woodlands while the huntsman was consigned to the 'fashionable' west of the country.[26] Surtees described Northamptonshire as being regarded as the 'admitted second best' to Leicestershire, but he was inclined to call it 'the *best* country in England'. The reason for his judgement was Northamptonshire's 'extensive' woodlands, which gave it 'a decided advantage over Leicestershire as a hunting country'. The advantage lay in the number of foxes that the country could provide, one of the aims of cub hunting being to disperse the foxes from the woodlands to the smaller coverts.[27] Surtees particularly praised the duke of Buccleuch's woodlands 'extending twenty miles end to end', where 'they may begin as early and hunt as late as any part of England, the New Forest not excepted' and where 'they generally kill twenty brace of fox before they disturb a cover in the Pytchley country'.[28] For all his enthusiasm for acres and acres of rolling grassland, Surtees regarded himself as belonging more to that group who rode to hunt, rather than those who hunted to ride. By the 1870s the interest in the different types of hunting country had polarised sufficiently to make it worth forming a separate hunt, the Woodland Pytchley, to concentrate on the type of hunting landscape to be found in north-east Northamptonshire.[29] There was a certain contradiction lying at the heart of the landscape requirements of modern foxhunting. The foxes themselves required the traditional hunting landscape of woodland and dense undergrowth as habitat, but their pursuers favoured smaller coverts, sparsely situated across

24. NRO, Althorp Chace Books: ML4431.
25. Elliott, *Fifty years' foxhunting*, p. 41.
26. Nethercote, *The Pytchley hunt*, p. 170.
27. Cecil, *Records of the chase*, p. 283.
28. Surtees, *Town and country papers*, pp. 188, 93–4.
29. Nethercote, *The Pytchley hunt*; Paget, *Althorp and Pytchley hunt*.

grass country, to encourage their prey to run along the desired 'lines' and give the opportunity for extended gallops.

Conclusion

This chapter has examined how two aspects of traditional hunting fared under modern conditions. As regards the traditional prey, deer continued to be hunted into the nineteenth century, but the methods used were very different to what had gone before. The ability to keep captive deer and to transport them to a convenient hunting location gave rise to a sport that was practised in situations where foxhunting was not feasible. This is the key to understanding the hunting of the carted deer: it was a 'needs must' substitute for fashionable foxhunting, not a poor stand-in for traditional deer hunting, which did not happen in our Northamptonshire study area. The county's forests could not rival the favoured Northamptonshire shires in terms of popularity, but they were valued by the fox hunts themselves, as both a training ground for young hounds and a reservoir for the supply of young foxes.

7

Horses and hunting

In the previous chapters the suggestion was made that if early hunting was about the hound, then later hunting, and particularly foxhunting, was about the horse. This chapter examines this assertion in more detail.

Horses in literature

Medieval hunting sources largely ignore the horse. For example, *The master of game* had extensive coverage of the types of prey that might be hunted, much on hounds and on how to train them, a great deal on the ways to seek out a stag and on the social formalities of the hunt, but the work contained not one word on the hunting horse.[1] The sixteenth century, however, saw the beginning of a period when horses themselves were considered to be a suitable subject of literature. Initially this enthusiasm was sparked by a continental, and particularly Italian, passion for high-school riding (from which modern-day dressage descended). The sixteenth century saw a growing number of works on the breeding and training of horses and on treating their ailments. The first writers on equestrianism had connections with the royal household. Thomas Blundeville had spent his youth at court. John Astey was a friend of Blundeville's and the son of a Gentleman Pensioner. Gervase Markham, who became probably the most prolific and popular author on horsemanship in the early modern period, was also related to one of Henry VIII's Gentleman Pensioners and his father was a friend of Francis Walsingham.[2]

Blundeville's first published book was an English translation and adaptation of the work of the Italian Federico Grisone. In 1565 Blundeville followed this with the larger and more original *Fower chiefest offices belongyng to horsemanshippe*. Blundeville was concerned with the quality of the native horses and had many suggestions for improving the stock, although his main interest was in horses for service (that is, for warfare), rather than in horses for hunting. Indeed, he went so far as to suggest that gentlemen's parks would be better dedicated to the breeding of horses than to the keeping of deer (which he described as 'altogether a pleasure without profite').

1. Edward of Norwich, *Master of game.*
2. J. Thirsk, *Horses in early modern England*, p. 17.

In the part of the book that dealt with breeding, Blundeville acknowledged that people required different types of horse for different purposes. Some wanted a 'breede of great trotting horses' for military use, some wanted 'ambling horses of a meane stature' for travelling long distances by road. He acknowledged here that some would have a race of 'swift runners to run for wagers, or to gallop the bucke or to serve for such like exercises of pleasure'. For the breeding of such a horse he recommended the use of a Turk or Barb stallion, particularly the latter, as he had a natural toughness. The writer observed that such 'extreame exercises as to gallop the bucke, or follow a long winged hawke – killeth yearlie in this realme many a good gelding'. The remainder of the *Fower chiefest offices* was dedicated to the breaking and riding of a horse intended for warfare or for high-school riding, and to dealing with vices that might develop in these horses. There is no further mention of the hunting or racing horse.[3]

By contrast, in the early seventeenth century Gervase Markham dedicated the third part of his book *Cavelarice* to 'the choice, training, and dyeting of hunting horses'. He was interested in the type of horse best suited both for riding after hounds and for use in hunting matches. He had specific recommendations to make as regards the type of hunting that readers should use to train their horses. Interestingly, Markham discounted the chase of the fox or the badger because 'for the moste part it continues in woody and rough grounds, where a horse can neither convenientlie make foorth his way, nor can tread without danger of stubing'. Markham approved of the pursuit of the buck or stag, especially 'if they bee not confyned within the limits of a parke or pale, but haue libertie to chuse their waies according to their own appetites, which of some Hunts-men is cald hunting at force', but he equally warned that this sport should be reserved for the exercise of horses of 'staid yeares' as it was too long and exacting for young horses. For the training of youngsters, the best by far was hare hunting, which provided chases of the right length and speed and took place between Michaelmas and April, when the sun was not too hot nor the ground too hard.[4]

Michael Baret gave advice on both hunting horses and 'running horses', but he saw a gentleman's interest in his hunting horses as being focused more on how to win hunting matches. For Baret the difference between a hunting horse and a running horse was not great, but 'only in continuance of labour, for this dependeth upon long and weary toyle; and that upon a quicke and speedy dispatch'. The hunting horse was more stretched both in terms of the distance that he was expected to run and the quality of the ground that he had to gallop over, but the training regime that Baret advised was very similar for both types of horse.[5] Thomas de Grey produced another book entirely dedicated to horses

3.   T. Blundeville, *The fower chiefyst offices belongyng to horsemanshippe* (London, 1566), p. 12.
4.   G. Markham, *Cavelarice*, Book 3 (London, 1607), p. 6.
5.   M. Baret, *An hipponomie or the vineyard of horsemanship* (London, 1618), pp. 51–73.

and horsemanship in 1639. In *The compleat horse-man and expert ferrier*, however, far from giving his readers guidance on the breeding and training of hunting horses, he went so far as to criticise their use in the sport. De Grey complained that the hunters 'overstraine the strength of their poore horses'. The sight of horses returning after a day's hunting would 'pitty the heart' of any horse lover, the mounts being 'mired, blooded, spurred, lamentabley spent and tyred out'.[6]

Later in the century William Cavendish, duke of Newcastle, produced probably the most famous work on horsemanship surviving from the early modern period. Cavendish was primarily concerned with training the horse for the 'mannage'. He talked of 'dressing' horses, in the sense of training them to perform various high-school movements, and it is from this type of riding that we derive the terms 'dressage' and 'manége' (the latter being an all-weather arena in which horses are trained). Cavendish made some allusion to hunting in passing, however, grouping together the sorts of horse that a man might use for hunting, hawking or travelling. He was certainly of the opinion that such horses had their place: 'I am always ready to buy for such purposes an old nagg of some hunts-man or falconer, that is sound'. Cavendish deemed such an animal to be 'a useful nagg' because he 'gallops on all Grounds, leaps over ditches and hedges'; such a horse was not, however, suited 'for a souldiers horse, nor the mannage'. Cavendish had no particularly high opinion of running horses either. These, he said, 'are the most easily found and of the least use'. Part of the trouble was the ground they were used to: 'commonly they run upon heaths (a green carpet)'. This made them unaccustomed to rough going and 'they run on the shoulders'; in modern parlance they were 'heavy on the forehand'. This is still considered an undesirable feature in a riding horse, with the preference being for a horse to power itself using its hind legs, not its forelegs.[7]

This survey of early equestrian literature suggests that the authors were not particularly concerned with hunting. They were as likely to describe the features of a horse required for hawking as one for hunting. This would seem to confirm the impression gained from the early writers on hunting: while horses were necessary for the sport, their role was not considered to be important enough to be treated separately. Where the early modern equestrian writers did give consideration to the hunting horse it was likely to be in relation to the considerations of hunting matches. This is significant when we come to consider the relationship of the developing sport of horse racing to the changing physiology of the horse and to the development of 'modern' foxhunting.

Hunting itself remained a popular literary theme, and there were books published in this period that covered both horses and hunting. In 1677 the first

6.   T. de Grey, *The compleat horse-man and expert ferrier* (London, 1639) (unnumbered introduction).
7.   W. Cavendish, duke of Newcastle, *A new method, and extraordinary invention, to dress horses, and work them according to nature* (London, 1667), pp. 110–11.

edition of Nicholas Cox's The gentleman's recreation appeared. This described the four gentlemanly sports of hunting, hawking, fowling and fishing. Like earlier works on hunting, the book said very little about the hunting horse per se, but the third edition, published in 1686, added an entire section devoted to the selection, feeding and training of a horse to be used for hunting and for running in hunting matches. This work repeated much of what Markham had to say on the subject at the beginning of the century.[8] Richard Blome had a somewhat wider view of gentlemanly recreations than Cox. The first part of Blome's The gentleman's recreation was an encyclopaedia of the arts and sciences, while the second part contained treatises on horsemanship, hawking, hunting, fowling, fishing and agriculture, with a short section on cock-fighting.[9] Although he talked of hunting horses in his section on horsemanship, Blome's advice on hunting comprised the standard fare: the types of hound that were available, how to hunt the various prey, how to treat the illnesses of hounds. Horsemanship and hunting were treated as two separate recreations.

Cox and Blome were both reprinted in the eighteenth century, and other works appeared in that century on the subjects of both hunting and on horsemanship, such as Thomas Fairfax's The compleat sportsman (1764) and William Osbaldiston's The universal sportsman (1792). These works were often derivatives of the books that we have already examined. Fairfax, for example, quoted Cavendish verbatim when describing how a colt should be kept in his early years. These authors repeated the pattern of treating horsemanship and hunting as two separate subjects.[10]

The sport of modern foxhunting came to have a large body of literature associated with it: magazine articles by 'celebrity' sporting correspondents, guides on where to hunt, novels based on the hunting field and antiquarian histories of famous hunts. These works contained much less emphasis on how to hunt and much more on where to hunt and with whom. Above all, there was more emphasis on what to hunt on. The Sporting Magazine, first published in 1792, covered all manner of sports through means of correspondents scattered the length and breadth of the country. Early issues contained articles on such diverse sports as boxing and cock fighting.[11] It carried accounts of every type of hunting: meetings of stag hounds, buck hounds and harriers, as well as of foxhounds, but by the 1820s it began to concentrate on foxhunting. In 1822 the magazine employed Charles Apperley, who took the pen name 'Nimrod', as a hunting correspondent

8.   Cox, Gentleman's recreation.
9.   Blome, Gentleman's recreation.
10. T. Fairfax, The compleat sportsman; or country gentleman's recreation (London, 1758); W. Osbaldiston, The universal sportsman: or, nobleman, gentleman, and farmer's dictionary of recreation and amusement (London, 1795).
11. For example, the October 1803 edition had two articles on boxing, but only some correspondents' reports on hunting meets. It did contain two articles on the health and welfare of horses. The Sporting Magazine, October 1803.

at not inconsiderable expense. By the early 1820s the magazine was the fourth best-selling monthly periodical in London, one writer crediting Nimrod's contributions with trebling the magazine's circulation.[12] Nimrod's pieces often took the form of reports on the various meets that he had attended. The emphasis was on the thrill of the chase and included detailed descriptions of the riding, the riders and their falls. Although he talked of the hounds and the men who hunted them, the horses were foremost in Nimrod's accounts. A man who understood the working of the hunt and the nature of the hounds would have a distinct advantage, but this was because it enabled him to achieve the aim of the foxhunter: to keep up with the hounds and be in at the death, and this was more for the sense of achievement than plain enjoyment of hunting *per se*.[13] Apperley was himself an accomplished horseman and although, as an inveterate snob, he would never describe himself as a horse dealer, he supported himself before his writing career took off by buying, training and selling hunters. Unlike earlier works on hunting at no point did Nimrod give advice on the breeding or keeping of hounds, or on the 'science' of hunting itself, but he did publish advice on the hunting horse. He collected together some of his writings from *The Sporting Magazine* and published them as a book entitled *Remarks on the condition of hunters* in 1837.[14]

Other writers followed in Nimrod's footsteps, of whom Surtees is probably the most famous. He started as a hunting correspondent for *The Sporting Magazine* around the time of Nimrod's rather acrimonious departure in 1829, assuming the pen name 'Nim South'. He had a rather different attitude to Nimrod, preferring to follow hounds away from the press of fashionable people in Leicestershire; if Nimrod could be described as an inveterate snob, Surtees could be described as an inverted one. Surtees was more interested in the hunting itself and, after inheriting the family estate in Durham, kept a pack of hounds himself. He too fell out with *The Sporting Magazine* and was one of the forces behind the founding of *New Sporting Magazine* in 1831. His Jorrocks character first appeared in the latter magazine. Surtees was rather more interested in hounds than Nimrod, and his accounts of runs included more details on the hunting than his predecessor's. He was well aware of the difference between those who rode in order to hunt and those who hunted in order to ride, and one cannot escape the impression that he approved rather more of the former.[15] Surtees's work, however, still bears more resemblance to Nimrod's than it does to the seventeenth- and early eighteenth-century works on hunting that we have described previously. His accounts were narratives, rather than prescriptions on the best ways to hunt, and paid much attention to those who

12. C. Cone, *Hounds in the morning: selections from The Sporting Magazine 1792–1836* (Lexington, KY, 1981), pp. 22–4.
13. Nimrod (C. Apperley) 'Riding to hounds', *The Sporting Magazine* (January 1823).
14. Nimrod (C. Apperley), *Remarks on the condition of hunters* (London, 1837).
15. Surtees says as much in his observations about a Dorset hunting parson: 'Dorsetshire: Mr. Farquharson's (1834–1835)' in Surtees, *Town and country papers*, p. 118.

attended various meets and the ways in which they were dressed. While he gave more descriptions of the hounds than the horses, the rideability of the hunting country remained paramount in his descriptions.[16]

Where writers did seek to provide instruction on the management of a hunt and its hounds the horse still played a larger role than in the earlier examples of the genre. Colonel John Cook published *Observations on fox hunting* in 1826. This, like Beckford's work of fifty years before, was written in the style of someone offering advice to a young gentleman seeking to establish his own hunt. Where it differed, however, was in its explicit acknowledgement of the importance of the horse to the success of the project. Cook might have rued the fact that an entire pack of hounds could be purchased for less than the price of a good horse, but he advised his student that mounting himself and his hunt servants was crucial to the aim of providing good sport and good entertainment for the gentlemen of the neighbourhood.[17]

Subsequent writers on hunting tended to follow in the footsteps of Nimrod and Surtees rather than those of Cook. They concentrated on reporting on real-life hunts rather than giving advice on how to hunt. The next famous correspondent was Henry Hall Dixon, who took the pen name 'The Druid'. He did not himself ride to hounds, but he took delight in reporting the escapades of those who did. The primary hunting coverage in both *The post and the paddock* and *Silk and scarlet* featured the recollections of the 'rough rider' Dick Christian, and naturally were very much more concerned with tales of hard riding than with hard hunting.[18]

Today Surtees is more famous for his novels, all of which have foxhunting at their centre. The nineteenth century also produced Whyte-Melville, who wrote both general works on horsemanship and foxhunting novels in the middle of the century.[19] The great Victorian novelist Anthony Trollope was himself an ardent foxhunter, and hunting scenes featured heavily in some of his works.[20]

This survey of hunting literature has served to illustrate two points: that the role of the horse was very much more important to later foxhunters than it was to earlier deer hunters, and that the literature of the nineteenth century was addressed to the very large 'field' that followed the hounds, rather than to the men who actually kept and hunted hounds. Some time between the seventeenth century and the early nineteenth century, the animal previously referred to as 'the hunting

16. We have already drawn upon Surtees's description of Northamptonshire's landscape and the 'stiffness' (difficulty) of its fences. 'The Pytchley (1833–1834)' in Surtees, *Town and country papers*, p. 90.

17. Cook, *Observations*, pp. 4, 58.

18. 'The Druid' (H. Hall Dixon), *The paddock and the post* (1857; London, 1862); Druid, *Silk and scarlet*.

19. For example: G.J. Whyte-Melville, *Market Harborough* (1862; London, 1984); Whyte-Melville, *Riding recollections*.

20. Trollope produced a set of hunting sketches, first published in the *Pall Mall Gazette*, in which he satirised the various followers of hounds. A. Trollope, *Hunting sketches* (London, 1865).

horse' became recognised by the term 'the hunter'. It is one of the arguments of this book that the changing nature of the horse, and the increased enthusiasm for riding hard to hounds, was one of the forces that drove the hunting transition; and thus we need to investigate the development of the horse between 1600 and 1850 in more detail.

Horse racing

A significant cultural development of the eighteenth century was the growing importance of the sport of horse racing. It has been described as 'the most rapidly developing and commercially oriented of eighteenth-century physical recreations'.[21] Horse racing as an organised sport was relatively young. Although horse racing certainly existed under the Tudors, it was to the reign of James I and the beginning of the ascendancy of Newmarket that the modern sport generally traces its origins. James and his son Charles both had hunting establishments at Newmarket. In his history of Newmarket and English racing the nineteenth-century writer Hore made various references to hunting matches and the losses and wins of sundry noblemen as they bet on the outcome. Hore usefully turned his attentions away from Newmarket and gave evidence of race meetings elsewhere in the country in the first two decades of the seventeenth century, at, for example, Chester, Croydon, Richmond, Lincoln, Salisbury, Derby, York and, significantly for students of Northamptonshire, Brackley.[22] Meanwhile, the 'earliest authentic and irrefutable occurrence' of racing at Newmarket in the reign of Charles I was the Gold Cup in 1634. Charles II himself rode in the races at Newmarket. Young Thomas Isham records in his diary being told that the king had ridden two heats at Newmarket 'and the Duke of Albermarle's horse had fallen'.[23]

The sport in the seventeenth and the early eighteenth centuries was very different from the sport of flat racing that we would recognise today. Hunting matches were a popular way of competing. These involved pitching two horses against each other across three heats. For each heat a 'train scent' was laid by dragging a dead animal (usually a cat) along the route it was desired the horses should take. Hounds were then loosed to follow the scent, and the horses would follow the hounds. Each rider had a judge, called a 'trier', who rode behind and ensured fair play. The triers directed where the train scent was laid, which was an effective way of delimiting a racetrack over the kind of open terrain where most races were staged. Horses also ran for plates, without the benefit of hounds to chase.[24] A plate typically accommodated more runners than a match but between four and eight seems to have been the common number. Again, the race was

21. P. Borsay, *The English urban renaissance: culture and society in the provincial town, 1660–1770* (1989; Oxford, 1991), p. 181.
22. Hore, *History of Newmarket*, 1, pp. 338–58.
23. Marlow, *Diary of Thomas Isham*, p. 165.
24. Fairfax, *Compleat sportsman*, pp. 62–4; Osbaldiston, *Universal sportsman*, p. 486.

staged in heats. A horse often ran three heats of up to four miles each, which was an endurance event compared to the distances covered by modern racehorses. Some plates were specifically for horses that hunted, but as time went on there was more emphasis on specialist racehorses, which were too precious to risk on the hunting field. There were also races for 'galloways', which were strong ponies. The racing calendars of the last quarter of the eighteenth century show that, by then, racing was beginning to assume a more recognisable form. There were still plates and other prizes being run for in heats at various racecourses around the country, but there were far more competitions comprising 'one heat' and many more sweepstakes, where the prize money came from the entry fees.[25]

Northamptonshire was well provided with race meetings. We have already alluded to the meetings held at Brackley in the seventeenth century. Thomas Isham's diary, covering 1672 and 1673, adds races at Harlestone, just to the north-west of Northampton, Irthlingborough, near Wellingborough, and Rowell (Rothwell).[26] Early in the following century the diary of Justinian Isham recorded race meetings at Borough Hill (near Daventry), Irthlingborough, Harlestone and Rothwell.[27] One of the Harlestone meetings included a race for galloways.[28] The 1729 racing calendar gave details of race meetings at Daventry, Kettering, Peterborough, Rothwell and Northampton, many of which included races for hunters and galloways. The 1769 racing calendar gave details of races held on Wakefield Lawn at Whittlebury, but these races do not seem to have become an established event.[29] By 1779 the calendar listed only Northampton and Peterborough as racing venues in the county.[30]

Horses bred for racing

The enthusiasm for horse racing led to a concentration on the breeding of horses for this purpose that culminated in the production of the English thoroughbred. It has been said that the thoroughbred in the eighteenth century 'helped to define Englishness in a country obsessed with horse racing'.[31] But the significance of the thoroughbred has been greatly understated by most historians. The impact of the breeding of this animal was wider than merely on the sports of racing or

25. James Weatherby, *Racing calendar: containing an account of the plates, matches, and sweepstakes, run for in Great-Britain and Ireland, &c. in the year 1774* (London, 1774).
26. Marlow, *Diary of Thomas Isham*, pp. 147, 153, 203.
27. NRO, Isham archive: IL2686.
28. J. Cheny, *An historical list of all horse-matches run, and of all plates and prizes run for in England and Wales (of the value of ten pounds or upwards) in 1729* (London, 1729), pp. 93–7.
29. B. Walker, *An historical list of horse-matches, plates and prizes, run for in Great-Britain and Ireland, in the year 1769* (London, 1770), p. 92.
30. James Weatherby, *Racing calendar: containing an account of the plates, matches, and sweepstakes, run for in Great-Britain and Ireland, &c. in the year 1779* (London, 1779), p. iv.
31. P. Edwards, *Horse and man in early modern England* (London, 2007), p. 31.

of hunting; the lessons learned laid the foundations for the great programme of stock improvement associated with the agricultural revolution in the latter half of the eighteenth century. While this fact has been acknowledged by specialists in the subject of stock breeding, it is largely unknown to a wider audience.[32]

Conscious attempts to manipulate and improve the standard of horses in England were made as early as the reign of Henry VII. He passed legislation, aimed at preserving the country's breeding stock, that sought to prevent the export of mares or stallions.[33] Henry's son also recognised that England's horses stood in need of some improvement. The pursuit of war required horses both to fight from and to pull baggage trains, and Henry VIII's warlike propensities led both to greater demand for horses and a diminution in supply. Further legislation thus sought to encourage the breeding of suitable equines. A law of 1535 dictated that those in possession of a park, or other enclosed ground with a circumference of a mile or more, should keep two mares capable of breeding foals to mature at a minimum height of 13 hands. The penalty for ignoring this law was a 40-shilling fine. There was a similar penalty for anyone who allowed these mares to be covered by stallions of less than 14 hands. A law of 1541 forbade anyone in named Midland and southern counties to turn loose any stallion under 15 hands in 'forest, chase, moor, heath, common or waste' where there were mares and fillies running. Furthermore, any females found in such places judged unlikely to bear sizeable offspring were to be killed. Henry had earlier passed legislation reinforcing his father's export ban, and had included Scotland in its scope. In 1541–2 nobility, gentry and churchmen were ordered to keep riding horses of certain ages and sizes. The exact requirements depended on the status and income of the man. The king himself set up a number of breeding studs in his parks as an example to his subjects, the most famous of which was at Tutbury, still in existence a century later.[34] Under Elizabeth the pressure to improve the supply of horses for service was maintained. In 1580 the queen set up the 'Special Commission for the Increase and Breed of Horses', whose remit was to oversee the enforcement of existing laws and to ensure that those required to keep horses for service were fulfilling these commitments. There is some evidence, however, that the nobles and gentlemen being so supervised were themselves quite interested in improving the breeding of horses.[35]

We have already observed that the sixteenth century saw the beginning of an explosion of literary interest in the subject of horses and horsemanship, and many of these works concentrated on breeding. The advice tended to follow the same pattern even if the specifics varied from author to author. For example, the readers

32. See below, p. 116, for a fuller discussion of this point.
33. A law of 1496 forbade the export of any stallions and of mares worth more than six shillings and eight pence. Sir W. Gilbey, *Concise history of the Shire horse* (1889; Liss, 1976), p. 21.
34. Gilbey, *Shire horse*, p. 21; Thirsk, *Horses in early modern England*, pp. 12–14.
35. Thirsk, *Horses in early modern England*, p. 16.

of both Blundeville and Markham had the various breeds of horse described to them and were advised on which they might choose as a sire or a dam according to the intended purpose of the offspring. They were also told what type of ground was suitable for stallion, mare and mare with foal at foot, and even how to divide their park accordingly (Markham also catered for the humbler breeder, in that he gave advice on the best places to tether a mare). Feeding was covered, as were the mechanics of covering the mare and of her foaling.[36]

Cavendish was a less derivative writer than his predecessors, and he was positively scathing about Blundeville's work, from the century before his own. However, he still had much to say on the various breeds of horses and which to use as sire and dam. He was primarily concerned with horses for the 'mannage' and, as we have previously seen, had a low opinion of horses bred for racing. Spanish horses were unrivalled as sires in his opinion (although he did recognise the value of eastern horses in breeding racehorses). While Cavendish strongly advised against the use of a stallion that the reader himself had bred (he believed that would lead to the production of 'cart horses' within three generations), he did suggest that his audience 'cannot Breed Better, than to Breed of your Own Mares that you have Bred; and let their Fathers Cover them; for there is no Incest in Horses: And thus they are Nearer, by a Degree, to the Purity, since a fine Horse Got them, and the same fine Horse Covers them again'.[37] Such inbreeding became the key to stamping an identity on sheep, pigs and cattle in the following century.

At the end of the seventeenth century, however, it seems that Cavendish's audience was more interested in breeding horses for racing, rather than for the school or war service. It was at this time that the foundations were laid for the production of the English thoroughbred, a creature in an advanced state of development long before Bakewell of Dishley produced the New Leicester sheep. Earlier works on horses gave only passing advice on the breeding of running horses. There was near unanimity, however, in suggesting that it was the eastern breeds of horse, identified variously as the Turk, the Barb and the Arab, that made the best sires when breeding for this purpose.[38] As the sport of horse racing rose in popularity after the Restoration so more and more gentlemen turned their attention to breeding horses that would win matches and wagers. They followed the advice of the writers on horsemanship and turned to the eastern horses for their foundation stock. All modern thoroughbreds include three early sires in the male line of their pedigrees: the Byerley Turk, the Darley Arabian and the Godolphin Arabian. The first of these was initially his owner's war horse (having reputedly been captured at the siege of Vienna in 1683 and later fighting at the

36. Blundeville, *Fower chiefyst offices*; Markham, *Cavelarice*.
37. Cavendish, *New method*, p. 93.
38. For example, Blundeville, *Fower chiefest offices*, p. 12; Blome, *Gentleman's recreation*, p. 2.

Battle of the Boyne); he was retired to stud in North Yorkshire until his death in 1709. The Darley Arabian was purchased at Aleppo and brought to England in 1704. He stood at Aldby Park near York until 1730 and sired the famous and influential horse Flying Childers. The Godolphin Arabian stood at stud in Cambridgeshire until his death in 1753. Other eastern stallions, such as the Dun Arabian and the Bloody Shouldered Arabian (imported from Turkey in 1715 and 1719 respectively), had early influence on racehorses but their lines have since died out in the thoroughbred, although they can be traced in the pedigrees of other breeds. Upwards of 200 stallions were imported into England in the late seventeenth and early eighteenth centuries.[39] These stallions were used on both eastern and English mares to produce a recognisable, and reproducible, breed of horse. Many of the bloodlines were recorded for posterity in the various racing calendars that appeared in the eighteenth century, as well as in the *General stud book* produced by James Weatherby in 1791.[40] This latter book traced the lineage of thoroughbred horses back to the late seventeenth century, and it was the foundation for the thoroughbred stud book which is produced by Weatherbys to this day. From these records, and from the studbooks of individual breeders, we get some picture of how close breeding was a tool used in stamping the desired features on a horse. Writing in 1756, the veterinary surgeon William Osmer observed that 'affinity of blood' was fine in the breeding of horses so long as it was 'not continued too long in the same channel'. As proof he cites the case of Flying Childers, 'perhaps the best racer ever bred in this kingdom', who had the sire Spanker twice in his dam's line.[41]

It is difficult to identify exactly when the term 'thoroughbred' was first used to describe the horses specifically bred for racing. In *A dissertation on horses* Osmer argued that the 'excellency' of particular racehorses was due to their conformation rather than to some invisible quality of 'blood'. The author did admit that all racehorses must be bred from 'foreign' (that is, eastern) stock, and referred to this group as 'high bred'.[42] Ten years later he appended a defence of this argument to a work on farriery. In this he used the term 'bred horse' to describe these animals. He later used the term 'half-bred' to describe horses that 'can boast of no blood or pedigree'.[43] In 1809 John Lawrence pondered the question of how early in the history of racing a certain breed of horse was fixed upon; he commented that, in his time, all horses intended for racing 'it is well known must be thorough-bred'. He

39. <http://www.tbheritage.com/HistoricSires/FoundationSires.html>. Accessed 15 December 2012.
40. For example, John Cheny's series of *An historical list of all horse-matches run* ran from 1729 to 1750; Reginald Heber's similarly titled series ran from 1751 to 1768; James Weatherby's *Racing calendars* ran from 1773 to 1800. All contained some information on breeding, as well as accounts of the races themselves.
41. W. Osmer, *A dissertation on horses* (London, 1756), p. 26.
42. Osmer, *Dissertation*, p. 7.
43. W. Osmer, *A treatise on the diseases and lameness of horses* (London, 1766), pp. 207, 209.

went on to define the term: 'in plain terms both their sires and dams must be the purest blood of Asiatic or African coursers exclusively, and this must be attested in an authentic pedigree, throughout whatever number of English descents'.[44] By the 1820s the term 'thoroughbred' had certainly entered the common parlance. Nimrod, for example, used it freely.

Modern historians who have looked at the 'improvement' of farm livestock in the eighteenth century have acknowledged the great influence of horse breeding. Some recognised that the requirements for different types of horse had effectively led to selective breeding even before the advent of the thoroughbred. Others have pointed out the proximity of hound and horse breeding programmes to later, more famous, livestock improvers.[45] The link that these historians have drawn between horse breeding and the drive to improve farming stock would have come as no surprise to its contemporaries. Writing towards the end of the eighteenth century, William Marshall described the improvement of Midland sheep that reached its apogee with Bakewell's New Leicester. Marshall acknowledged that the exact method used by Bakewell was unknown, but maintained that he had probably bred by 'selecting individuals from kindred breeds'. Elsewhere, the writer tells us, breeders had used outcrossing in an attempt at breed improvement, but in the Midlands 'superior stock' had been raised by breeding 'not from the same line only, but from the same family'. This technique had acquired a phrase to describe it: 'breeding inandin', but in a footnote Marshall informed the reader that the term was not of Midland origin. He gave Newmarket as its birthplace, where the practice had been established by the breeders of racehorses.[46]

Few writers have looked at the question of animal breeding in depth and there is some disagreement among those that have. For example, some have denied that there was much inbreeding involved in the early history of the thoroughbred, while

44. J. Lawrence, *History and delineation of the horse* (London, 1809), p. 98.
45. Thomas commented that 'by the end of the eighteenth century cattle, sheep, foxhounds and even pigeons were being bred with comparative attention'. Thirsk commented that 'for want of proof, one can only hazard guesses when exactly the lessons learned from horse breeding influenced breeders of other livestock', but she thought that it was 'no accident' that Bakewell's Dishley farm was in 'good hunting country'. This is a thought echoed by J.R. Walton who suggested, in his study of pedigree in cattle, that Bakewell may have been 'strongly influenced' by Hugo Meynell, who had been breeding improved foxhounds a mere six miles away. Walton went on to remark on the geographical proximity of areas of 'improvement for profit' with existing sites of 'improvement for pleasure'. He went so far as to suggest that selective breeding was more successful for animals such as foxhounds, hunters and racehorses where 'richer land owners made direct use of the animals' utility functions'. Thomas, *Man and the natural world*, pp. 59–60; J. Thirsk, 'Agricultural innovations and their diffusion', in J. Thirsk (ed.), *Agrarian history of England and Wales, 1640–1750*, 2 vols (Cambridge, 1985), 2, p. 578; J.R. Walton, 'Pedigree and the national cattle herd *circa* 1750–1950', *Agricultural History Review*, 34 (1986), pp. 153–4.
46. W. Marshall, *The rural economy of the midland counties*, 2 vols (London, 1796), 1, pp. 340, 250.

others accept its role.[47] As we have seen, the contemporary writers on equestrian matters did not necessarily agree with each other in their recommendations as to breeding strategy, and it is hard to know whether their prescriptions were closely followed in any case. One of the major problems in judging breeding advice is that writers had no knowledge of genetics, so that the justifications that they employed were inevitably fanciful. In his work on early modern animal breeding Russell described how early writers on horse breeding turned to the classics for inspiration, and from these sources came theories as to whether the mare or the stallion engendered form, or whether it was the environment in which horses were bred that directly affected both form and function (with the implication that both would be lost if long removed from their native environment). But whether by accident or design, the formula of using imported eastern stallions on native-bred mares (themselves with varying degrees of eastern blood) was successful in producing the ultimate equine athlete. So successful was it that the breed was subsequently exported around the world and enabled the growth of horse-racing industries from the United States to Australia. Even without a knowledge of phenology, genology and heredity, seventeenth- and eighteenth-century racehorse breeders found a way of breeding for performance and breeding true to type.

Thoroughbreds and hunting

It was asserted above that the production of the thoroughbred was a major factor in the transformation of hunting between the years 1600 and 1850. It is now time to examine the impact of the thoroughbred upon the sport of hunting.

The writer Nimrod had no doubt as to what type of horse was required for hunting at the beginning of the nineteenth century, and particularly for hunting in the shires. In his account of the history of the sport he detected the greatest change as having taken place 'in the horse called the hunter'. Nimrod admitted that a good half-bred horse was sufficient for the job a hundred years before, but a horse of that description would never 'carry the modern sportsman, who rides well up to hounds, on a good scenting day, over one of our best hunting countries'; such an animal 'would be powerless and dangerous before he had gone across half a dozen Leicestershire enclosures'. Nimrod advised his readers to mount themselves on a thoroughbred horse, or what he terms a 'cock-tail', which in modern parlance is a three-quarters or seven-eighths thoroughbred.[48] Lawrence described the required animal thus: 'the hunter, is either a thorough-bred Horse of sufficient substance, or one with a considerable shew of blood, and with good action; for example, got by a racer out of a half-bred, or three-part-bred mare; or

47. N. Russell, *Like engendering like: heredity and animal breeding in early modern England* (Cambridge, 1986), p. 104; P. Willet, *The Thoroughbred* (London, 1970), p. 30.
48. Nimrod, *Chace*, pp. 7–9.

any horse, mare, or gelding of sufficient powers and action'.[49] Youatt echoed this view: 'In strong, thickly inclosed countries, the half-bred horse may get tolerably well along; but for general use the hunter should be at least threequarters bred, perhaps seven-eighths.'[50] Cook, although more of a hound man than a horse man, had come to the same conclusions as Nimrod, Lawrence and Youatt, commenting that 'many fox-hunters prefer thorough-bred horses, others cock-tails; I always give preference to the former'. It is worth noting that Cook had reached his conclusions hunting in Suffolk and in Essex; he was not a 'shire' man, but he still found thoroughbred horses to be superior hunters in terms of jumping ability and stamina.[51] Neither extraordinary speed nor particular jumping ability had been required in the horses employed in earlier forms of hunting, and writers such as Markham had seen the chief virtue of a hunting horse as being able to cover a variety of terrain safely. Even in hunting matches it was endurance and ability to cover rough ground that could be more useful than sheer speed, and matches were made between horses of comparable abilities rather than being a straightforward competition to find the fastest.[52] All the later writers were agreed, however, that hunting, whether of fox, deer or hare, had become much faster and more furious and so required a horse bred for speed.

Nimrod's account of his earlier horse-dealing days gives a picture of the type of horse that he was able to sell as a hunter. These included horses that he raced while a soldier in Ireland and then brought back to England. One such horse broke his knees on the passage and was only then fit to make a whipper-in's horse ('breaking the knees' is an injury to the skin and soft tissue rather than the bone and results in unsightly scarring, but does not necessarily lead to permanent lameness). Not all thoroughbreds would make good hunters; when first in Leicestershire Nimrod found himself in possession of two ex-racehorses, one with the venerable Eclipse in his bloodlines, but he found them both 'absolute failures' and 'without any mercy for my life and limbs' and so packed them off to London to see what they would fetch. On the other hand he failed to take the opportunity to buy a racehorse called Fisherwick, who was sold cheaply to another dealer due to foot problems and was subsequently purchased by the fourth earl of Jersey for 300 guineas.[53]

All the hunting writers who recommended a horse to ride out hunting recommended a thoroughbred.[54] There was apparently a degree of resistance to this, with some preferring a part-bred horse or 'cock-tail', but Delmé Radcliffe

49. Lawrence, *Delineation*, p. 117.
50. W. Youatt, *The horse, with a treatise on draught* (London, 1831), p. 51.
51. Cook, *Observations*, p. 60.
52. Baret, *Hipponomie*, pp. 51–60.
53. Nimrod (C. Apperley), *My horses and other essays* (London, 1928), pp. 7, 12, 14.
54. For example, Nimrod, *Chace*, pp. 7–9; Cook, *Observations*, p. 60; Delmé Radcliffe, *Noble science*, p. 64.

countered that the 'taste for the highest bred is daily gaining ground'. He was convinced that a 'race-horse, with bone and substance sufficient to qualify him for the rough and smooth encounter of crossing a country, is, beyond all comparison, superior to the best cock-tail that can be produced'.[55] A weight-carrying thoroughbred attracted a premium. For the ten- to twelve-stone man acquiring a good hunter was not difficult, but a weight-carrying horse commanded a much higher price. According to Delmé Radcliffe, 'horses equal to higher weight, and possessing any knowledge of their business, are not to be had for under three figures'.[56] William, second earl of Sefton, who took over mastership of the Quorn from Meynell, was credited with promoting the solution to the problem of heavy men riding thoroughbred, or part-thoroughbred, horses. Although riding at about twenty stone, he would have several horses in the field, ridden by lighter grooms, and made frequent swaps between them. For the Druid, horseflesh was one of Sefton's primary interests: 'Lord Sefton cared very little for hounds, but his stud was superb, and he never had less than three horses out in a day.'[57] The use of second, or even third, horses was widely adopted by those who could afford a large stud of hunters. The aspirational mount for the foxhunter was a substantial thoroughbred, and, although many continued to ride part-breds, there can be no doubt that the thoroughbred horse had a powerful influence on the horse called the hunter.

Horseriding skills

Horses and horsemanship had long been central to the status and identity of England's elite. At the beginning of the early modern period the type of horse and the kind of horsemanship were very much connected with the military role of the mounted knight. But this was soon to change as gunpowder and shot came to predominate on the battlefield. The man in full armour mounted on a heavy horse was becoming obsolete as emphasis moved to infantry supported by lightweight, more manoeuvrable, cavalry.[58] The horse's importance did not fade, however; early modern life continued to be 'saturated with horses and horse culture'.[59] Although this importance embraced many different types of equine, performing all kinds of task for those at all levels of society, the horse remained most conspicuous as an expression of power and status. Those at the upper end of the social scale had the wealth and leisure time to develop new methods of asserting their position through the equestrian arts.

---

55. Delmé Radcliffe, *Noble science*, p. 64.
56. Delmé Radcliffe, *Noble science*, p. 63.
57. Druid, *Silk and scarlet*, p. 252.
58. Boehrer has investigated how the changing role of the mounted knight was reflected in Shakespeare's plays: B. Boehrer, 'Shakespeare and the social devaluation of the horse', in K. Raber and T. Tucker (eds), *The culture of the horse: status, discipline and identity in the early modern world* (Basingstoke, 2005), pp. 91–111.
59. Raber and Tucker, *Culture of the horse*, p. 1.

Figure 7.1 Seventeenth-century riding position. Detail from *The Manag'd Horse* after Jan Wyck, published by R. Blome (c.1683–85) © Trustees of the British Museum.

Figure 7.2 The English hunting seat. Detail from *Clerical and Lay* by Henry Alken Snr.

The advent of *haute école* riding was one response to the changing role of the horse. Originating in Italy, and soon gaining ground in France, it became a way of demonstrating superiority through close control of a large and powerful animal performing intricate and impressive movements (which were claimed to have their origin in military tactics). Most of the seventeenth-century equestrian books that we described earlier contained instructions on riding such movements as the *capriole*, the *terre à terre* and the *courbette*. High-school riding was the primary focus of Cavendish's books. He was convinced that he had perfected the knowledge, and that his advice was superior to his English (not to mention Italian and French) predecessors. While such riding was widely accepted as a way for the elite to demonstrate their physical and mental prowess to themselves, to each other and to the 'inferior' ranks of society, another form of horsemanship was rapidly gaining ground in England: one that had its origin on the racecourse and found widespread expression on the hunting field.

To ride a horse at speed required a different type of equitation than that demanded by the manége. The illustrations in Blome's section on horsemanship show the rider to have an upright posture, with straight legs in long stirrups and a deep saddle with a high pommel and cantle (Figure 7.1). This was the posture needed to ride a horse in extreme collection: with the hind legs well underneath the animal and the energy finding expression in elevation rather than in forward movement. This was demonstrably not the way to ride a horse when a gentleman wanted to win a hunting match or other race; this required a different saddle design and a different 'seat' on the horse, based more on how the Turks rode their horses (Figure 7.2).[60] In the case of both the eastern horse and the eastern riding style, the English imported it, changed it and produced something that they considered to be superior to the original. Whereas the nobility had, in the medieval period, shared a common military function across Europe predicated on their mounted role in battle, the English elite now self-consciously separated themselves from continental horse culture. The wealthy and the powerful increasingly used the horse to express their status, and their common identity, on the racecourse and in the hunting field, while in the remainder of western Europe the emphasis remained on high-school riding.

Foxhunters found ways to express the significance of horseriding to their status and identity. We have already described the nature of the literature that accompanied modern foxhunting, and its concentration on the rider and the horse rather than the huntsman and the hound. The anecdotes that were popular with these writers demonstrated an obsession with the 'derring-do' of the hard riders

60. Landry has traced the development of what came to be called 'the English hunting seat' and described how English horsemen adopted, and adapted, the short stirrups and forward posture of the Turkish rider. D. Landry, *Noble brutes: how Eastern horses transformed English culture* (Baltimore, MD, 2009), pp. 44–73.

that began to characterise the sport from the beginning of the nineteenth century. Nimrod shared his vision of the essentials of foxhunting in his fictionalised account of a Leicestershire run. This follows the progress of a well-mounted visitor from the 'provinces' experiencing his first hunt in the 'shires'. From early in the chase the reader is left in no doubt as to the potential dangers this newcomer faced: 'two horses are seen loose in the distance – a report is flying about that one of the field is badly hurt, and something is heard of a collar-bone being broken, others say it is a leg; but the pace is *too good* to enquire'.[61] The pace being too good for anyone to stop and ask, let alone stop and help, is a chorus repeated throughout the account. The Druid found that Dick Christian's reminiscences of hard riding in Leicestershire and Northamptonshire were popular with his readers. Christian recounted experiences such as the time he attempted to leap a flock of sheep huddling by a fence he needed to jump. The horse cleared the sheep but hit the top of the rail and somersaulted. Unhurt, Christian remounted, and was in at the death. He reckoned himself lucky if he took only three falls in a day.[62] The foxhunter aspired to have the skill and daring to keep with the hounds no matter how fast they ran and what obstacles they encountered. It was not done to complain too much of one's own injuries, or to be too concerned with the mishaps of others if the run was good (and it was exceedingly bad form if one of those 'others' complained at this treatment). These characteristics, displayed on the hunting field, were taken to demonstrate a man's character in a wider field of endeavour. In his memoirs George Osbaldeston (master of numerous hunts in the first half of the nineteenth century, including the Quorn and the Pytchley) was scathing about Charles, Lord Middleton's performance as a horseman, and asserted that the said lord was not much of a performer in the bedroom either.[63] The dash and courage required to follow hounds across country was also considered essential to the training of a soldier. Delmé Radcliffe described foxhunting as a 'national utility', and quoted the celebrated soldier Lord Lynedoch commenting that 'he should not have been the soldier he is, had he not been bred a fox-hunter'.[64] Soldiers from Northampton and Weedon figured largely in the Pytchley field, and the Blues had founded the covert of the same name.[65]

Foxhunting's writers were also convinced of their superiority as riders to their continental cousins. Nimrod was critical of French horsemen and French

---

61. Nimrod, *Chace*, p. 37.

62. Druid, *Scarlet and silk*, pp. 3, 7.

63. G. Osbaldeston, *Squire Osbaldeston: his autobiography*, ed. E.D. Cuming (Bungay, 1927), pp. 52–3.

64. Delmé Radcliffe, *Noble science*, p. 5. Thomas Graham, first Baron Lynedoch, had a renowned military career in the French Revolutionary and Napoleonic wars.

65. See above, p. 86. N. Mansfield has recently suggested that the popularity of foxhunting had a bad effect on cavalry officers, arguing that it made for recklessness on the battlefield, where control was needed. N. Mansfield, 'Foxhunting and the Yeomanry: county identity and military culture', in R.W. Hoyle (ed.), *Our hunting fathers: field sports in England after 1850* (Lancaster, 2007), pp. 241–56.

horses. The worst features were the length of the stirrups and the absence of the rising trot: 'his system of riding – not rising to the action of the horse by the aid of his stirrups – destroys enjoyment of his most ordinary, and enduring pace, the trot'. The postilion was 'awkwardness and sloth' personified, with 'his awkward seat – his carcase bumping, his feet scarcely touching the stirrups from the extreme length of the leathers'. None of this was helped by the design of the French saddle: 'the pommel is of uncalled-for height, tipped with brass, and so is the cantle', but the stirrups were worse: 'the leathers make their appearance through holes in the flaps, and the buckles are so placed that they come in contact with the rider's thigh. Then they are placed more to the rear than ours, so as to be almost in a perpendicular line with the rider's body.' This was very different from the flat-seated, forward cut saddle of English design, so suited to riding fast across country. Neither could Nimrod understand why the French shunned the thoroughbred, preferring Yorkshire carriage horses to thoroughbreds as sires for their cavalry horses. It was no surprise to him that most French travel was conducted at a mere five miles per hour, with eight miles per hour as an absolute maximum.[66]

Conclusion

We have journeyed from a period when horses were seen as a necessary tool of hunting, but not its major focus, to a time when horses were the primary concern of most followers of the sport. In the sixteenth and seventeenth centuries hunting advice was likely to centre on the prey and the hounds used to pursue it. By the nineteenth century the horses, and the exploits of their riders, took centre stage. The growing popularity of horse racing, itself arising from 'hunting matches', drove the experiments in breeding which led to the creation of the ultimate equine athlete: the English thoroughbred. Lessons learned were eventually used to 'improve' many other animals, including the foxhound. Faster horses required faster foxhounds, and increasing pace led, in turn, to many more mounting themselves on the thoroughbred. In the 1820s Nimrod could reflect on how much faster hunting was than 100 years previously. By the 1870s the witnesses to the parliamentary enquiry into the state of the horse industry could talk of the blistering pace of contemporary hunters compared with those of 50 years before.[67]

66. Nimrod, *My horses*, pp. 118–25.
67. Nimrod, *Chace*, pp. 7–9; Parliamentary Papers HCPP, 1873, XIV.

8

The chase goes out of fashion: hunting and the polite society

It has been argued above that the hunting transition had its roots in the eighteenth century and that causality lies in the changes in the landscape that happened in this period. But the eighteenth century also witnessed a great cultural shift, and it is worth examining whether this was a factor in the change in hunting prey and hunting practices.

The end of the seventeenth and the beginning of the eighteenth centuries witnessed the emergence of 'polite society'. This is a considerable subject in its own right, but notions of politeness can be summarised as a self-conscious break from older ideals of appropriate behaviour and courtly ideals. Superficially it was concerned with manners and how people in the upper strata of society behaved towards one another. But historians have detected far more wide-ranging social and cultural movements underpinning these developments. These reflect a shift from the medieval culture of 'courtesy', through early modern 'civility', to eighteenth-century 'politeness'.[1] Associated with this was a movement from the hierarchical household of lordship, which emphasised vertical relationships between master and servants, towards a culture which laid more stress on the horizontal relationships between men of similar standing (although it has also been argued that polite society in some ways involved broadening the definition of the 'elite').[2] There was also a political dimension to this. Politeness and urban society were associated with the Whigs, while the rural country interest was associated with the Tories.

These developments had some impact on the sport of hunting. Seventeenth-century hunting manuals that were united in portraying the hunting of deer and other quarry as an appropriate pastime for a gentleman were still being

1. A. Bryson, *From courtesy to civility: changing codes of conduct in early modern England* (Oxford, 1998); M. Vale, *The gentleman's recreations: accomplishments and pastimes of the English gentleman 1580–1630* (Cambridge, 1977).
2. P. Langford, 'The uses of eighteenth-century politeness', in *English politeness: social rank and moral virtue, c. 1400–1900, Transactions of the Royal Historical Society*, 12 (2002), p. 311.

reprinted in the early eighteenth century.[3] But other books appeared around this time seeking to instruct gentleman how to behave, and these denigrated country pursuits, particularly hunting.[4] These views found literary expression well into the eighteenth century, from the essays of Addison and Steele in *The Spectator* through to novels such as the picaresque adventures produced by Fielding and Smollett. The country squire who dedicated his life to hunting and the hound became a figure of fun at best and a boorish villain at worse.

Notions of politeness and civility might have been firmly rooted in London, but they had resonances in the provincial towns. This was a period that has been described as one of urban renaissance, in which towns and cities underwent transformations in culture, producing their own fashionable meeting places in the forms of assemblies, theatres, walks and race meetings, and when leisure began to become a commodity in its own right. A hierarchy in the development of provincial towns has been identified. At the apex were the fashionable spa towns, such as Bath and Tunbridge Wells, but the county towns also developed significant social importance, and these were followed in turn by some of the market towns.[5]

There were contradictions aplenty to be detected in this cultural shift. Hunting continued to be popular with the higher echelons of society, and this was as true of members of the Whig government as the Tory opposition. Walpole himself was an enthusiastic sportsman, and, as we have seen, the Whig second duke of Grafton was heavily involved in the foundations of foxhunting as a modern pastime. Moreover, the very members of the gentry who might have been ridiculed as 'country squires' were themselves important to the development of fashionable society in the provincial towns. The landed interest was still, at this time, the foundation of society, and was traditionally associated with hunting.[6] So, although it may have been ridiculed, hunting maintained a significant presence. Indeed, by the end of the century hunting had been reborn in a new guise and its fortunes were very much on the rise.

This is the background against which we must trace the decline of the traditional forest- and park-based pursuit of the deer and the rise of foxhunting to become a fashionable and aspirational pastime. I am going to suggest that

---

3. A second edition of Blome's *Gentleman's recreation* appeared in 1710. Cox's *Gentleman's recreation* was reprinted in 1706 and 1721.

4. Carter commented that 'attention was drawn throughout this period to the unacceptability of expressions of male violence, such as dueling and hunting, on which instruction had often been provided in early modern guides to gentlemanly education'. P. Carter, *Men and the emergence of polite society, Britain 1660–1800* (London, 2000), p. 71.

5. Borsay, *English Urban Renaissance*, pp. 4–11.

6. As Deuchars observed, 'hunting as sport required and proclaimed the availability of land, the freedom and time to exploit it, and, very often, an economic status derived from a dependent class beneath'. S. Deuchar, *Sporting art in eighteenth-century England: a social and political history* (Yale, 1988), p. 2.

hunting adjusted, adapted and absorbed many of the cultural shifts that went on in the eighteenth century, and its new shape was formed by these very developments.

Changing attitudes to hunting

In our examination of early modern hunting techniques we drew upon early modern literary sources. As well as giving insight into the methods employed, these works also shed some light on how participants thought and felt about the sport, and the place that hunting was perceived to occupy in the wider culture. The authors of the hunting manuals commonly took time to expound on the value of their subject both in the life of the individual and in a broader context. Blome reflected at length on the health-giving properties of hunting: 'Hunting is (or at least ought to be) a pleasing and profitable exercise intended to make us strong and active and to recreate and delight the mind.'[7] Markham had more specific advice for those who wanted to use hunting as a means of keeping fit. The hunter should acquire the type of hounds most suited to his exercise requirements: the biggest and slowest hounds for those wishing to exercise on foot, the slowest of the middle-sized hounds for those on horseback. If a man was more infirm and could only manage to walk and not run, then beagles were recommended.[8] It was not only writers on hunting who recognised the sport's health-giving properties; Robert Burton had hunting and hawking as one of the possible cures for melancholy 'because they recreate the body and the mind'.[9]

The other great benefit that hunting was thought to bring was training for warfare. Cockaine found that hunters 'by their continuall travaile, painfull labour, often watching, and enduring of hunger, of heate, and of cold are much enabled above others to the service of their prince and Countrey in the warres'.[10] Blome wanted his readers to consider the requirements of war even when choosing their hunting horses. He did not recommend horses that were too fine because they would not do for war service.[11] King James clearly had hunting's military application in mind when he derided hunting with greyhounds as 'not nearly so martial' a game as *par force* hunting.[12] Blome echoed this in recommending that horsemen of a 'warlike nature' ought to choose 'such sorts of hunting as are most capable to answer these ends', which, in his opinion, was most likely to be hunting the stag, the buck or the fox.[13]

The sources quoted so far are practically unanimous in the approval of hunting as a suitable occupation for a gentleman (although Burton observed that

7.   Blome, *Gentleman's recreation*, p. 7.
8.   Markham, *Countrey contentments*, pp. 12–14.
9.   R. Burton, *Anatomy of melancholy* (Oxford, 1621), p. 340.
10.   Cockaine, *Short treatise*, p. 2.
11.   Blome, *Gentleman's recreation*, p. 7.
12.   James, *Basilicon Doron*, p. 144.
13.   Blome, *Gentleman's recreation*, p. 7.

the English nobility hunted so much it was 'as if they had no other meanes, but hauking and hunting to approve themselves Gentlemen with').[14] Towards the end of the seventeenth century, however, there began to emerge some dissonant voices, casting doubt on the value of country sport. Richard Allestree's *The gentleman's calling* expounded on the natural advantages bestowed upon the gentleman and on the way in which he should put these advantages to use. When considering the free time that the gentleman was lucky enough to enjoy, Allestree had some stern warnings concerning 'recreations'. While admitting that some 'divertisement' was necessary for the body of a man, he condemned as reprehensible the 'excess and inordinacy of it'. Allestree reflected that some gentlemen made the sports of hawking and hunting into their 'calling'. They never considered that being a falconer or a huntsman was a 'mean vocation'.[15] Allestree was writing from a religious and a moral viewpoint, while other critics of hunting were to condemn hunting because it was unfashionable, not because it was ungodly. But one thing both sets of critics agreed on was that it was not hunting *per se* that was bad, but rather the following of the sport to excess.

The *Tatler* and *The Spectator* magazines, the results of the collaboration of Joseph Addison and Richard Steele, have been credited with setting much of the initial tone and agenda of 'polite society'. *The Tatler* was published three times a week from 1709 to 1711. *The Spectator* appeared daily between 1711 and 1712 and thrice weekly in 1714. *The Tatler* has been viewed as the more 'up-market' publication, aimed at the clientele of the coffee house, while *The Spectator* was addressed more to the morning tea table and to civil servants and merchants (although there was some overlap in the lists of subscribers of the two periodicals).[16]

In *The Spectator* the authors created Sir Roger de Coverley, the archetypal Tory hunting squire. Sir Roger, we are told, was the scourge of the local foxes in his youth. In his older years he had given up foxhunting, but he kept a pack of 'stop-hounds'. Readers were treated to an account of Sir Roger hunting hare with these dogs. He remained keen enough on sport to be out hunting nearly every day during the visit of the narrator of these tales.[17] Sir Roger was written about with some affection – it was not a scathing portrait by any means – but as a character he represented the old-fashioned and the amusing. The reader is left in no doubt this hunting squire stood for the somewhat laughable society of a bygone age.

The episodes in *The Spectator* concerning Sir Roger and his friends have been described as a forerunner to the development of the novel in literature.[18] Looking forward to the 1740s, and the novels of Henry Fielding, we find yet more examples of the hunting squire, sometimes as a figure of fun and sometimes as a villain.

14. Burton, *Anatomy of melancholy*, p. 340.
15. R. Allestree, *The gentleman's calling* (London, 1660), p. 106.
16. A. Ross, *Selections from The Tatler and The Spectator* (London, 1982), p. 37.
17. R. Steele and J. Addison, *Sir Roger de Coverley*, ed. J. Hampden (London, 1967), p. 68.
18. Ross, *Selections*, p. 55.

In *Joseph Andrews* the eponymous hero was 'bred up' in the sporting country ways, working in the squire's kennels and his stables before being elevated to the post of footman. There are one or two references to sporting squires of the de Coverley ilk, such as Sir Oliver Hearty, who would 'sacrifice everything to his country' except 'his hunting'.[19] But the biggest villain in the novel, the would-be ravisher of the heroine, was a fanatical hunter. The travellers had the misfortune to cross his path when he was out in pursuit of the hare, and he set his hounds upon the parson for his own amusement. This squire was a spoilt and indulged child and 'from the age of fifteen he addicted himself entirely to hunting and other rural amusements'.[20]

Similarly, *Tom Jones* had a hunting squire as a major character. Squire Western, the father of the heroine, was more a comical figure than a villain, but was nonetheless an exemplar of the type: a man totally obsessed with his country sports. Fielding repeatedly tells us how much Western loved his daughter, but she had second place to horses and dogs.[21] Western crashed his way through the novel, nearly always announcing his presence with a hunting cry, and was seemingly incapable of describing anything without a hunting analogy. When he encountered Jones at the Inn at Upton, he exclaimed 'We have got the dog fox, I warrant the bitch is not far off.'[22] Smollett's *Humphry Clinker*, although 22 years later than *Tom Jones*, has similar references to disreputable hunting characters. One of his protagonists had the 'misfortune' of being second brother to a man who was 'a fox-hunter and a sot'. The elder brother neglected his affairs, insulted and oppressed the servants and 'well nigh ruined the estate'.[23]

The literary sources that we have cited illustrate clearly the attitude towards hunting and other 'country sports' that was prevalent in fashionable and polite society. Its proponents were, at best, figures of fun and, at worst, were cast in the role of villain. When advising his illegitimate son on how to behave in society, the earl of Chesterfield was similarly disparaging about such sports. For him, hunting numbered among the pleasures that could 'degrade a gentleman' as much as 'some trades could do'. The earl echoed the earlier opinions of Allestree (although from a very different moral viewpoint) in that he maintained that 'rustic sports' – which included fox-chases and horse races – were 'infinitely below the honest and industrious professions of a tailor and a shoemaker'.[24]

However 'out of fashion' hunting may have become, for hunters to have become such stock figures in literature there must still have been much hunting

19. H. Fielding, *The history and adventures of Joseph Andrews and his friend, Mr Abraham Adams* (1742; London, 1999), p. 157.
20. Fielding, *Joseph Andrews*, p. 247.
21. H. Fielding, *The history of a foundling, Tom Jones* (1749; Oxford, 1998), p. 130.
22. Fielding, *Tom Jones*, pp. 477–8, 760.
23. T. Smollett, *The expedition of Humphry Clinker* (1771; Oxford, 1998), p. 321.
24. Philip Stanhope, earl of Chesterfield, *Lord Chesterfield's letters to his son and others* (1929; London, 1975), p. 97.

going on. It also seems that the hunters themselves were sensible of the criticism. The end of Stringer's *The experience'd huntsman* is given over to a discussion between 'Mr Townly' and 'Mr Worthy' in which the latter stood up for hunting and argued that 'hunting is not a diversion so unbecoming a scholar so unsuitable to the politeness of a Gentleman' as Mr Townly imagined.[25] It has been suggested that there was something of the mentality of an embattled minority among enthusiasts of the chase in the eighteenth century. There were two trends: one promoting an insular, specialised culture that was 'incomprehensible' to outsiders, and the other seeking to return hunting to the mainstream by justifying the sport in terms of its social benefits.[26]

The adaptation of hunting to polite society

The concept of the 'polite society' is a complex one. We have already suggested that it had a deeper significance than merely prescribing a code of manners. It has been described as a concept with a 'meaning and implications that open doors into the mentality'.[27] Naturally such an important shift in the culture of the country has been the cause of investigation, and some debate, among historians. In particular, there have been discussions as to what extent the polite society represented the culmination of sixteenth- and seventeenth-century developments or, rather, a complete, self-conscious break from the past.[28] An important point for our purposes is that the whole concept of politeness was inextricably linked with leisure.[29] Hunting was a leisure activity

25. Stringer, *Experience'd huntsman*, p. 297.
26. Deuchar, *Sporting art*, p. 93.
27. Langford, 'The uses of eighteenth-century politeness', p. 311.
28. Anna Bryson has argued for continuity. She traced a move away from hierarchical households towards social groups based on a degree of informal equality, and allied these developments to the ascendance of the metropolis. Despite Stuart efforts to ensure that landowners stayed on their land, rather than becoming purely a court aristocracy, by 1632 it was suggested that the greater part of the gentry wintered in London. In the seventeenth century the 'naive astonishment and ineptitude' of the country gentleman visiting London for the first time was already providing a comic stock character. Other historians, however, have stressed the self-conscious break with the past. Carter, for example, emphasised features by which advocates of politeness distinguished it from existing codes of behaviour: it was distinctive and so they gave it a new label. Evidence supporting Clark's view can be found in *The Spectator*, where the narrator described the transition as a 'very great revolution'. The 'modish world' found too great a constraint in the old form of manners which involved 'several obliging Deferencies, Condescensions and Submissions' and had therefore thrown most of them aside. Bryson, *Courtesy to civility*, p. 131; P. Carter, 'Polite "persons": character, biography and the gentleman', in *English Politeness: social rank and moral virtue, c. 1400–1900*, *Transactions of the Royal Historical Society*, 12 (2002), p. 335; Steele and Addison, *Roger de Coverley*, p. 81.
29. As Tosh expressed it 'Leisure was the most fundamental precondition of politeness, the mark of a gentleman being either a man living on private means, or someone on whom business did not weigh too heavily.' J. Tosh, 'Gentlemanly politeness and manly simplicity in Victorian England',

and, in examining its relationship with the concept of the polite society, we are concerned with changing attitudes to leisure.

There are several strands in the debate on politeness that are significant when examining the relationship between the cultural shift that occurred in the eighteenth century and the transition that happened in the methods and location of hunting. These are the move away from the central position of the hierarchical household towards a more stratified form of social relationships, the conscious attempt to break away from formal and rigid modes of behaviour that were deemed to be 'old-fashioned', the increasing importance of urban above rural society and, lastly, the central place of leisure time and the means by which a gentleman filled it.

Traditional hospitality

The investigation of traditional hunting methods above provided examples of the types of hierarchical household from which eighteenth-century polite society was breaking away. This structure is illustrated in Smyth of Nibley's account of life in the Berkeley household and the instructions on how the young gentlemen retained as servants in the great household should behave themselves in various circumstances.[30] This type of organisation was also reflected in hunting itself in, for example, the highly formalised structure of the Royal Buckhounds, with offices such as sergeants, yeomen prickers and grooms.[31]

Hunting was intertwined with the traditional concepts of hospitality. The essential role that hunting played in the entertainment of foreign dignitaries under both Elizabeth and James I illustrates its symbolic role as a display of royal power. Elizabeth's entertainments in particular were lavish and formal. Perhaps unsurprisingly, therefore, the identification of hunting with hospitality rippled down through society. Nobles and gentlemen used their deer parks for the entertainment of their guests. Nicholas Breton's countryman described how some lords invited their tenants and their neighbours to join them in hunting when the harvest was safely home.[32] And those not entitled to hunt in their own right might avail themselves of a spot of illicit hunting to celebrate such events as weddings or christenings.[33]

in English Politeness: Social Rank and Moral Virtue, c. 1400–1900, Transactions of the Royal Historical Society, 12 (2002), p. 462.

30. Smyth, Berkeleys, 2, pp. 365–6.
31. Borsay described a set of recreational practices and ceremonies in the early modern period that were accessible to, and participated in in different ways, by all levels of society. Critical for him was that, as a result of 'polite and improving commercial culture', these pastimes became 'deeply unfashionable'. P. Borsay, A history of leisure: the British experience since 1500 (Basingstoke, 2006), p. 102.
32. N. Breton, The courtier and the gentleman (London, 1618), p. B.
33. Manning, Hunters and poachers, pp. 9, 18–19.

The entertainment provided by the hunt was a way for country magnates to define their patriarchal status, and it also played an important part in the bringing together of kinsfolk and neighbouring landowners. We can see in the early seventeenth-century journal of Nicholas Assheton how neighbours and kin would band together to hunt the stag.[34] But by the late seventeenth century landed families were moving away from the practice, if not the rhetoric, of the old-style hospitality. They were reducing the numbers of servants they kept and spending at least a part of the year in London.[35] The literary sources that set the agenda for the polite society could be as critical of old-fashioned hospitality and manners as they were of old-fashioned country pursuits. *The Spectator* devoted an entire article to the subject of country manners and the inconvenience they caused a man used to the more relaxed manners of the city. The rules of precedence on who walked first or last and who sat where at dinner were troublesome to the writer, who had known 'my friend Sir Roger's dinner almost cold before the company could adjust itself to the ceremonial'.[36]

The new sociability

The antiquated manners and ideas of hospitality were replaced with new ideas of sociability. The dining table in the great hall was replaced as a social focus by the coffee house and the club. Clubs and societies had their origins in London, but developed in the eighteenth century to become national social institutions, spreading through the provincial towns. Northampton, for example, had a florists' feast, a ringing society, a Masonic lodge and a philosophical society. Elsewhere in the county the towns of Kettering, Wellingborough and Daventry also benefited from the existence of clubs. The clubs and societies had a role in bringing together old and new elite groups: gentry, professional men, traders and, to a lesser extent, merchants.[37]

The sport of hunting had been very much associated with the traditional world, and traditional sociability, but there is some evidence that the sport was adapting itself to the newly emerging trends of the eighteenth century. The Charlton hunt in West Sussex has claimed for itself the position of the first organised fox hunt. It had its foundations in a pack of hounds kept for chasing the fox in the late seventeenth century by the duke of Monmouth. In the first half of the eighteenth century it counted men who were prominent at court and in politics among its followers, including the dukes of Grafton and Richmond. In 1720 some 28 members of the hunt subscribed towards the building of a banqueting hall in the village of Charlton, and in 1738 the hunt followers formed themselves

---

34. N. Assheton, *The journal of Nicholas Assheton* (Manchester, 1848), pp. 39, 54, 57.
35. P. Clark, *British clubs and society 1580–1800: the origins of an associational world* (Oxford, 2000), pp. 32, 29.
36. Steele and Addison, *Roger de Coverley*, p. 82.
37. Clark, *British clubs*, pp. 84, 90, 450.

into a 'regular society'. The club was founded when the gentlemen who followed the hunt met for dinner in the Bedford Head Tavern in London.[38] A decade or two later (the exact date is unknown) the Pytchley Hunt Club was founded in Northamptonshire. The club had as its headquarters Pytchley Hall, from which it took its name. The hall was lent to the club, rent-free, so long as they kept it in repair and paid the taxes, and was sizeable enough to accommodate twenty members and their servants at any one time, and offer stabling for their horses. The earliest list of members, from 1766, included the duke of Grafton and Earl Spencer among its number.[39] We have already described the hunting confederacy which the earl of Cardigan formed in 1730 with the third duke of Rutland and the fourth earl of Gainsborough, among others. Unlike the Charlton and the Pytchley, this association lacked a club building, with the confederacy instead moving the hounds, and its social focus, from the Lincolnshire/Leicestershire border to Rutland, and ultimately to Northamptonshire, as the season progressed.[40]

The Charlton and the Pytchley clubs were organised along similar lines. New members were nominated by an existing member and then balloted in, a black ball being sufficient for exclusion. The members of both clubs could invite friends to partake of the clubs' hospitality, albeit for a limited time. Both clubs held their annual meetings in London. The Charlton and Pytchley rules were all about regulating the club: how its costs were defrayed and how the membership was ordered. In contrast, the rules of Cardigan's hunting confederacy were concerned with the hunting itself. It was essentially an agreement between ten individuals about how horses and hounds were maintained. The agreement did make provision for hunt servants which, in addition to a steward, a huntsman and six whippers-in, included two cooks, but these were catering for the hounds, not the humans.[41]

Both types of organisation, hunting club and hunting confederacy, mark a break with the past. The archetypal model of a hunt had been the pack of hounds kept by a gentleman, who invited his friends and neighbours to join in, and there were still many examples of this type of arrangement in the eighteenth century. Justinian Isham's diary reveals him hunting around Lamport in Northamptonshire in the autumn and winter of 1709/10 and inviting friends to join him.[42] It was one of the defining characteristics of 'modern' foxhunting, however, that it gradually left behind the model where both hounds and hospitality were entirely at the pleasure of some local landowner in favour of one where hunt followers paid subscriptions for the support of the hunt. Certainly the hounds themselves were most often the personal property of the master – for example, from 1763 Lord Spencer owned the

---

38. Rees, *Charlton Hunt*, pp. 1–4.
39. Paget, *Althorp and Pytchley hunt*, pp. 70–71.
40. Wake and Champion-Webster, *Letters of Daniel Eaton*, p. 153.
41. Wake and Champion-Webster, *Letters of Daniel Eaton*, p. 153–4.
42. NRO, Isham archive: IL2686.

Pytchley hounds – but other expenses, such as the rent of the fox coverts and the payment of the earth stoppers, were met out of funds contributed by subscribers. In 1798 the Pytchley club spent £124 7s 6d on renting fox coverts, and in 1800 the bill for stopping fox earths came to £15 15s 0d.[43] This reflected another facet of the development of leisure in the eighteenth century: the use of subscriptions as a way of jointly funding sports or entertainments.[44]

The clubs and societies that burgeoned in the eighteenth century have been viewed as an overwhelmingly urban phenomenon.[45] The Charlton and Pytchley hunt clubs were both based in villages, but these were unusual. This brings us to another theme of the cultural history of the eighteenth century: the phenomenon that has been described as the 'urban renaissance'. While many of the new modes of behaviour had their origins in London, the eighteenth century witnessed their spreading outwards into the provincial towns. Several themes have been identified as characterising this urban renaissance: a physical transformation, as classical architecture and new modes of urban layout came to prominence; an economic buoyancy which produced surplus wealth; and the expansion of the so-called 'middling sort' in society. Northampton has been used as an exemplar of many of these developments. The town's horse fair, which was of national significance, put Northampton firmly on the map as a thriving trading community. The number of trades and crafts in the Northampton district rose from 45 in the period 1562–1601 to 83 in the period 1654–1705, reaching 114 between 1716 and 1776. In addition, the great fire of 1675 meant that Northampton began to be rebuilt in the fashionable classical style much earlier than other towns.[46]

But the aspect of the urban renaissance that most concerns the present study is that which has been described as the 'commercialisation of leisure'.[47] This was the process whereby theatres, assembly rooms, walks, pleasure gardens, coffee houses and similar innovations became central to the lives of the social elite in provincial towns and surrounding areas. Again, Northampton could boast several of these amenities. It had an assembly which met on a weekly basis and in 1722 it boasted two coffee houses.[48] Provision was made for promenading and public display in the form of walks laid out across the Cow Meadow in 1703 and between St Thomas of Canterbury's Well and Vigo Well in 1784.[49]

The early eighteenth-century diary of Justinian Isham illustrates how one

---

43. Paget, *Althorp and Pytchley hunt*, p. 73.
44. Borsay saw the widespread adoption of subscription systems in the eighteenth century as a 'crucial development', providing a 'halfway house' between the patron of traditional culture and the modern anonymous market place. Borsay, *Leisure*, p. 19.
45. Clark argued convincingly for the urban nature of clubs: Clark, *British clubs*.
46. Borsay, *Urban renaissance*, p. 45.
47. J.H. Plumb, *The commercialisation of leisure in eighteenth-century England* (Reading, 1973).
48. Borsay, *Urban renaissance*, pp. 145, 153.
49. *VCH Northamptonshire*, 3, p. 23.

young Northamptonshire gentleman enjoyed leisure pursuits and socialising both at home and in the metropolis. The diary started in the spring of 1709 with our diarist in London. In addition to frequent dining with friends and acquaintances, he fitted in seven plays and an opera. After returning to Lamport at the end of May the social pace scarcely slackened: 2 June saw Isham at the races at Borough Hill near Daventry, rounded off with a visit to the Wheatsheaf, where the dancing continued all night. A few weeks later there was a trip to Deene Park, where Isham bowled and inspected the dog kennels. In July he attended the assizes in Northampton (the assizes commonly provided a social focus for county towns in this period). August saw an excursion to the Wellingborough races, followed by dining at 'the ordinary' with a good deal of company. The races were clearly a major attraction for the diary's author, as elsewhere he mentioned attending Harlestone races and even travelling to York for the races there.[50]

The urban focus

We have made the point that hunting had lost much of its status as an elite pursuit and indeed had become a subject of some derision, but the urban-based leisure revolution did include some provision for hunting. In this period towns developed a relationship with hunting either directly, by supporting town hunts, or indirectly, by servicing the needs of local hunts. The towns of Preston, York, Leeds, Liverpool, Beverley and Bristol kept their own packs of hounds (unfortunately there seems to be no evidence of any town hunts in Northamptonshire).[51] Having already had a glimpse of how hunting adapted to the culture of the club that gained such ground in the eighteenth century, we can usefully examine how hunting adapted to the more urban focus of leisure and culture that emerged in this period.

To some extent it had always been possible for a town dweller to hunt. We have already described Henry, Lord Berkeley, 'daily hunting' while living in London with his mother as a young man.[52] In the great town versus country debate that occupied the *English courtier and the cutrey gentleman*, Vallentine assured Vincent that, in the city, 'if you will hauke or hunt, there are Faukners and hunters enough'.[53] Back in Northamptonshire the Pytchley, which had its origins firmly in the eighteenth century, had its urban adherents. The late eighteenth-century lists of followers in the Althorp Chace books often included parties of gentlemen from Northampton, among whose number was one Mister Hillyard who, in November 1786, 'had a bad fall but was not much hurt altho' he cried a good deal'.[54] As foxhunting developed, its social context became more public and fashionable,

50. NRO, Isham archive: IL2686.
51. Borsay, *Urban renaissance*, pp. 178–9.
52. Smyth, *Berkeleys*, 2, p. 281.
53. Anon., *The English courtier, and the cutrey gentleman* (London, 1586), p. Mi.
54. NRO, Althorp Chace Books: ML4429.

and so the role of towns as service centres for the sport was enhanced.[55] But if the eighteenth century laid the foundations, it was in the early nineteenth century that a town could become a national focal point for the sport of foxhunting, which was the mantle that Melton Mowbray, in Leicestershire, assumed. Quorndon Hall, the residence of Hugo Meynell, was near to the town of Loughborough, and it was this town that first attracted a seasonal visitation of foxhunters; as 'rough rider' Dick Christian put it: 'in Mr. Meynell's time the company used to be at Loughborough'.[56] In 1762 Leicester hosted the county's hunt ball, with catering provided by Meynell's cook.[57] Around the turn of the century, however, the 'company' began to move to Melton Mowbray. Dick Christian attributed this to the duke of Rutland's publication in 1804 of a map of the Quorn, Cottesmore and Belvoir hunt countries: 'Melton was just at the centre, so they came there after that.'[58] Using Melton as their base, the foxhunters could hunt six days a week over the grassland that was fast winning fame as 'the shires'. In its early days Melton saw the establishment of a number of foxhunting clubs. Unlike the Pytchley and Charlton clubs, however, these were not connected to a particular hunt and were town, not village, based.

None of the Northamptonshire towns allied themselves so closely with foxhunting. Those men of fashion who wanted to experience the Pytchley country in west Northamponshire were most likely to base themselves just over the Leicestershire border in Market Harborough, the town that probably came closest to rivalling Melton's status as foxhunting metropolis. Although not as well placed as Melton Mowbray, it was possible to hunt with two fashionable packs when based there. From Harborough the foxhunter could reach many Pytchley meets and just about all those of the South Quorn/Tailby Hunt. Meets of other notable, but not quite 'top-drawer', packs, such as the North Warwickshire and the Atherstone, were also accessible. Writing later in the century, Brooksby advised the foxhunter that Market Harborough 'is glad to welcome you to its comfortable hostelries and unlimited stabling'; echoing Nimrod's earlier assessment of Melton, he reflected that Harborough owed 'all its position in the world to its attractiveness as a hunting quarter'.[59] For those wishing to hunt with the Pytchley, Brooksby recommended Rugby, Weedon, Northampton or Market Harborough as bases. Of these, Rugby was deemed the most popular. Northampton, Brooksby reckoned, 'hitherto has not been much frequented'; like Weedon, it was chiefly famous as soldiers' quarters. For the Woodland Pytchley, Kettering, Thrapston or Oundle could be suitable bases, but although all three 'might invite visitors' 'few come'.[60]

55. Borsay, *Urban renaissance*, p. 179.
56. Druid, *Silk and scarlet*, p. 67.
57. Borsay, *Urban renaissance*, p. 179.
58. Druid, *Silk and scarlet*, p. 67.
59. Brooksby, *Hunting countries of England*, 1, p. 166.
60. Brooksby, *Cream*, pp. 131–5.

Our investigation of the relationship between hunting and towns has taken us rather further on in time than the rest of this chapter. But it is important to note that, when foxhunting reached the peak of its popularity in the nineteenth century, it was already comfortable in being associated with an urban setting. Whereas hunting had previously been associated with parks and royal forests, the newly emerging sport came to be identified with a particular area of the country and with particular towns. That is not to say that foxhunting did not take place elsewhere, because it was ubiquitous, but the truly fashionable hunted the Midland shires. That this development could happen was due in part to the development of better communications in the eighteenth century. In the same way that better roads allowed other urban centres to 'specialise' in the provision of certain types of leisure, so there could be a dedicated foxhunting area.

The resurgence of the rural ideal

In its consideration of the emergence of the ideals of the polite society, this chapter has tended to concentrate on the period when the urban ideal was embraced and the rural rejected. It has not been an intention to argue that the rural interest was totally overshadowed, however. There was certainly tension between the two ideals in this period: we have portrayed a cultural transition whereby the more traditional forms of social interaction were attacked as unfashionable and *passé*.[61] But the countryside remained vitally important to the very people – gentlemen and aristocrats – who were most concerned with fashion, politeness and social propriety. We have quoted from the letters of Earl Fitzwilliam to his steward, and from Lord Cardigan's steward to his master. This correspondence exists because their lordships were spending so much of their time in London, but their Northamptonshire estates were essential to the funding of this metropolitan lifestyle.[62] The elderly earl of Winchelsea was evidently enjoying the opportunities London life offered for intellectual pursuits, subscribing to the publication of a great many books, but his 1723 journal also recorded the receipt of 'wood money', 'buck money' and other returns from his Northamptonshire park.[63] Sir Justinian Isham was spending the winter seasons in London, fulfilling his duties as a member of parliament, but still valued the country sports that Lamport offered enough to have injured himself quite badly by falling

---

61. As Clark commented, 'rural society was not only seen as boring, backward, and dirty, but as populated by crypto-jacobites pursuing old-fashioned sports'. Fletcher talked of a 'genuine clash of cultures' and of how city dwellers found it impossible to appreciate the seriousness with which the country gentry and their tenants took the whole business of country sports. Clark, *British clubs*, p. 182; A. Fletcher, *Gender, sex and subordination in England 1500–1800* (Yale, 1995), p. 329.

62. Clark reckoned that Fitzwilliam was receiving well over £8000 a year from his Norfolk and Northamptonshire estates. Clark, *British clubs*, p. 145.

63. NRO, Finch Hatton archive: FH282.

from his horse while hunting the hare in 1725.[64] It can be seen that the country estates of these lords and gentlemen remained important to them as sources of both income and occasional entertainment.

Towards the end of the eighteenth century the tide of fashion was beginning to turn and country life was once more being seen as desirable. This was manifested in the visual arts, where a nostalgia for the supposedly rural life of Old England emerged in the 1760s and had become a 'thriving business' by the 1790s. This was a reversal of the distaste for what was perceived to be the 'medieval', and therefore awkward and barbaric, in the earlier decades of the century. Indeed, something of a cult of the countryside emerged around this time; by the 1770s town dwellers were beginning to 'idolise' the country cottage, with a degree of anti-urbanism emerging by the end of the eighteenth century.[65] The diaries of John Byng (later Lord Torrington) give some evidence of this. Commencing one of his trips around the country in 1794, he observed that 'I have for many years stated my haste, in spring, to get out of London (with pleasure I could quit thee for ever) seizing every opportunity to renovate myself by country air.'[66] This was part of a much wider cultural shift in the way landscape came to be regarded. Where countryside had previously been admired, it was as a landscape tamed and made productive by man.[67] Morton, in his 1712 description of Northamptonshire, was proud that the county had 'no naked or craggy rocks, no rugged and unsightly mountains'.[68] Robert Andrews, who set out from the East Midlands on a tour of the west in August 1752, recorded in his journal after leaving the Black Mountains in Wales that 'it was very agreeable, after travelling some time thro a country affording only the wild and scanty productions of nature to see again the returns of agriculture'.[69] In contrast, the end of the eighteenth century brought Romanticism, and wilderness and mountains came to be appreciated and sought out. Travellers began to explore Britain's wilder fringes. John Byng was escorted up Cader Idris in 1784 by a man who was a 'seasoned' guide, and was later able to describe enthusiastically the 'wildness' of Charnwood Forest in Leicestershire, with its 'pleasant dips, and many romantic scars and rocks'.[70] Perhaps one of the most widespread manifestations of this

---

64. NRO, Isham archive: IL1917.
65. Deuchar, *Sporting art*, p. 154; Thomas, *Man and the natural world*, pp. 248, 251; Borsay, *Leisure*, p. 210. The author quotes Rosalind Sweet describing how the assumed barbarity of the Middle Ages acted as a fan to the polite and commercial society of eighteenth-century Britain.
66. Bruyn Andrews, *Torrington diaries*, 4, p. 1.
67. Thomas observed that to the agricultural propagandists of the early modern period 'untilled heaths mountains and fens' were 'a standing reproach'. Thomas, *Man and the natural world*, p. 254.
68. Morton, *Northamptonshire*, p. 20.
69. NRO, Robert Andrews' journal: A280.
70. Bruyn Andrews, *Torrington diaries*, 2, p. 158.

shift in sensibilities is to be found in the landscape park, which concealed views of cultivation behind vistas of the seemingly wild.[71]

Conclusion

This chapter has explored the period that was crucial to the hunting transition in terms of how certain sections of society thought and felt about the sport. Hunting undoubtedly fell out of favour in some quarters, and socially and culturally influential quarters at that, where it was viewed as an outdated and antiquated pastime. By the end of the eighteenth century, however, the fortunes of the sport were once more on the rise. During the course of the century hunting had adapted to many of the changes that had affected elite leisure. It was organising itself on a subscription basis, along the same lines as many gentleman's clubs, and it was fully ready to exploit the amenities now offered by provincial towns.

Among the distinguishing features of modern foxhunting were the large number of mounted followers it attracted and the increasingly public nature of the sport. Whereas hunting had traditionally been very much at the pleasure of the wealthy owners of the hounds, the hunt members now could influence, if not dictate, when and where the hunt met and what type of landscape it encompassed. These followers tended to be largely interested in the riding, and preferred the type of grassland offered by the shires. It was this group that helped foxhunting to attain the pre-eminence it achieved in the nineteenth century.

71. Thomas suggested that this fashion was, in part, a reaction to the very success of agricultural revolution. As the landscape came to be more ordered and regular, so the disordered came to be valued. Thomas, *Man and the natural world*, p. 254.

9

Conclusion

The aim of this book has been to examine the transition from deer hunting to foxhunting that occurred between 1600 and 1850 in the context of the landscape of Northamptonshire, and to evaluate whether the traditional explanation for the transition stands up to scrutiny. The traditional explanation had tied the transition to change in the landscape: loss of woodland habitat led to loss of deer, and therefore there was nothing left to hunt. The fox was identified as a suitable replacement, a prey that would enable the elite to continue with their favoured pastime of hunting from horseback. The earliest source for this argument appears to be W. Scarth Dixon's 1912 book *Hunting in the olden days*. Scarth Dixon was a foxhunter rather than a historian, but his account of the transition gained currency and has been repeated in subsequent accounts up to and including Griffin's *Blood sports* in 2007.[1]

An examination of the royal forests of Northamptonshire has not shown the kind of large-scale diminution in woodland in the period 1600–1850 that would have driven a hunting transition based on necessity, however. Whittlewood and Salcey Forests remained very much the same size and shape over this period. In Rockingham even disafforestation did not lead to a radical reduction in woodland. Landowners continued to find wood and timber the best use for what could be agriculturally marginal forest lands. Where the woodlands remained, so did the deer, and the forests were still managed to provide habitat for them. Insofar as the deer population can be traced, it seems to have recovered from a mid-seventeenth-century crisis by the beginning of the eighteenth century, before foxhunting emerged in its 'modern' form. It was in the period after 1850, and after the establishment of foxhunting as a dominant country sport, that the woodlands of Northamptonshire finally went under pasture and plough, and man attempted to clear the deer from the landscape. Up until that time, if the will remained to hunt deer then there were still deer to hunt.

A recent examination of Rockingham Forest supports the findings of this book by showing a survival of woodland. But the project also illustrated a significant

---

1. Scarth Dixon devotes an entire chapter to 'The Passing of the Red Deer'. Scarth Dixon, *Hunting*, pp. 20–27; Griffin, *Blood sport*, pp. 108–10.

diminution of wood pasture from the medieval to the early modern period.[2] It could be argued that, perhaps, a crisis in deer population should be pushed backwards in time, and that the deer had already been depleted, and the landscape of pursuit restricted, by the late medieval period. Such an investigation is outside the chronological scope of this work, but it should also be observed that the hunting transition did not occur until the eighteenth century. The move from deer hunting to foxhunting did not happen when the wood pasture was turned over to arable agriculture, but much later, so any explanation of the hunting transition that linked it with this change in landscape would necessarily have to account for the fact that the transition took more than 250 years to take effect.

The exploration above of the diverse methods used for hunting deer has demonstrated the role that the park played in the sport. The pursuit of deer was not necessarily a fast and furious horseback chase, and much sport and entertainment could be had within the park pales. We have found evidence for a resurgence in park-making in the county of Northamptonshire and beyond in the early modern period. We have also demonstrated that these parks continued to be stocked with deer, even if the park's form and function changed in other ways. Again, if there was the will to continue with hunting as carried out in the sixteenth and seventeenth centuries, the prey and the environment to facilitate this were certainly available.

The fox required a similar habitat to the deer; it favoured woodland and, in particular, woodland with dense undergrowth. The landscape of foxhunting was, however, characterised by grassland: this was the terrain required to chase the fox across at speed. As the sport of foxhunting grew in popularity its proponents had to make special efforts to preserve the prey and ensure that there were sufficient foxes to hunt. These efforts included the renting of land and the creation of purpose-made fox coverts. Foxes still inhabited the woodland retreats of Northamptonshire's royal forests, but this landscape did not become a centre for the new sport because it was not so good to ride across. It is an irony that, while the traditional explanation had hunting changing because foxes were plentiful, and deer were not, the hunters of the fox were constantly confronted with a potential shortage of prey. They had to take steps, including the manipulation of the landscape, to ensure that there would be foxes to hunt.

An understanding of the methods used to pursue both deer and foxes has proved crucial to interpreting the hunting transition and its relationship with the landscape. Deer hunting was heterogeneous in its methods: deer could be pursued from horseback, driven past stands to be shot or coursed by greyhounds, but all of these involved the participation of trained dogs. Modern foxhunting was homogeneous in its methods: it involved fast pursuit on horseback. Even the most comparable form of deer hunting, the *par force* hunt, was significantly

2.   Foard et al., *Rockingham Forest: an atlas*, pp. 73–158.

different to the form of foxhunting that rose to such popularity in the eighteenth and nineteenth centuries. Great importance was placed on finding a suitably prestigious stag to hunt and ensuring that the hounds stuck to that exact animal. The hunt depended on the active participation of many men on foot: to lead couples of hounds to places along the expected line of the hunt where they could be loosed in relays, to help control the hounds and to assist them over any unsurmountable obstacles. The whole affair was slower by far than the modern foxhunt and had different priorities. The horse was an important player but by no means a central focus of the sport: it played a comparable role in medieval or early modern falconry. In foxhunting, on the other hand, the priority for the majority of the participants was the sheer thrill of a fast horseback chase. This contrast seems to have been missed by many writers studying early modern hunting techniques. They have expected to find evidence of an essentially equestrian sport, and when they discover that an activity predicated on long, fast gallops was not feasible in some environments, such as deer parks, they have disputed whether these really were hunting arenas. They have questioned whether the sport that would have taken place there could actually be classified as hunting, or whether it was some sad, faded descendant of a more energetic medieval predecessor. But I believe that this is to fundamentally misunderstand the nature of early modern hunting. The sport was about the hound, not about the horse. The acknowledged highest form of the sport was known as *par force des chiens*, not *par force des chevaux*.

The examination of literary sources has shown hunting to have been held in high regard in the sixteenth and seventeenth centuries. It was one of the activities that defined a nobleman or a gentleman. There is also evidence that people were not only reading about hunting, they were participating too. Regardless of the fact that some modern commentators have questioned whether what occupied the early modern hunter constituted 'real hunting', there was little doubt that the participants viewed it as such. Hunting did lose much of its cultural *caché* at the beginning of the eighteenth century, however. The thrill of the chase seemed to hold little appeal for fashionable, metropolitan polite society. Hunting became the pastime of the hopelessly outdated Tory squire ensconced in his rural retreat, a figure of fun or of derision. But in the course of the eighteenth century hunting adapted, and by the beginning of the nineteenth century foxhunting was not only the indisputably most popular form of hunting, it was well on its way to becoming a cultural icon. Hunting by then, however, was quite a different sport. It had become what we regard it to be today: a primarily equestrian sport.

The social position of hunting was transformed along with its methods. Modern foxhunters congratulated themselves on the social inclusivity of their sport (albeit such inclusivity was extremely limited to modern eyes). As the nineteenth century progressed the hunting field swelled to include men employed in trade and industry, as well as the landed elite. Farmers and graziers also had a significant presence and, although they were not regarded as the social equals of the foremost of the hunt followers, the importance of their active cooperation in allowing the hunt to cross their land was acknowledged. Both rural and urban labouring classes were well represented in the foot followers of the hunt, even if their presence might not always have been appreciated.

An important part of the explanation for why the nature of hunting changed so much lies in the popularity of horse racing and the breeding of the thoroughbred horse. With the arrival of this supreme equine athlete, men (and women) wanted to experience the thrill of riding such a creature across the country. The very nature of riding itself changed in this period. Englishmen abandoned the long stirrup leathers and deep-seated saddles of high-school riding, and developed 'the English hunting seat', with its shorter stirrups and flat-seated saddle. The hunting seat facilitated fast, forward riding, and the jumping of obstacles at speed. Following behind came the development of the side saddle with the 'leaping head', which held women in a secure position such that they could retain decorum while riding just as fast, and jumping just as high, as the men.[3] The central role of the horse explained the very different landscape that provided the theatre for the new form of hunting. What its participants required, above all else, was grassland over which to gallop. The enclosure history of Northamptonshire, along with the conversion to grazing, led to a portion of the county becoming part of the hallowed shires: the foremost location of an incredibly fashionable and aspirational pastime.

The sport of deer hunting itself was transformed to incorporate the type of chase so beloved by foxhunters. The practice of transporting a captive deer by cart to a hunting ground and then recapturing it at the end of the chase has been taken by hunting historians as further proof of the decline of deer stocks that supposedly drove the hunting transition. But the location of many nineteenth-century deer hunts and contemporary accounts of the sport suggest that it was, in fact, viewed as a poor substitute for foxhunting, rather than as a poor substitute for the idealised sport of deer hunting. Nineteenth-century deer hunts were primarily located near the capital, where a man could get away from business for a few hours' hunting, and in Norfolk and Suffolk, where the shooting interest militated against the establishment of foxhunting packs. The hunts themselves used foxhounds rather than old-fashioned stag hounds, and the principal virtue of the carted deer was in the provision of a certain, and comparatively short, pursuit.

This work has revisited the traditional explanation of the transition that took place in the sport of hunting in the period 1600 to 1850. The hunting transition was tied to the landscape, but in a different way to that generally described. Hunting did not simply react to a negative – the diminution of woodland and disappearance

---

3.   By the mid-nineteenth century the dashing and fearless female rider after hounds had become a stock character in fiction. For example, the hero of *Orley Farm* is injured when he unwisely follows the crack rider Miss Tristram over a bank and double ditch. A. Trollope, *Orley Farm* (1861; Oxford, 2008) pp. 287–8.

of deer – rather, it transformed itself into a different sport for cultural reasons and exploited landscape changes to enhance the experience. In addition, the central position of the horse has been demonstrated. The breeding of the thoroughbred predated the breeding of the fast foxhound as well as the widespread switch to the fox as the primary prey of hunters. Modern foxhunting was a new sport, and marked a distinct break with tradition, precisely because, for the majority of participants, the horse was more important than the hound.

Bibliography

Manuscript sources

Leicester, Leicestershire and Rutland Record Office (LRO)
Swiss No. 7 Hunting Map: DE2055/1
Hartopp papers: 8D39/7377; 8D39/7382
Hunting appointment cards, DG9/2802
Letter, Charles Dormer to Fortescue Turville: DG39/1099
Letter, Mr Clowes to Charles William Packe: DE5047/113/1; DE339/350–3

The National Archives (TNA)
MR 1/314
MR 1/359
MR 1/1653
MPE 1/938
MPE 459
MPEE 104

Northamptonshire Record Office (NRO)
Althorp Chace Books: ML4428 (1773–77); ML4429 (1777–90); ML4430 (1790–1807);
    ML4431 (1807–08)
Brooke of Oakley archive: B(O)327/27; B(O)313/21; Brooke vol. 163
Brudenell archive: Bru Map 126; Bru.I.xiii.1; Bru.I.xiii.2; Bru.I.xiii.3; Bru.I.xiii.4a;
    Bru.I.xiii.4b; Bru.I.xiii.5b; Bru.I.xiii.5c; Bru.I.xiii.17; Bru.I.xiii.24a
Charles King Chace Book: 1800–08, YZ2586; 1817–19, YZ2588
Clipston parish records: 206p/247
Coales (Aldwinckle Lodge) archive: C(AL)10; C(AL)12
Computation of damage done in the underwoods of Whittlewood forest: ZB707/4
Dryden (Canons Ashby) archive: D(CA)406; D(CA)719
Finch Hatton archive: FH272; FH282; FH1433; FH2056; FH2457; FH2646; FH2829;
    FH2858; FH2954; FH3141; FH3842; FH3843; FH4248; FH4389
Fermor Hesketh archive: Fermor Hesketh N Bundle 7
Grafton archive: G399/16/6; G1662; G2017; G2464–G2471; G3867; G3951/23; G3980;
    G3982; G3999; G3999/3; G4000; G4050/2; G4079/50/1; G4104; G4139/3; G4252
Henry Dryden's diary 1839–1842: ZA477

Isham archive: IL1917; IL2686; IL3115

Langham archive: L(C)32–35; L(C)646; L(C)681; L(C)688; L(C)693; L(C)695; L(C)697; L(C)1082

NRO Maps: Map 2905; Map 2865; Map 3105; Map 4093; Map 4096; Map 4097; Map 4210; Map 5965; M(CM) 595

NRO Wills: 20.7.1773; 19.9.1783; 13.9.1793; 15.2.1794; 9.2.1797; 9.5.1810

Puppy cards: YZ3494

Quarter Session Records: QSR1/173/24

Robert Andrews' journal: A280

Survey of Whittlewood Forest by Richard Davis of Lewknor: NPL3044

Westmoreland of Abethorpe archive: W(A) box4/parcel VIII/no 1; W(A) VI 2/23; W(A) VI 2/25; W(A) VI 2/26; W(A) 6 VI 2/36; W(A) 6 VI 2/0

Wilson's diary: ZA3801; ZA8011

Parliamentary Papers

HCPP, 1873, XIV
Commons Journal, 46
Commons Journal, 47

Contemporary printed sources

Anon., The English courtier, and the cutrey gentleman (London, 1586).

Anon., The memoirs of Dick the little poney supposed to be written by himself (London, 1800).

Allestree, R., The gentleman's calling (London, 1660).

Baret, Michael, An hipponomie or the vineyard of horsemanship (London, 1618).

Bearn, W., 'On the farming of Northamptonshire', Journal of the Royal Agricultural Society of England, 13 (1852), pp. 44–113.

Blome, R., The gentleman's recreation (London, 1686).

Blundeville, Thomas, The fower chiefyst offices belongyng to horsemanshippe (London, 1566).

Breton, Nicholas, The courtier and the gentleman (London, 1618).

Brooksby (Pennell-Elmhirst, E.), The cream of Leicestershire: eleven seasons' skimmings, notable runs and incidents of the chase (London, 1883).

Brooksby (Pennell-Elmhirst, E.), The hunting countries of England, their facilities, character and requirements, 2 vols (London, 1878).

Bryant, Andrew, Map of the county of Northampton from actual survey in the years 1824, 1825 and 1826 (London, 1827).

Burton, Robert, Anatomy of melancholy (Oxford, 1621).

Camden, W., Britannia or a geographical description of Great Britain and Ireland, 2nd edn (London, 1722).

Cavendish, William, Duke of Newcastle, A new method, and extraordinary invention, to dress horses, and work them according to nature (London, 1667).

Cheny, John, An historical list of all horse-matches run and of all plates and prizes run for in England and Wales (of the value of ten pounds or upwards) in 1729 (London, 1729).

Cockaine, Thomas, A short treatise of hunting (London, 1591).

Cox, N., The gentleman's recreation (London, 1674).

Delmé Radcliffe, F.P., The noble science (London, 1839).

Donaldson, J., *General view of the agriculture of the county of Northampton, with observations on the means of its improvement* (Edinburgh, 1794).

Drakes gazetteer and directory of the counties of Leicester and Rutland (Sheffield, 1861).

'The Druid' (Dixon, H.H.), *Silk and scarlet* (London, 1859).

Elliott, J.M.K., *Fifty years' foxhunting with the Grafton and other packs of hounds* (London, 1900).

Elyot, Thomas, *The book named the Governor* (London, 1531).

Fairfax, Thomas, *The compleat sportsman; or country gentleman's recreation* (London, 1758).

Gascoigne, George, *The noble arte of venerie or hunting* (London, 1575).

Grey, Thomas de, *The compleat horse-man and expert ferrier* (London, 1639).

Heber, Reginald, *An historical list of all horse-matches run and of all plates and prizes run for in England and Wales* (London, 1751–68).

Holinshed, *Chronicles of England, Ireland and Scotland* (London, 1587).

Lawrence, J., *History and delineation of the horse* (London, 1809).

Leland, John, *The itinerary of John Leland the antiquary*, 9 vols (Oxford, 1768–9).

Manwood, John, *A treatise of the forrest lawes* (London, 1598).

Markham, G., *Cavelarice* (London, 1607).

Marshall, W., *The rural economy of the midland counties*, 2 vols (London, 1796).

Mastin, J., *The history and antiquities of Naseby* (Cambridge, 1792).

Monk, J., *General view of the agriculture of the county of Leicester* (London, 1794).

Morton, J., *Natural history of Northamptonshire* (London, 1712).

Moscrop, W.J., 'A report on the farming of Leicestershire', *Journal of the Royal Agricultural Society of England*, 2nd ser., 2 (1866), pp. 289–337.

Nimrod (Apperley, C.), *The horse and the hound* (Edinburgh, 1843).

Nimrod (Apperley, C.), *Remarks on the condition of hunters* (London, 1837).

Nimrod (Apperley, C.), 'Riding to hounds', *The Sporting Magazine* (January 1823), pp. 178–84.

Norden, J., *Speculi Britannie pars altera or a delineation of Northamptonshire* (London, 1720).

Osbaldiston, W., *The universal sportsman: or, nobleman, gentleman, and farmer's dictionary of recreation and amusement* (Dublin, 1795).

Osmer, W., *A dissertation on horses* (London, 1756).

Osmer, W., *A treatise on the diseases and lameness of horses* (London, 1766).

Owen, W., *An authentic account published by the king's authority, of all the fairs in England and Wales* (London, 1756).

Pitt, W., *General view of the agriculture of the county of Leicester* (London, 1809).

Pitt, W., *General view of the agriculture of Northamptonshire* (Northampton, 1809).

Ribblesdale, Lord, *The queen's hounds and stag-hunting recollections* (London, 1897).

The Sporting Magazine, November 1803.

Stringer, A., *The experience'd huntsman* (Belfast, 1714).

Thomas Jones' diary (Derby, 1816).

Trollope, A., *Hunting sketches* (London, 1865).

Walker, B., *An historical list of horse-matches, plates and prizes, run for in Great-Britain and Ireland, in the Year 1769* (London, 1770).

Weatherby, James, *Racing calendar: containing an account of the plates, matches, and sweepstakes, run for in Great-Britain and Ireland, &c. in the year 1774* (London, 1774).

Weatherby, James, *Racing calendar: containing an account of the plates, matches, and sweepstakes, run for in Great-Britain and Ireland, &c. in the year 1779* (London, 1779).

Youatt, W., *The horse, with a treatise on draught* (London, 1831).

Young, A., *The farmer's tour through the east of England*, vol. 1 of 4 (London, 1771).

Printed sources

Assheton, N., *The journal of Nicholas Assheton* (Manchester, 1848).

Beckford, Peter, *Thoughts on hunting in a series of familiar letters to a friend* (1781; Lanham, MD, 2000).

Berners, Juliana, *English hawking and hunting in 'The Boke of St Albans': a facsimile edition of sigs a2-f8 of 'The Boke of St Albans'* (Oxford, 1975).

Boswell, James, *Life of Johnson* (1791; Oxford, 1998).

Bruyn Andrews, C. (ed.), *The Torrington diaries*, 4 vols (London, 1934–8).

Calendar of State Papers Domestic: James I, 1603–1610 (London, 1857).

Calendar of State Papers Domestic: James I, 1619–1623 (London, 1858).

Calendar of State Papers Domestic: James I, 1623–1625 (London, 1859).

Calendar of State Papers Domestic: Charles II, 1660–1661 (London, 1860).

Calendar of State Papers Domestic: Charles II, 1661–1662 (London, 1861).

Calendar of State Papers Domestic: Charles II, 1663–1664 (London, 1862).

Calendar of State Papers Domestic: Elizabeth and James I, Addenda 1580–1625 (London, 1872).

Calendar of State Papers Domestic: Elizabeth, 1601–1603, with Addenda, 1547–1565 (London, 1870).

Calendar of State Papers Domestic: Interregnum, 1649–1650 (London, 1875).

Calendar of State Papers Domestic: Charles II, March 1682–1683 (London, 1932).

Cecil (Tongue, C.), *Records of the chase* (1854; London, 1922).

Cobbett, William, *Rural rides* (1830; London, 1950)

Cone, C. (ed.), *Hounds in the morning: selections from* The Sporting Magazine *1792–1836* (Lexington, KY, 1981).

Cook, Colonel John, *Observations on fox hunting* (1826; London, 1922).

Defoe, Daniel, *A tour through England and Wales*, 2 vols (London, 1928).

'The Druid' (Dixon, H.H.), *The paddock and the post* (1857; London, 1862).

Edward of Norwich, *The master of game*, eds W.A. and F.N. Baillie-Grohman (1909; Philadelphia, PA, 2005).

Fielding, Henry, *The history and adventures of Joseph Andrews and his friend, Mr Abraham Adams* (1742; London, 1999).

Fielding, Henry, *The history of a foundling, Tom Jones* (1749; Oxford, 1998).

Fiennes, Celia, *The illustrated journeys of Celia Fiennes*, ed. C. Morris (London, 1982).

Fiennes, Celia, *The journeys of Celia Fiennes* (London, 1983).

Hainsworth, D.R. and Walker, C. (eds), *The correspondence of Lord Fitzwilliam of Milton and Francis Guybon, his steward 1697–1709* (Northampton, 1990).

Hawkes, John, *The Meynellian science or fox-hunting upon system* (1808; Leicester, 1932).

James, King, *Basilicon doron* (1599; Menston, 1969).

Markham, G., *Countrey contentments* (1615; New York, 1973).

Marlow, N. (trans.), *The diary of Thomas Isham of Lamport, 1671–73* (Farnborough, 1971).

Nimrod (Apperley, C.), *The chace, the road and the turf* (1837; London, 1927).

Nimrod (Apperley, C.), *My horses and other essays* (London, 1928).

Nimrod (Apperley, C.), *Nimrod's hunting tours* (1835; London, 1926).

Osbaldeston, G., *Squire Osbaldeston: his autobiography*, ed. E.D. Cuming (Bungay, 1927).

Palk Collyns, C., *Notes on the chase of the wild red deer in the counties of Devon and Somerset* (1862; London, 1902).

Phoebus, Gaston, *Livre de chase*, commentary by W. Schlag (London, 1998).

Ross, A. (ed.), *Selections from The Tatler and The Spectator* (London, 1982).

Smollett, Tobias, *The expedition of Humphry Clinker* (1771; Oxford, 1998).

Smyth, J., *The Berkeley manuscripts: lives of the Berkeleys*, ed. J. MacLean, 3 vols (Gloucester, 1883).

Stanhope, Philip, earl of Chesterfield, *Lord Chesterfield's letters to his son and others* (1929; London, 1975).

Steele, R. and Addison, J., *Sir Roger de Coverley*, ed. J. Hampden (London, 1967).

Surtees, R.S., *Town and country papers* (R.S. Surtees Society, 1993).

Trollope, A., *Orley Farm* (1861; Oxford, 2008).

Wake, J. and Champion-Webster, D. (eds), *The letters of Daniel Eaton to the third earl of Cardigan 1725–1732* (Northampton, 1971).

Whyte-Melville, G.J., *Market Harborough* (1862; London, 1984).

Whyte-Melville, G.J., *Riding recollections* (1875; London, 1985).

Secondary sources

Acton, A., 'Getting by with a little help from my hunter: riding to hounds in English foxhound packs', in N. Kowalsky (ed.), *Hunting philosophy for everyone: in search of the wild life* (Oxford, 2010), pp. 80–92.

Albion, R.G., *Forests and sea power: the timber problem of the royal navy, 1652–1862* (1926; Annapolis, MD, 2000).

Almond, R., *Medieval hunting* (Stroud, 2003).

Barker, T. and Gerhold, D., *The rise and rise of road transport, 1700–1990* (Basingstoke, 1993).

Beaumont James, T. and Gerrard, C., *Clarendon: landscape of kings* (Macclesfield, 2007).

Beaver, D.C., *Hunting and the politics of violence before the English civil war* (Cambridge, 2008).

Berry, E., *Shakespeare and the hunt* (Cambridge, 2002).

Bevan, J., 'Agricultural change and the development of foxhunting in the eighteenth century', *Agricultural History Review*, 58/1 (2010), pp. 49–75.

Birrell, J., 'Deer and deer farming in medieval England', *Agricultural History Review*, 40/2 (1992), pp. 112–26.

Birrell, J., 'Hunting and the royal forest', *L'uoma e la Foresta Secola XIII–XVIII* (1995), pp. 437–57.

Boehrer, B., 'Shakespeare and the social devaluation of the horse', in K. Raber and T. Tucker (eds), *The culture of the horse: status, discipline and identity in the early modern world* (Basingstoke, 2005), pp. 91–111.

Bond, J., 'The park before the palace: the sixteenth and seventeenth centuries', in J. Bond and K. Tiller (eds), *Blenheim: landscape for a palace* (Gloucester, 1987), pp. 55–66.

Borsay, P., *The English urban renaissance: culture and society in the provincial town, 1660–1770* (1989; Oxford, 1991).

Borsay, P., *A history of leisure: the British experience since 1500* (Basingstoke, 2006).

Bovill, E.W., *The England of Nimrod and Surtees* (London, 1959).

Bovill, E.W., *English country life 1780–1830* (London, 1962).

Brander, M., *Hunting and shooting: from earliest times to the present day* (London, 1971).

Brereton, J.M., *The horse in war* (Newton Abbot, 1976).

Brownlow, J., *Melton Mowbray queen of the shires* (Wymondham, 1980).

Bryson, Anna, *From courtesy to civility: changing codes of conduct in early modern England* (Oxford, 1998).

Cantor, L. and Squires, A., *The historic parks and gardens of Leicestershire and Rutland* (Newton Linford, 1997).

Cantor, L.M., 'The medieval parks of Leicestershire', *Transactions of Leicestershire Archaeological and Historical Society*, 46 (1970–1), pp. 9–24.

Carr, R., 'Country sports', in G.E. Mingay (ed.), *The Victorian countryside*, vol. 2 of 2 (London, 1981).

Carr, R., *English foxhunting: a history* (1976; London 1986).

Carter, P., *Men and the emergence of polite society, Britain 1660–1800* (London, 2000).

Carter, P., 'Polite "persons": character, biography and the gentleman', in *English politeness: social rank and moral virtue, c. 1400–1900, Transactions of the Royal Historical Society*, 12 (2002), pp. 333–54.

Cartmill, M., *A view to a death in the morning: hunting and nature through history* (1993; Harvard, 1996).

Clark, P., *British clubs and society 1580–1800: the origins of an associational world* (Oxford, 2000).

Clayton, M., *Foxhunting in paradise* (London, 1993).

Colyer, R.J., 'Some aspects of cattle production in Northamptonshire and Leicestershire during the nineteenth century', *Northamptonshire Past and Present*, 5 (1973), pp. 45–54.

Cook, T., *A history of the English turf* (London, 1901).

Cox, J.C., *The royal forests of England* (London, 1905).

Crofts, J., *Packhorse, waggon and post: land carriage and communications under the Tudors and Stuarts* (London, 1967).

Cummins, J., *The hound and the hawk: the art of medieval hunting* (1988; Edison, 2003).

Dale, T.F., *The history of the Belvoir hunt* (London, 1899).

Deuchar, S., *Sporting art in eighteenth century England: a social and political history* (Yale, 1988).

Dunlop, I., *Palaces and progresses of Elizabeth I* (London, 1962).

Edwards, P., *Horse and man in early modern England* (London, 2007).

Edwards, P., 'The horse trade of the midlands in the seventeenth century', *Agricultural History Review*, 27/2 (1979).

Edwards, P., *The horse trade of Tudor and Stuart England* (1988; Cambridge, 2004).

Edwards, P., Enenkel, K.A.E. and Graham, E. (eds), *The horse as cultural icon: the real and the symbolic horse in the early modern world* (Leiden, 2012).

Ellis, C.D.B., *Leicestershire and the Quorn hunt* (Leicester, 1951).

Falk, B., *The royal Fitzroys: dukes of Grafton through four centuries* (London, 1950).

Finch, J., 'Grass, grass, grass: fox-hunting and the creation of the modern landscape', *Landscapes*, 5/2 (2004), pp. 41–52.

Finch, J., 'Wider famed countries: historic landscape characterisation in the midland shires', *Landscapes*, 8/2 (2007), pp. 50–63.

Fitter, C., 'The slain deer and political imperium: As You Like It and Andrew Marvell's "Nymph Complaining for the Death of Her Fawn"', *Journal of English and Germanic Philology*, 98 (1999), pp. 193–218.

Fletcher, A., *Gender, sex and subordination in England 1500–1800* (Yale, 1995).

Fletcher, J., *Gardens of earthly delight: the history of deer parks* (Oxford, 2011).

Fletcher, N., 'Hart's desire', *Gastronomica*, 1/3 (2001), pp. 77–81.

Foard, G., Hall, D. and Britnell, T., *The historic landscape of Rockingham Forest: its character and evolution from the 10th to the 20th centuries* (2003), <http://www.rockingham-forest-trust.org.uk/RF%20pdfs/Rockingham%20Forest%20Project%20final%20report.pdf>. Accessed 13 December 2012.

Foard, G., Hall, D. and Partida, T., *Rockingham Forest: an atlas of the medieval and early modern landscape* (Northampton, 2009).

Fox, H.S.A., 'The people of the wolds in English settlement history', in M. Aston, D. Austin and C. Dyer (eds), *The rural settlements of medieval England: studies dedicated to M.W. Beresford and J.G. Hurst* (Oxford, 1989), pp. 77–101.

Gash, N., *Robert Surtees and early Victorian society* (1993; Surtees Society, 1996).

Gerhold, D., *Carriers and coachmasters: trade and travel before the turnpikes* (Chichester, 2005).

Gilbey, Sir W., *Concise history of the Shire horse* (1889; Liss, 1976).

Gillies Shields, J., *Old Tom of Tooley – father of the Quorn: his life and times* (n.p., 1998).

Grant, R., *The royal forests of England* (Stroud, 1991).

Griffin, E., *Blood sport: hunting in Britain since 1066* (New Haven, CT, and London, 2007).

Hall, D., 'Enclosure in Northamptonshire', *Northamptonshire Past and Present*, 9/4 (1997–8), pp. 351–67.

Hall, D., 'The woodland landscapes of southern Northamptonshire', *Northamptonshire Past and Present*, 54 (2001), pp. 33–46.

Harding, P.T. and Wall, T. (eds), *Moccas: an English deer park* (Peterborough, 2000).

Harris, E., *Oak: a British history* (Macclesfield, 2003).

Hill, C., *Liberty against the law: some seventeenth-century controversies* (London, 1996).

Hingston, F. (ed.), *Deer parks and deer of Great Britain* (Buckingham, 1988).

Hoppitt, R., 'Hunting Suffolk's parks: towards a reliable chronology of imparkment', in R. Liddiard (ed.), *The medieval park: new perspectives* (Macclesfield, 2007).

Hore, J.P., *The history of Newmarket and the annals of the turf*, 3 vols (London, 1886), pp. 146–64.

Hore, J.P., *The history of the royal buckhounds* (Newmarket, 1895).

Hoskins, W.G., *Leicestershire: an illustrated essay on the history of the landscape* (London, 1957).

Hoskins, W.G., *The making of the English landscape* (1955; London, 1985).

Huggins, M., *Flat racing and British society 1790–1914: a social and economic history* (London, 2000).

Isaacson, R., *The wild host: the history and meaning of the hunt* (London, 2001).

Itzkowitz, D., *Peculiar privilege: a social history of foxhunting, 1753–1885* (Hassocks, 1977).

Jones, R. and Page, M., *Medieval villages in an English landscape: beginnings and ends* (Macclesfield, 2006).

Landry, D., *The invention of the countryside: hunting, walking and ecology in English literature, 1671–1831* (Basingstoke, 2001).

Landry, D., *Noble brutes: how eastern horses transformed English culture* (Baltimore, MD, 2009).

Langford, P., 'The uses of eighteenth-century politeness', in *English politeness: social rank and moral virtue, c. 1400–1900, Transactions of the Royal Historical Society* 12 (2002), pp. 311–31.

Langton, J., 'Forests in early-modern England and Wales: history and historiography', in J. Langton and G. Jones (eds), *Forests and chases of England and Wales c.1500–c.1850* (Oxford, 2005), pp. 1–9.

Liddiard, R., 'Medieval designed landscapes: problems and possibilities', in M. Gardiner and S. Rippon (eds), *Landscape history after Hoskins: medieval landscapes* (Macclesfield, 2007), pp. 201–14.

Liddiard, R. (ed.), *The medieval park: new perspectives* (Macclesfield, 2007).

Linnell, J.E., *Old oak: the story of a forest village* (London, 1932).

MacGregor, A., 'The household out of doors: the Stuart court and the animal kingdom', in E. Cruickshanks (ed.), *The Stuart courts* (Stroud, 2000), pp. 86–117.

Madden, D.H., *The diary of Master William Silence: a study of Shakespeare and of Elizabethan sport* (1897; New York, 1969).

Manning, R.B., *Hunters and poachers: a social and cultural history of unlawful hunting in England, 1485–1640* (Oxford, 1993).

Mansfield, N., 'Foxhunting and the Yeomanry: county identity and military culture', in R.W. Hoyle (ed.), *Our hunting fathers: field sports in England after 1850* (Lancaster, 2007), pp. 241–56.

Marvin, G., 'English foxhunting: a prohibited practice', *International Journal of Cultural Property*, 1/4 (2007), pp. 339–60.

Marvin, G., 'Living with dead animals? Trophies as souvenirs of the hunt', in N. Kowalsky (ed.), *Hunting philosophy for everyone: in search of the wild life* (Oxford, 2010), pp. 107–17.

Marvin, G., 'A passionate pursuit: foxhunting as performance', *The Sociological Review*, 51 (2003), pp. 46–60.

Middleton, I.M., 'The origins of English fox hunting and the myth of Hugo Meynell and the Quorn', *Sport in History*, 25/1 (2005), pp. 1–16.

Mileson, S.A., *Parks in medieval England* (Oxford, 2009).

Mingay, G.E., *English landed society in the eighteenth century* (London, 1963).

Moore-Colyer, R., 'Aspects of horse breeding and the supply of horses in Victorian Britain', *Agricultural History Review*, 43/1 (1995), pp. 47–60.

Moore-Colyer, R., 'Woods and woodland management: the bailiwick of Rockingham, Northamptonshire c.1700–1849', *Northamptonshire Past and Present*, 9/3 (1996–7), pp. 253–8.

Munsche, P.B., *Gentlemen and poachers: the English game laws 1671–1831* (Cambridge, 1981).

Neeson, J.M., *Commoners: common right, enclosure and social change in England, 1700–1820* (1993; Cambridge, 1996).

Nethercote, H.O., *The Pytchley hunt past and present* (London, 1888).

Nichols, J., *The progresses, processions, and magnificent festivities, of King James the First*, 4 vols (London, 1828).

Nichols, J., *Progresses, public processes &c of Queen Elizabeth*, 3 vols (London, 1823).

Overton, M., *Agricultural revolution in England: the transformation of the agrarian economy 1500–1850* (Cambridge, 1996).

Page, W. (ed.), *The Victoria history of the counties of England. A history of the county of Buckingham*, vol. 2 (London, 1908).

Page, W. (ed.), *The Victoria history of the counties of England. A history of the county of Northampton*, vol. 3 (London, 1930).

Page, W. (ed.), *The Victoria history of the counties of England. A history of the county of Sussex*, vol. 2 (London, 1907).

Paget, G., *The history of the Althorp and Pytchley hunt 1634–1920* (London, 1937).

Partida, T., 'The early hunting landscapes of Northamptonshire', *Northamptonshire Past and Present*, 60 (2007), pp. 44–60.

Pettit, P.A.J., *The royal forests of Northamptonshire: a study in their economy 1558–1714* (Gateshead, 1968).

Phillips, A.D.M., *The underdraining of farmland in England during the nineteenth century* (Cambridge, 1989).

Plumb, J.H., *The commercialisation of leisure in eighteenth-century England* (Reading, 1973).

Pluskowski, A., 'The social construction of medieval park ecosystems: an interdisciplinary persepective', in R. Liddiard (ed.), *The medieval park: new perspectives* (Macclesfield, 2007), pp. 63–78.

Raber, K. and Tucker, T. (eds), *The culture of the horse: status, discipline and identity in the early modern world* (Basingstoke, 2005).

Rackham, O., *Ancient woodland: its history, vegetation and uses in England* (London, 1980).

Rackham, O., *An illustrated history of the countryside* (London, 1994).

Rackham, O., *Trees and woodland in the British landscape: the complete history of Britain's trees, woods and hedgerows* (1976; London, 2001).

Rackham, O., *Woodlands* (London, 2006).

Rees, S., *The Charlton hunt: a history* (Chichester, 1998).

Richardson, A., *The forest, park and palace of Clarendon, c.1200–c.1650: reconstructing an actual, conceptual and documented Wiltshire landscape* (Oxford, 2005).

Riden, P. (ed.), *The Victoria history of the counties of England. A history of the county of Northampton*, vol. 5 (Woodbridge, 2002).

Ridley, J., *Fox hunting* (London, 1990).

Ritvo, H., *The animal estate: the English and other creatures in the Victorian age* (Harvard, 1987).

Roberts, B. and Wrathmell, S., *Region and place: a study of English rural settlement* (London, 2002).

Russell, N., *Like engendering like: heredity and animal breeding in early modern England* (Cambridge, 1986).

'Sabretache' (Barrow, Albert Stewart), *Monarchy and the chase* (London, 1948).

Scarth Dixon, W., *Hunting in the olden days* (London, 1912).

Schumer, B., *Wychwood: the evolution of a wooded landscape* (Charlbury, 1999).

Serjeantson, R.M. (ed.), *The Victoria history of the counties of England. A history of the county of Northampton*, vol. 2 (1906; London, 1970).

Shirley, E.P., *Some account of English deer parks* (London, 1867).

Shoard, M., *A right to roam* (Oxford, 1999).

Spencer, C., *The Spencer family* (London, 1999).

Stamper, P., 'Woods and parks', in G. Astill and A. Grant (eds), *The countryside of medieval England* (Oxford, 1988), pp. 128–48.

Steane, J.M., *The making of the English landscape: the Northamptonshire landscape* (London, 1974).

Steane, J.M., 'The medieval parks of Northamptonshire', *Northamptonshire Past and Present*, 5/3 (1975), pp. 211–33.

Sykes, N., 'Animal bones and animal parks', in R. Liddiard (ed.), *The medieval park: new perspectives* (Macclesfield, 2007), pp. 49–62.

Tate, W.E., 'Inclosure movements in Northamptonshire', *Northamptonshire Past and Present*, 1/2 (1949), pp. 19–33.

Taylor, A., 'Pig-sticking princes: royal hunting, moral outrage, and the republican opposition to animal abuse in nineteenth- and early twentieth-century Britain', *History*, 89 (2004), pp. 30–48.

Taylor, C., 'Ravendale Park, Derbyshire and medieval deer coursing', *Landscape History*, 26 (2004), pp. 37–57.

Theis, J., 'The "ill kill'd" deer: poaching and social order in *The Merry Wives of Windsor*', *Texas Studies in Literature and Language*, 43 (2001), pp. 46–73.

Thirsk, J., 'Agricultural innovations and their diffusion', in J. Thirsk (ed.), *The agrarian history of England and Wales*, vol. 5 of 8 (Cambridge, 1985), pp. 533–89.

Thirsk, J., *Horses in early modern England, for service, for pleasure, for power* (Reading, 1978).

Thomas, K., *Man and the natural world: changing attitudes in England 1500–1800* (1983; London, 1984).

Thompson, E.P., *Whigs and hunters: the origin of the Black Act* (London, 1975).

Tosh, J., 'Gentlemanly politeness and manly simplicity in Victorian England', in *English Politeness: Social Rank and Moral Virtue, c. 1400–1900*, Transactions of the Royal Historical Society, 12 (2002), pp. 455–72.

Tubbs, C.R., *The New Forest: an ecological history* (Newton Abbot, 1968).

Vale, M., *The gentleman's recreations: accomplishments and pastimes of the English gentleman 1580–1630* (Cambridge, 1977).

Vamplew, W., *The Turf: a social and economic history of horse racing* (London, 1976).

Wade Martins, S., *Farmers, landlords and landscapes: rural Britain 1750–1800* (Macclesfield, 2004).

Walton, J.R., 'Pedigree and the national cattle herd circa 1750–1950', *Agricultural History Review*, 34 (1986).

Whitehead, G.K., *Hunting and stalking deer in Britain through the ages* (London, 1980).

Wilkinson, D., *Early horse racing in Yorkshire and the origins of the Thoroughbred* (York, 2003).

Willett, P., *The story of Tattersalls* (London, 1987).

Willett, P., *The Thoroughbred* (London, 1970).

Williams, J., 'Hunting, hawking and the early Tudor gentleman', *History Today*, 8 (2003), pp. 21–7.

Williamson, T., *Polite landscapes: gardens and society in eighteenth-century England* (Stroud, 1995).

Williamson, T., *The transformation of rural England: farming and the landscape 1700–1870* (Exeter, 2002).

Williamson, T. and Taigel, A., *Parks and gardens* (London, 1993).

Woodward, F., *Oxfordshire parks* (Oxford, 1982).

Worsley, G., *The British stable* (New Haven, CT, and London, 2004).

Yelling, J.A., *Common field and enclosure 1450–1850* (London, 1977).

Young, C., *The royal forests of medieval England* (Leicester, 1971).

Index